RECLAIMING
THE
BLACK BODY

RECLAIMING
THE
BLACK BODY

· *Nourishing the Home Within* ·

ALISHIA MCCULLOUGH, LCMHC

THE DIAL PRESS / NEW YORK

Published in the United States by The Dial Press, an imprint of Random House, a division of Penguin Random House LLC, New York.

THE DIAL PRESS is a registered trademark and the colophon is a trademark of Penguin Random House LLC.

ISBN: 9780593447482
Ebook ISBN: 9780593447499

Printed in the United States of America on acid-free paper

randomhousebooks.com

2 4 6 8 9 7 5 3 1

First Edition

Book design by Caroline Cunningham

This book is dedicated to all of the versions of myself that courageously and continuously took the road less traveled, allowing each unknown step to unfold into my own becoming. This book would not have manifested without the favor and wisdom of God(dess), my ancestors, and my birth and chosen families. This is for my fellow healers and culture shifters, and all of those who dream and live with liberation in your hearts. We collectively birthed this work.

TABLE OF CONTENTS

AUTHOR'S NOTE

THERE ARE TIMES WHEN it feels like the universe knows a culture shift is necessary, so it creates conditions that challenge us to transform. I believe the events of 2020 were our wake-up call. None of us could have predicted that both a global pandemic and a series of senseless killings of Black people at the hands of a system whose job it is to protect us would become conduits for change. But each brought to light social ills we could no longer ignore.

Covid-19 cut a swath through our country that year, leaving a trail of chaos, uncertainty, and grief in its wake as we all grappled with the many unknowns about the virus, and with the millions of lives that were eventually lost. One would think that this unique experience we were all going through would have brought us closer together as human beings. But the same anti-Black indoctrination I'd seen in my work as a mental health therapist not only continued to pop up, but appeared to get worse.

When articles began to appear that questioned why Covid death tolls were higher in Black communities compared with other races, the narrative immediately became that our higher rates of health issues were to blame. It was also suggested that this phenomenon was happening to us because Black people are "overweight" or "obese." Once again, the onus was placed on us to debunk these myths. Many Black folks in the field had to point out that poor health care options and low-income jobs are really what had put Black communities at higher risk. Those who had access to money, transportation, and social capital were better able to isolate, and to call out from work or work from home. But for those living in low-income Black communities that wasn't an option. Having to use public transportation to get to work, for example, forced people to put themselves at risk as they exposed themselves to areas where the virus was highly transmittable.

During this time, the white-dominated eating disorder field chose to deal with Covid by focusing on helping people feel better about their pandemic weight gain. The internet was full of messages that said it's okay that you put on a few extra pounds—"After all, we are in a global pandemic," as if being in a pandemic was the only acceptable excuse for someone to gain weight.

As some of us folks in the field tried to call attention to and deal with the racial disparities connected to Covid, another crisis took over our communities: the terrorism and murders of Black folk by police and racist people. I remember waking up every day in survival mode, holding my breath as I watched the news to see who had been harmed this time. The constant barrage of police brutality and other racist incidents had many of us feeling isolated, hopeless, and burned out.

Toward the beginning of the pandemic, I made the decision to leave a job where the impacts of systemic and personal racism were literally holding my nervous system in a consistent state of hyperarousal. For the first time in my life, I did not have a plan, so I took a job in a group private practice with the hopes that I could pick up a bit of income during that tumultuous time. As the pandemic and racial trauma persisted, I felt that my work as a mental health and eating disorder therapist must also include speaking out against social injustice and oppression. I needed a space where I could share my voice and my experiences so that I wouldn't feel like I was constantly screaming into an echo chamber.

This was around the time when Black therapists who spoke up about racism in my field stood out like unicorns in a stable of white horses. When I first got into this work I was one of four Black eating disorder providers in my area, and out of those four I was the only one who was using language like "decolonizing" eating disorders and discussing the implications of trauma, racism, and oppression showing up in our bodies. There were many times when white eating disorder providers questioned my competence—and whether I deserved to be in the field at all—because I challenged the status quo. I consistently spoke out about the impact of cultural issues and embraced a holistic view when discussing healing. Still, I and a few courageous others put ourselves and our careers on the line to tell the truth about our experiences in the industry. (This, I should also mention, was around the same time that an eating disorder conference was scheduled to be held on a slave plantation.)

Whenever we'd talk about the issues we and our clients of color were experiencing, we were often dismissed, silenced, and labeled as being too controversial. A white provider even once told me that I was "taking too much of a granular lens," and that I needed to focus on "the standard"—which in her mind was the white, thin women who were being represented as having eating disorders. As my colleagues and I pushed back and refused to conform to the way things had always been, many of us were blackballed. Still, we continued to advocate for systemic and institutional change for our clients and ourselves.

This growing tension between those of us who were challenging the status quo and those who were working overtime to uphold it came to an inflection point in 2020, as police violence toward Black bodies became endemic. It was hard to show up in my Black body every day and deal with my own fears, uncertainty, anger, grief, and frustration with the state of affairs in America, while also having to show up and hold space for clients who shared their personal trauma and grief associated with the war on Black bodies—from the pandemic to police brutality. At the time I had a white supervisor and did not feel safe discussing the nuances of what it was like for me to wake up in terror, wondering if the Black men in my life were going to make it to where they were going, or if friends and family would contract a deadly virus because they didn't have the option to work from home.

It was hard to talk about how I was holding in my body not only my own grief, but the rage of my ancestors and the myriad feelings of my Black clients every single day, session after session. It was hard to talk about the white people who'd just discovered that racism existed and were now purposefully seeking out Black therapists to help them process and work through their white privilege. Having to hold space for white people to become undone in confidential therapy sessions, while we ourselves were not okay, added to our trauma. We were forced to compartmentalize in order to show up. It was a lot—and often *too* much.

The breaking point for me: the murder of Botham Jean. Jean was a twenty-six-year-old accountant who was killed by an off-duty Dallas Police Department patrol officer named Amber Guyger. Guyger entered his apartment in Dallas, Texas, allegedly claiming she had confused it for her own apartment. She said she fatally shot Jean because she thought he was a burglar. I remember sitting on the couch in my living room speechless as the news circulated through the media. During a time of the pandemic when we were being mandated to stay inside and had curfews for when we could and could not leave the house, here was a situation in which a Black man minding his own damn business was killed in his own home. Yet, the media centered the story on the white woman's perceived fear. There was little to no show of concern for how Jean's life, dreams, and future had been cut short.

A few weeks later, we learned about the circumstances surrounding the death of Ahmaud Arbery, who was murdered by two white men in a racially motivated hate crime while jogging. He was simply existing and moving in his body while Black. There was a flurry of other killings–Tony McDade, Breonna Taylor, and then the murder that caused an international uproar and countless uprisings: George Floyd. It was all too much to process. These murders received widespread press, but there were many more that we did not hear about. I had clients showing up for sessions who were telling me how they were Tased, gassed, and/or arrested for protesting or, worse, that they had lost a loved one to police violence or a hate crime. It was devastating. I was afraid, and I felt powerless.

As an outlet I began to post on Instagram about what was happening in the world and speaking out even more about the intersections of racial trauma and eating disorders. I felt that racism was at the epicenter of eating disorders, yet that conversation was completely missing from my formal education and work environments. And so I created a social media page centered on eating disorders and anti-racism.

It attracted a lot of Instagram followers who were dietitians and traditional eating disorder therapists, most of whom were white, which surprised me. As I continued to post about the intersectional injustices faced in Black, Indigenous, and People of Color communities, I gained even more engagement, and soon connected with other people from all over the world who were also engaged in addressing issues of body liberation, eating disorders, social justice, and anti-oppression work. It felt good to find community and connect with people who shared similar experiences. For the first time I felt validated and heard, and I met with other Black providers who would often check in with one another weekly to see how we were coping with everything that was going on.

In May 2020, I was invited to participate in a live stream meeting with the originators of the Covid-19 Eating Support Community. The number of people who were presenting with clinical eating disorders significantly increased during the pandemic, and as our routines changed, many people were distressed about their changing bodies. So, the group hosted weekly live stream sessions on social media to support people who were struggling, with the intention of holding space for folks who may need to eat with someone else present and be affirmed around their experiences. After the live stream, I was invited to be a consultant for this online community and to support them with ideas around how to be more inclusive and anti-oppressive.

It was on this Zoom call where I met my colleague and friend Jessica Wilson, who is a dietitian based in Sacramento, California. I was immediately drawn to Jessica, because she was direct and not afraid to share her opinion. It was the first time I was in a role where I had my voice heard among white people, and in a room with another Black woman who was professional and poised but did not play into respectability politics. After the Zoom meeting, Jessica and I exchanged numbers, and we kept in contact. We'd have conversations about our frustrations with the state of the world and how what we were experiencing on a macro systemic level was also showing up on a micro and interpersonal level within the eating disorders field. We'd had enough of white narratives and voices dominating the field, and wanted to do something big to address what was happening.

We decided that we would start a social media movement aimed at centering the voices of Black and Brown people, thinking it would be a good opportunity to connect with other professionals and content creators who were in solidarity with centering and uplifting melanated people. We started off with a post that read, "So often social justice–oriented accounts center the white narrative. White people use their positionality to profit from the people who are most impacted by systems of oppression, and marginalized folks are often pushed to the margins of social media. We want to center the voices and lived experiences of folks of color doing this work and challenge you to #AmplifyMelanatedVoices."

We then asked folks to "mute the white noise" during the week of June 1–June 7, 2020; this involved using a feature on Instagram at the time that would allow someone to temporarily mute a page. Then we asked them to follow, listen, and support pages of Black and Brown creators on social media. We asked participants to re-post content from BIPOC (Black, Indigenous, and other People of Color) content creators on their grid and in their stories, to tag the creators, and most important, once the week was over, to reflect on what was different for them during that week. People were encouraged to pay Black creators for their labor on social media, and we offered reflection prompts and action items for folks to engage in.

Our goal was to target eating disorder and body liberation com-munities to bring about change and awareness; however, the move-ment reached way more people than we anticipated. We included social media accounts to follow based on people we had personally learned from and been in community with within our small online circles. But we were not prepared for the seismic impact the Am-plify Melanated Voices (AMV) movement would have. We inspired nine thousand new posts on Instagram within the first day alone. Within a matter of days, I went from having a few thousand follow-ers to hundreds of thousands of followers from all over the world, sharing about our movement, reposting our content, and telling us about how inspired they were by what we were doing. We had un-knowingly posted our initial message one day after the Black soli-darity squares began to circulate on social media in support of the Black Lives Matter movement.

My direct messages were full of people reposting my content, and a simple Google search showed that multiple media platforms were covering our movement. Overnight, I went from being a mental health therapist who was using social media for my own healing and connection to others to a global voice for anti-oppression and mental and emotional wellness.

In the weeks that followed, Jessica and I received backlash and threats from offended white people, as well as praise for what we had created. Many BIPOC folks from many industries told us that they felt heard, were seeing changes in their workplaces, had right-fully earned long-overdue promotions, and were receiving finan-cial donations and opportunities because of the AMV movement. I had people reaching out to me from places as far-reaching as Ger-many and Australia to ask how they could donate and raise aware-ness on a community organizing level within their locations.

Within the health industry, many companies decided that it was time—as well as trendy and socially lucrative—to hire Black con-sultants and to rightfully direct promotions and leadership oppor-tunities to Black and other non-white communities. Organizations such as the Association for Size Diversity and Health became in-tentional about shifting its leadership to center fat Black women, femmes, and gender-expansive folks. We were swept up in the wave of social media activism, while also physically marching and showing up in the streets for our Black lives.

As a therapist and the primary provider in my household, I was in a strange position in that I was constantly going out into the streets to protest, but also acutely aware that this could result in arrest and subsequently threaten my job security and professional license. Social media activism offered another sustainable route to ensure that my voice was heard. This kind of community activism was my self-care and self-love practice throughout 2020. It was how I chose to take back my autonomy, and I began to feel more liberated within my body. It also helped me feel as if I was making a difference because of my sphere of influence and the way I was supporting the holistic well-being of more people in my commu-nity through direct actions such as making financial donations and helping folks access resources.

The overwhelmingly positive reaction to the Amplify Melanated Voices movement proved to me that body liberation and activism cannot, and should not, be separated. We cannot simply love our-selves into body liberation or be positive enough about our bodies to reduce or deconstruct systemic oppression. The liberation within our bodies requires us to get uncomfortable and to take the leaps of faith required to create movements that center our Black voices and experiences. This especially goes for those who have already been pushed to the margins within their Black existence— namely, gender-expansive, disabled, LGBTQIA++, larger-bodied, fat, and low-income folks. When I think about all the efforts that have been made to address the deeper layers of body oppression, I feel especially uplifted by the work done by Black people in the field, those who have figured out how to marry their lived experiences of the issues that we are facing as Black people with activism.

I believe working in concert with another Black woman who unapologetically took up space and always showed up authentically on both a personal and professional level taught me how to show up in a similar way. It began an inner movement within me. It was through these life-changing interactions, working side by side with other Blacks, Indigenous folks, and People of Color, that I was able to unpack the indoctrination of my past. I think about the network of support I found in Black online eating disorder consultation groups who let me know that working with my clients through the lens of anti-oppression was not only appropriate, but imperative to their healing.

Each transformative experience has emboldened and inspired me to foster that same sense of liberation in others. The book you now hold in your hands is a testament to this transformation—and I hope it will be the continuation of yours.

INTRODUCTION

A S A YOUNG PERSON, I remember thinking, *If I can change my body through the food that I eat, then I can achieve the perfect shape and size.* I believed that controlling my food and body image would grant me access to safety and acceptance, as well as a sense of empowerment and freedom that I didn't have as a young Black girl in the South. When I was growing up in Little Washington, North Carolina, a coastal town in the eastern region of the state, there were certain expectations of little girls that were made clear to me from early on. How I dressed, how I spoke to others, even what and how I chose to eat were constantly scrutinized. I could plainly see that the women I grew up around associated health and desirability with body size. There was this belief that a woman who was "put together" was slim, and that slimmer women were better able to keep their men from wandering.

I began to internalize the messages I was receiving. I found myself teetering between a longing to be just desirable enough to feel like I fit in with my peers and the idea that if I took up less space, I could prevent myself from being sexualized by older men. I don't think I am alone in these experiences, and would argue that many young Black girls share similar feelings.

Caught between these two ideas, I decided that I had to demonstrate to someone—my family, my peers, society—that I was disciplined about my eating habits. I had to prove to myself that I had control over my body. I learned that eating less was something that was expected of women, and that we should feel shame about indulging in the more pleasurable foods we desired. Food restriction became my go-to coping strategy in times of emotional distress.

Of course, believing that I was solely responsible for everything that happened to me was a lie forced onto me by society. When I was younger, I wasn't aware of the insidious ways white culture and institutions can make Black women feel less than human. I had been conditioned to think that the way people saw me was all my fault and that something was wrong with *me*. I didn't understand how the messaging of mainstream culture, which is rooted in systemic oppression, had a powerful hold on my beliefs about myself. Because I had been socialized to believe the lie, I began to suppress my inner trauma.

Obsessing over what and how I ate became a way for me to try to gain a sense of freedom, boundaries, belonging, safety, and value not often afforded to Black girls. But my body goals were unrealistic. Every time I'd indulge in foods that had been labeled as "bad," every time I couldn't achieve the slim yet "thick-in-all-the-right-places" body type I'd see in the teen magazines, and every time I "failed" on a diet, I would think that I was not good enough. I told myself that if I could just work a little harder and have more willpower, I could meet my goals. This mindset only sent me spiraling into a cycle of food deprivation. During these moments, all I cared about was making myself smaller. I developed a fear of taking up space within my own body.

THE ILLNESS WE DON'T TALK ABOUT

Eating disorders are biopsychosocial-spiritual conditions that impact people of *all* genders, *all* sexual orientations, *all* races, religions, spiritualities, ethnicities, abilities, body shapes, and weights. National surveys estimate that 24 million Americans are impacted by eating disorders, and that 70 million people are affected worldwide. The study of eating disorders as a clinical issue is relatively new: Major advances were mostly made in the 1980s, but behaviors we describe as eating disorders have been documented as far back as the religious practices of the twelfth and thirteenth centuries.

Having an imbalanced relationship with food doesn't look the same for everyone. For some, it's about compulsive dieting, or not eating enough, thereby denying your body the nutrients it needs in order to thrive. For others, it can look like binge eating, purging and compulsive behaviors, vomiting, laxative misuse, fear or discomfort around certain smells, taste, colors, and textures, consuming non-edible things, or being fixated on consuming only "healthy" or "clean" food. These disruptions of our regular eating patterns can often lead to a clinical eating disorder.

What I didn't realize when I was growing up—but what I now know is true—is that as a young woman, I was teetering on the precipice of a full-blown eating disorder.

While eating disorder awareness and treatment has been amplified in white communities—particularly among cisgendered able-bodied white women—practitioners, scholars, and researchers estimate that Black communities experience higher rates of eating disorders and disordered eating than the overall population. Most treatment of eating disorders in Black and other communities of color either lacks research and/or is underfunded, though there has been some recent research devoted to studying these communities.

Although the research is still in its early stages, here are some facts I can share with you: A 2011 study showed that Black teenagers are 50 percent more likely to exhibit bulimic behavior than white teenagers. Another study in 2000 found that recurrent binge eating is more common among Black women than white women. And a 2003 study discovered that Black people are less likely to be asked by a doctor about eating disorder symptoms when self-reporting eating/weight concerns. Only 17 percent of clinicians identified Black women's eating behaviors as problematic. In contrast, 44 percent of clinicians identified white women's eating behavior as problematic, and 41 percent identified problematic eating behaviors in Hispanic women.

Compared with white women, Black women and femmes tend to experience a disproportionate amount of trauma, violence, marginalization, discrimination, and adverse childhood experiences, compounded by misogynoir and racism—all of which can amplify eating disorder symptoms by increasing imbalanced eating behaviors and stress. We also know that social factors can create disparities in our relationship to food, things like: a lack of access to affordable and diverse food options based on our zip code; lack of access to clean water; stress; lack of sleep; socioeconomic status; illness; a family history of food scarcity; or a lack of affirming body movement options. These kinds of personal experiences have a *direct* correlation to the development of eating disorders in Black communities.

Clearly, there is some real unpacking to be done here—and the stakes couldn't be higher. Black communities are suffering under the weight of eating disorders at disproportionate rates. It's a public health crisis no one is talking about—a silent threat endangering our communities, body by body.

WHAT EATING DISORDERS LOOK LIKE FOR US

Throughout this book you will see me use the terms "eating imbalance" and "imbalanced eating" to describe the eating challenges in our community, in place of "eating disorder." When we view other diagnostic conditions such as anxiety and depression, we say that they cause imbalances in the brain and that with the support of medications or homeopathic remedies those suffering from these disorders are able to create more balance. Why do we not describe eating issues this way? "Disorder" concludes that something is out of order, and often places blame on the individual as a result. In the context of eating, this implies that there are some who are just not equipped to nourish themselves, or who don't know how to be in relationship with their body.

Instead, I view these issues more holistically. In many Indigenous practices, illness and disease are not described as being disordered, but rather in disharmony with the body, and healers look at a variety of influences that cause or contribute to that disharmony. It is not that our eating is disordered, it's that our relationship to our bodies and how we have come to nourish ourselves has become fragmented and created imbalance within us. This fragmentation did not just happen spontaneously—it is a direct result of the colonizing, supremacist culture that we live in, the same one that has wreaked havoc on marginalized communities for centuries. A part of healing our relationship with eating, then, is restoring the balance within us, which is a process that must take into account not only our history, but our relationship to the land, animals, and plants and to the cyclical nature of being nourished completely.

When we are out of balance, we tend to reach for familiar coping strategies and adaptive responses even when they are harmful to us. My fear is that, until we are liberated from the societal disparities that plague our communities, we will likely continue down this perpetually destructive path. Reframing the conversation in ways that validate the history and lived experiences of those who struggle with eating imbalances is one way to shift the paradigm and redefine these challenges on our own terms. And so, you will see that effort to shift and reframe on display in these pages through the use of this alternative language.

When it comes to eating imbalances and Black communities, many doctors either don't recognize the symptoms or discriminate in their treatment of them. Far too often we're not represented when clinical studies on the subject are being conducted. There are also those in the medical profession who attach a stigma to size and weight or make certain assumptions about Black beauty ideals. All of this can lead our communities to distrust the health care system.

In fact, we often enlist support only after our symptoms are extremely impacting our ability to function in society. In my own professional experience, prior to my practical field studies through academia, I never thought to look at my own relationship with food and eating through a diagnostic lens. All of my coursework included examples of thin white women. It wasn't until I started working with clients that I began to see more representation of eating imbalances in communities that were not white. It was only then that I started unpacking and investigating how the symptoms showed up in my own body and within my community.

In the work I've done as a mental health therapist over the last nine years, I have observed that eating imbalances show up differently in Black communities. Societal oppression has deeply impacted our ability to truly be in our bodies. The pressure put upon both Black women and femmes in particular to conform to certain beauty and desirability standards has had an undeniable influence on how we've learned to exist and survive. We've significantly internalized beliefs about ourselves that are oppressive, then passed down those same beliefs within our own families and communities— generation after generation.

But because as a community many of us do not know enough about eating imbalances, did not grow up discussing them, and have been disconnected from even talking about our bodies reflectively, we have never become accustomed to using language to articulate what we are experiencing, let alone to make the connection that these experiences are intrinsically interwoven with modern-day, body-based oppression. We have not yet fully reckoned with a history designed to demonize the Black body—its size, shape, color; the foods we eat; and how we stay healthy. Taking all of these factors into account, more attention must be paid as to why Black people are showing up with eating imbalances more and more often in our communities.

Even the word "disorder" implies stigma, and comes from a Western mental health care system that has historically excluded and harmed Black people. This, in part, explains why we don't often talk publicly about our experiences. Why share your hurts, vulnerabilities, and concerns with a system that has largely proven to harm you? Instead, our traumas have been normalized within our communities. They silently feed into larger patterns of behavior that can very often lead to imbalanced eating behaviors as a means to cope.

For far too many Black Americans, our relationships with our bodies have become conflicted. Our ancestors endured physical beatings, emotional torture, and spiritual demonizing and erasure. Many were forced to disconnect from their bodies and put on a cloak of "strength" to persevere through harsh and inhumane experiences. There was silence around their suffering, and they were forced to mentally escape their own bodies in order to survive. Today, our bodies hold on to the ways our ancestors learned to endure trauma. What we do not consciously remember or address from the past is stored in the body and begins to reveal itself to us through the body over time.

There are multiple ways our ancestral survival strategies manifest within the bodies of Black people in the present day, most notably as emotions of unprocessed grief, rage, and internalized shame. In Black communities, we are encouraged not to talk about difficult things and to sweep issues that happen in the family and community under the rug—which often leaves individuals isolated in the immensity of the trauma.

We know, however, that this pattern did not just organically appear in Black communities. It is a symptom of our collective trauma experience, one side of our collective story. It is the legacy of enslavement that tore families apart, separating us from land and food and leaving many of us helpless, depressed, hopeless, and without a place to call home. It is the colonization that exploited, erased, and enacted multilayered genocide onto us. It is capitalism that made men, women, kindred, and children the property of a vile transatlantic slave system. The Zulu word Ubuntu means "I am because we are." It is the idea that we are all connected, and that our individual experiences offer a collective story, both past, present, and future.

As a people, we have spent more than five hundred years internalizing the trauma that we've experienced, largely without any help or support. As a result, it has begun to show up in our bodies. Our behaviors are a direct response to being ripped away from our loved ones and divorced from our culture and personhood. Because of this violent disruption, we often do not recognize our own nonverbal cues—the hums, the grunts, the vibrations our body uses to express our feelings. Cultural systems of oppression—white supremacy, colonialism, capitalism—only contribute to our feelings of disconnection, amplifying the separation we experience with one another and the fragmentation we may be experiencing within ourselves.

WHY I DO THIS WORK

I never could have predicted that my experiences as a young girl would lead to a career path that is my life's passion: helping women and non–male identified folks come back home to their bodies so they can experience true healing and liberation. But my journey from mental health therapist to somatic healer, author, and culture shifter has been a long and winding road that started with learning theory, research, and treatment modalities created by old white men. Many of the Westernized teachings of these pioneers upheld racist, sexist beliefs that informed their approach to psychology and diagnosis. To become a therapist, I found that I had to assimilate to this narrow, whitewashed way of understanding and working in the mental health field.

For years I showed up in relationship with my clients and in my mostly white workplaces with this skewed, white-centered orientation. Because my training program did not offer a holistic view, my tools were limited. Even with my intrinsically strong social justice values, and bringing in my own marginalized experiences, I practiced traditional colonized therapy with my clients at the beginning of my career because at the time, that was the only training I'd received.

However, as the mental health field continued to grow, I became exposed to learning opportunities such as the Black Mental Health Symposium, Decolonizing Therapy with Dr. Jennifer Mullan, and Decolonizing Therapy for Black Folk by Dr. Shawna Murray-Browne, which supported the holistic approach I was seeking. As I learned more about non-Western healing, I began to see myself and my community in the work. It expanded my mind and, as time went on, I began to question and unlearn the ways I was taught to show up, conceptualize, and understand mental health conditions. I started to de-pathologize what I had learned in the past by moving away from the medical model that labels people as problems.

Instead, I began to take on a more humanistic approach that considered the ways that systems designed through hate contribute to the oppressive conditions that were manifesting in our minds, bodies, and spirits. I began to push back on existing diagnostic language and adopt a comprehensive and holistic picture of what I was contending with. At the same time, I began the process of discovering how to return to my own body and establishing safety.

This led me to do a deep dive into ancestral practices and initiations, and Indigenous healing wisdom of the African diaspora. It also prompted me to explore my identity within those ancient intelligent systems. I went through a process of completely rejecting Western teaching and began to learn from Black, Indigenous, Asian, Brown, and dual-heritage elders and teachers and from communities native to the global south. As time has gone on, I have taken a more integrative approach, blending what I gained in my Western education with what was waiting to be remembered by returning back to indigenous and ancestral wisdom and science. This well-rounded approach to mental health has allowed me to see true healing in myself and in my clients that I did not initially experience when working solely with Westernized education.

In this process I have redefined myself not just as a mental health therapist, but as a healer, a title that I feel encompasses a more expansive definition of my understanding of mental and holistic health. By weaving together Western, Indigenous, ancestral, cultural, spiritual, systemic, historical, energetical, somatic, and embodied stories of how we exist and relate to our bodies, I was able to birth my business BlackandEmbodied, which is grounded in the essence of healing and reclaiming wholeness.

While in graduate school for clinical mental health therapy, I had the opportunity to work individually and with groups of people of all backgrounds, shapes, sizes, races, and ethnicities. And I began to see some common themes emerge. A lot of my Black clients were coming to therapy without having eaten that day, due in part, I observed, to a deep-rooted belief that they did not deserve to be nourished. Many of my clients either had inconsistent access to food or expressed discomfort in their relationship with food. A number of them also discussed how difficult it was to talk about and actually be in their bodies.

Upon further exploration, I found that many of the women I counseled were exhibiting some of the symptoms typically associated with disordered eating, such as restrictions, binges, purges, being labeled as "picky eaters," laxative misuse, and rigid fitness regimens. They would often say, "Oh, that's just the way I eat," and shrug it off. When I began to discuss eating imbalances or body image concerns with them, it usually elicited responses ranging from complete silence and shutting down in their body language to expressing that they felt overwhelmed and hurrying to change the subject.

As I grew in my practice as a mind-body-spiritual healer and mental health therapist, and expanded my lens on how I could approach the work more inclusively, I knew I had to create more safety within my therapeutic relationship with clients. I began to mirror for them what it looks like to show up during sessions in fullness, simply by the way I held space. On an emotional level, I did not approach our sessions as if I were the expert of their lived experience. Instead, I let them know that I valued what they had to offer, and that my role was to hold safe and affirming space, facilitate growth, and guide them into healing with the wisdom they already held within their bodies. I listened and approached each person as an individual rather than grouping people's experiences together or making assumptions. I got comfortable with being imperfect, and offered co-creative statements like "Let's explore that together," instead of pretending that I had all the right answers.

Showing up fully also looked like wearing my natural hair and minimal or no makeup, holding space for levity, and using African American Vernacular English (AAVE) and other cultural references that resonated with many of my clients, while professionally connecting over shared experiences of existing in our Black bodies. I let them know that all parts of them were welcome in the session and they did not need to compartmentalize themselves or perform for my acceptance, and I mirrored this in my behavior as well. I encouraged them to be present in their bodies so that we could get into the deeper work of healing.

Once they felt safer and developed the skills to be sensitive to their emotions a bit more, they began to talk about body image and how some of their eating patterns stemmed from negative beliefs they'd inherited and experienced from a white-dominant culture that taught them to be at war with their bodies. At the end of our sessions, many shared that it was their first time opening up to someone or even talking about their bodies in this way.

As these clients began to share their stories, their emotional responses ranged from sadness, shame, numbness, and anger to perfectionism, fear of rejection, self-doubt, self-neglect, and un-processed grief. They described feeling hopeless and overwhelmed within their bodies without having any means of understanding where those feelings started or what to do with them. They did not trust themselves or their intuition—their inner guidance—and they had poor boundaries. In short, they had fallen out of touch with themselves.

The women and femme-identified clients I continued to meet with talked about the inner and outer conflicts they felt, particularly around sexuality. They felt constantly sexually objectified while also simultaneously uncomfortable with the idea of taking agency over their own sexuality and sensuality for fear of being shamed, judged, or harmed. They talked about their bodies being viewed as offensive or disruptive, of being othered in society, particularly if they were in a larger or fat body. They talked about existing in a world where they experienced invisibility and erasure as Black women and femmes, about being the only Black person in their workspaces, or about being passed over for opportunities and promotions despite having the experience in comparison to white peers with less experience.

They also talked about feeling both hyper-visible in and scrutinized by society, as if everything they were doing was being monitored and policed by some invisible force that dictated how they could move and exist in their bodies. For example, if a Black person did something negative, they felt they had to bear the blow-back of being lumped in together with that person. They believed they had to always be on guard and perfect, and how even that was never enough. They described the mental and emotional gymnastics of trying to assert themselves, set boundaries, and use their voice, while also not wanting to be labeled as aggressive, hard to work with, or uppity for fear of losing their livelihood.

I saw myself in these women and femmes and found myself offering help with more intentionality to make sure that they felt supported in their treatment. For so many, the topic of eating or body image was new terrain. They were so accustomed to others talking about eating or body image through the lens of dieting or body shaming and were shocked that I did not do the same. The way I showed up without judgment, offering a new, compassionate perspective was a part of the work of creating safety. I wanted to offer their bodies a safe environment to feel and process their trauma responses so that they could be felt and released. I became intentional about making space for them to describe the layers of body trauma they had experienced. I wanted them to know that I viewed them in the fullness and multidimensionality of who they are.

These clients were dealing with a host of intersectional issues—daily microaggressions, misogynoir, racism, family trauma, financial strain, and/or gender-based violence—often with little to no support. Many described feelings like it was all too much, and admitted that they were constantly overwhelmed, burned out, or barely just getting by day to day. The impact of stress and trauma from all they had experienced had begun to manifest physically in their bodies as inflammation, illness, autoimmune issues, hypertension, blood sugar issues, chronic health conditions, gut issues, skin issues, stress, hair loss, chronic fatigue, sleep issues, and inconsistent eating patterns.

In the Black community there is a saying: "Don't look like what you've been through." These clients had internalized that saying to their own detriment. They wore the Strong Black Woman persona in their social circles as leaders, caregivers, and confidantes, and outwardly exuded the energy of Black Excellence and Black Girl Magic. And yet, once inside our safe space, many of them sat in tears, talking about the heaviness of having to be strong and keep everything together perfectly, or constantly having to show up for others but not receiving that in return. They also described the pressure they felt from their families, in their intimate relationships, and through cultural and social conditioning.

I often worried about leaving my Black clients at the institutions where they were being treated. Most providers who treat eating imbalances are white. The therapy groups in inpatient facilities and residential treatment centers are typically white as well. Even if there is a person of color in the environment, the structure and methods of treatment are often still drenched in white-dominated recovery models. It is estimated that 70 percent of doctors receive less than five hours of eating disorder–specific training in medical school. It's no surprise, then, that health care providers often lack cultural competence—or any awareness of how eating imbalances show up in Black bodies. Because of this, I often assisted my clients with navigating the medical system. I was concerned about the additional pressure they would experience having to advocate for themselves, and would sometimes step in when doctors attempted to patronize or dismiss the idea that their Black bodies could be affected by eating imbalances, too.

As a therapist, healer, culture shifter, and human being, I am passionate about highlighting the illness of eating imbalances within Black communities, because these conditions have the second highest mortality rate of any mental health issue following opioid addiction. Black people will not "recover" from eating imbalances in the same systems that oppress us. These environments, even with the best of intentions, only exacerbate our trauma and delay the healing process. While we currently have literature that addresses *Fearing the Black Body: The Racial Origins of Fat Phobia* by Sabrina Strings, and *Killing the Black Body: Race, Reproduction, and the Meaning of Liberty* by Dorothy E. Roberts, I feel it is now time to build on the important work already done and begin to reclaim the Black body.

Reclaiming the Black Body breaks the silence around how eating imbalances and negative body image are injected into Black communities by the white-dominant culture. For many people who struggle with these conditions, food is either "good" or "bad," "healthy" or "unhealthy," and we internalize this duality as a part of who we are as people. Rather than talking to someone who can help us find better ways to cope and heal, we have allowed this binary and stigmatizing approach to limit the way we nourish our bodies holistically. When we are too ashamed to talk about what is hurting us and how that impacts on our relationship with food, we begin to lean into learned behaviors and trauma responses that are familiar to us, even if they do not help us regulate ourselves and cope with difficulties.

My goal in writing this book, and in sharing my story and the stories of the courageous Black women, femmes, and non-men I have supported in healing along the way, is to call attention to the ways the lives of both individuals and entire communities have been disrupted by our imbalanced relationship with eating. I also want to deepen our understanding of eating imbalances and examine how they show up specifically in Black bodies so that we are better able to recognize the signs.

This book threads together the stories, leadership, and activism of so many people. It represents a tapestry of knowledge, showing what happens when a community comes together to make meaningful change and collectively creates something bigger than the sum of our parts. These pages represent a collection of voices and learnings that have shaped me into the person and practitioner I am today. The work does not, cannot, happen alone. You will note that at the beginning of each chapter, I've included a quote from the many sources and scholars I am inspired by, because I feel that the best way to amplify marginalized voices is to center them.

The long-held cultural messages that tell us "What happens in the house stays in the house" or "Push it under the rug and move on" has never served us well. Eating imbalances are expressions of the harm we have endured in North America and continue to internalize, even when we can't exactly pinpoint what's wrong. It is my hope that this book serves as a much-needed balm by offering suggestions for a pathway to restoration and healing within our bodies—a way back to ourselves.

WHAT TO EXPECT ALONG
THIS JOURNEY

A S YOU READ EACH chapter, you may discover descriptions and examples of trauma that resonate with you. Oftentimes the trauma is a seed that has been planted that tells us that we are not good enough, or that our bodies are inherently "bad." In these moments, I encourage you to offer yourselves grace and compassion as you unpack what you may find to be difficult experiences. Through this work, we can begin to get to the root of this pain. We can learn to understand and acknowledge the seeds that have grown to consume our bodies in Black communities: white supremacy, capitalism, colonialism, fatphobia, and so much more. Together, we can work to uproot these seeds that do not serve us and begin to plant new ones that are more in alignment with our true selves.

Safety, dignity, belonging, and autonomy can live in our bodies when we create a healing environment by listening to our nervous system—the system that connects our brain and body. Regulating our nervous system is not just about being calm; it is about being able to connect to the body in the present moment so that it can carry out the processes that help our body to thrive.

Healing as part of a village and with others helps us remember and reclaim a sense of interconnectedness, hope, and possibility, which are essential to healing. Throughout the book, you will learn how to reconnect with your body, how to stay attuned to what it is communicating, and how to respond with compassion, grace, and love to cultivate the fertile ground for coming back home to your body. You will learn how to reframe and transform internalized, self-limiting beliefs and behaviors by reclaiming healing modalities grounded in our culture and ancestral practices. And you will come to understand that liberating our bodies is not only revolutionary, but also frees up more of our energy so that we can feel whole within ourselves.

In an ideal world, we would show up each day with more presence and an awareness of our triggers. We'd be more connected to ourselves and one another. When we continue to carry within our bodies the trauma of systems that have told us we have to accept things the way they are, it affects our emotional, physical, and spiritual selves. We ignore our issues altogether, or put bandages on wounds that require proper nurturing and healing. We must either choose to empower ourselves, or acquiesce and become stuck in the circumstances of oppression.

Some folks may be unfamiliar with taking a deeper look at the subjects we'll be discussing in these pages: fatphobia, healthism, weight stigma, anti-fat bias, critiques of fitness and exercise spaces. You may immediately ask, Are you trying to tell us not to focus on our health? Are you saying that working out means we are engaging in white supremacy? To that I say, No, not at all!

If working out or eating a certain way is life-affirming for you and your body, then I am in total support of it. I believe the bigger issue is that we live in a culture that doesn't give us a choice, that skews data and science in favor of capitalism and cultural oppression. My goal is to support as many people as possible by examining these systems with a critical eye. Only then can we make choices that align with our core values and have access to possibility. As long as those choices and possibilities are not coming at the expense of someone else's access and liberation, by all means—continue to do what feels right for you.

A few more notes before we begin: Within my body, I hold identities that have been both marginalized and privileged by society. This book is written from the lens of a Black cisgendered woman. While I am healing from an autoimmune condition, I am physically able-bodied, I have an advanced academic degree, and I am currently in a body that has been privileged due to my size. Throughout the book I will use the terms "women" and "femmes"; however, the purpose of this book is to center the experiences of non-men and those who have been oppressed by misogyny and misogynoir while existing in this patriarchal society. I also recognize that femmes may not identify with gendered pronouns. I want to name and honor that while also sharing that I will use "she"/"her" pronouns when speaking about my experience, and the preferred pronouns given to me by folks mentioned in this book. This is not to exclude femmes from the conversation; I ask for grace, as this book is intended to uplift the vast experiences of non-male-identified folks.

When discussing "white supremacy culture" or "whiteness," I am not solely referring to white people. I am simply acknowledging that race is a social construct, meaning that it is a human-invented classification system. It was developed as a way to define physical differences between people, but has more often been used as a tool of oppression and violence. Race was invented to place people associated with whiteness at the top and people associated with Blackness at the bottom. It arrived as a collaborative consensus among people who held power at the time of its invention, but it is not based in science.

Isabel Wilkerson, author of *Caste: The Origins of Our Discontents*, puts the idea this way, placing "race" at the center of a powerful sociopolitical contract: "A racial caste system is the ranking of human value that sets the presumed supremacy of one group against the presumed inferiority of other groups." She provides a global view of the ways in which caste has shaped this country and a complex argument for the ways in which Blackness and whiteness have been artificially constructed, arguing that our bodies signal "traits that would be neutral in the abstract but are ascribed life-and-death meaning in a hierarchy favoring the dominant caste whose forebears designed it. Race is what we can see, the physical traits that have been given arbitrary meaning and become shorthand for who a person is. Caste is the powerful infrastructure that holds each group in its place."

Some people may say, Well, why don't we just stop identifying with racial categories? And while I wish it were that simple, race isn't something we can learn or think our way out of, or simply remove; it is a generations-old practice that has biopsychological symptoms for all who have been conditioned into it. While it may be a human design, it has had serious cultural, generational, psychological, biological, and environmental impacts. Author and somatic abolitionist Resmaa Menakem adds an additional layer of depth to this concept. He says, "The race question is a species conversation first because it was a debate as to whether Black people were even a part of the human species, and then they took that conversation and grafted it onto pigmentation through pigmentocracy."

Menakem believes that as a culture we have to abolish the idea that white body supremacy is standard. The whole historical, ancestral, generational, social, and genetic practice of race that exists is hinged on its association with white bodies—white bodies that are superior to Black bodies; white bodies that are more intelligent, more desirable, more naturally equipped to succeed than Black bodies.

The concept of race falls apart when white bodies are separated from the equation. What needs to be "fixed" are not the bodies of Black and Indigenous folks and People of Color but the disease that lives within the white bodies that then manifests itself as

trauma in others. We have experienced five hundred years of embodied emotional charge. When it comes to race, that emotional
charge travels through our bodies the moment we begin to open
up the conversation. In order to correct this, we must first scruti-
nize its effects from a body-based level.

I am very intentional about not moralizing health. It is my belief
that you are not more valuable as a human being because you are
healthier or less valuable because you are unhealthier; however,
our overall society does not view health this way and creates binary
categories around health and wellness. Quite frankly, the way we
define health in our society is outdated, limiting, and rooted in
discrimination against people who are disabled, fat, non-white, and
lower-income. I say this while seeking to offer truths about the
origins of how disease and illness show up in our bodies and to
describe the impacts that living in a racialized system has had on
our bodies.

When addressing disability, I do not view it in a rigid and binary
way, nor do I define it through what is "normal" vs. "abnormal," as
I recognize that ability and disability are transient social identities
and experiences and that, at some point, many of us will live with
some form of disability, illness, or disease. Much of society centers
and rewards people who are non-disabled, particularly those who
are outwardly so. We have been taught to ignore that experiencing
disability is also an internal experience, particularly for those with
chronic, acute, and mental health conditions. We live in a society
that constantly works to "fix" those who are disabled, and to ask
them to conform to productivity and functionality ideals based in
white supremacy culture and capitalism.

When discussing fatphobia, know that I have been intentional
about centering and uplifting the voices of larger-bodied and fat
Black people whose lived experiences of fatphobia and discrimination have been mostly marginalized. They have been gracious
enough to offer their wisdom through interviews and consultations
for this book. I will acknowledge them and recommend that read-

ers engage with their work and learn directly from their lived experiences as well.

I also do not use the word "fat" to label someone else's body without their consent. Some see it as derogatory, while others see it as a word to reclaim from the dominant culture that has used this word to oppress and victimize larger-bodied people. While everyone has their own comfort level with this word, it may be emotionally activating for some, and I want to be mindful of that. I do not speak for all Black women and femmes; I am the expert of *my* experience and bound to make mistakes when discussing others'. While you will see a lot of me in this book, I will also speak from my work as a mental health therapist who specializes in healing eating imbalances in Black communities. It is rare for someone to bring this specific lens into this work, and I feel blessed to be a steward of this path.

Throughout this book I will discuss culture and systemic issues that impact our ability to fully be in our bodies. When I think about this, I view it as a toxic pond that we are all swimming in. Some of us are better able than others to recognize and deconstruct the way that the systems show up in our lives; however, my goal is to help us recognize that we are *all* wading around in contaminated waters, so that we can begin the process of relocation away from this poisonous environment. We can work together, collectively, to treat the spaces where we are living and breathing. What sets this book apart from other mainstream conversations on eating imbalances is that I recognize the way that trauma has physically, spiritually, energetically, collectively, and systemically shown up in our bodies. Even if all of the systems of oppression were dismantled or abolished tomorrow, we would still have a lot of internal work to do.

Western mental health defines the disruption that we have with food and our bodies as a clinical eating "disorder." My goal is to de-pathologize and decolonize the way we speak about issues we face within our communities. I do not view our eating and body relationships solely through the lens of Western mental health, which tends to individualize the issues and place people into diagnostic categories. I view the disruption that we have with food and the fragmentation that we experience in our body as a result of living in an oppressive racialized society that operates under colonialism and capitalism.

Throughout this book I address the current impacts of those systems on our Black bodies. And while I may sometimes use the terms "eating disorder" or "disordered eating," it is only to unpack and deconstruct what we have experienced through the shared language that is available to us at this time. I implore us and challenge myself to investigate new, expansive, and liberating ways that we can describe our eating patterns and relationships to our bodies.

I will also refer to terms such as spirit or spirituality; they are not to be conflated with Westernized religion. When I refer to "spirit" I am referring to the animating essence within all living things, and when I am referencing spirituality I am approaching the conversation from an indigenous African perspective, which is a holistic concept that stemmed from the historical, cultural, and religious heritage of Africa and that includes folktales, beliefs, rituals, and culture, among other things. There may be a variety of feelings and sensations that come up with this terminology and orientation; all of those reactions hold their own validity. I do not expect for everyone to agree or align around this topic; however, I do want to clarify the orientation from which I am approaching my writing and therapeutic practice.

I will offer a variety of guided experiences and activities at the end of each chapter, so even if only one of them works for you, or if you come up with something that works for you on your own, that's perfectly fine. Not every tool throughout the book will work for everyone, because everybody is unique and needs different things. I invite you to put my suggestions into action at your own pace and capacity. If something doesn't work, there's no need to feel ashamed; instead, I hope you opt to approach an internal response like "This is not for me" with self-compassion.

Finally, I give myself full permission and grace to not know everything. As a human being, I am constantly in a state of evolving. My understanding of eating imbalances and the body is likely to deepen and expand as I move through life. A teacher of mine once shared that the work we do inside of ourselves requires us to be deeply embodied reflections of our values and healing, so that when those systems no longer have a hold on us, we are able to create something new. As a lifelong learner, I hope that this book is a manifestation of the work that I have embodied up until now. As I continue to evolve and gain access to more wisdom and insight, my work will shift alongside my learnings.

A FEW KEY TERMS AND CONCEPTS
TO SITUATE US

T HERE MAY BE TIMES along this journey that I utilize certain terminology that may be unfamiliar to you. I will always explain what I mean when I am using certain words, phrases, or expressions. Since I've already referred to a few of the terms that you will see me use frequently throughout the book, allow me to briefly define them.

EATING DISORDER VS. EATING IMBALANCE While I have personally begun to transition from the word "disorder" to the word "imbalance" when describing the complex relationship that we have with food, there will be places in the book where I intentionally use "disorder" to delineate periods during which I was still viewing eating through that lens, or to signify the field that still uses this word. Using "imbalance" is an expansion on the work and also a way to de-pathologize the connection that we have to eating.

COLONIZATION is the policy of a nation seeking to extend control or retain authority over Indigenous people or territories, generally with the aim of economic dominance. This dominance is obtained through force, manipulation, violence, and genocide, and its goal is to benefit from the colonized country or landmass. This totalitarian control fosters disruption of the native plants and animals that people eat, the land and villages they inhabit, the culture they embody, the spiritual systems they practice, the medicines they use, and the familial relationships, language, and stories that form the basis of their communities. In their place, colonizers impose their own religion, economics, worldviews, and medicinal practices on those being oppressed. Colonization occurred everywhere and impacted Black, Brown, and Indigenous communities throughout the world. However, in this book I will focus on the European influence on those Black people who are descendants of the African diaspora and whose ancestors experienced enslavement and/or colonization.

In order for colonization and enslavement (which is the act of reducing human beings to property and completely controlling their actions, thoughts, emotions, and/or lives) to thrive, it required the subjugation of Black bodies. The first step of colonization was to demonize and create fear around anyone who was non-white, while creating a hierarchy that placed those labeled as "white" at the top and those thought of as "Black" at the bottom. This hierarchy also enforced the belief that you had to assimilate into the dominant culture to survive, and that to do so, it was imperative to surpress your own cultural existence. This happened first in Europe, then spread to America and was carried out through the commodification of Black folks as slaves. According to John W. Ashe, the president of the United Nations General Assembly, "The Transatlantic slave trade . . . for 400 years deprived Africa of its lifeblood for centuries and transformed the world forever." This impact and the residue of colonization and enslavement still show up today as the foundation of our systems, institutions, cultures, and personal indoctrinations.

CAPITALISM is an economic and political system in which a country's trade and industry are controlled by private owners for profit, rather than by the state. As Tricia Hersey, the artist and theologian best known as the founder of The Nap Ministry, has written, "Capitalism was created on plantations; the roots of it are violence and theft."

TRAUMA is the response to a deeply distressing or disturbing event that overwhelms an individual's ability to cope, causes feelings of helplessness, and diminishes one's sense of self and ability to feel a full range of emotions. It lives in our cells, bones, postures, and muscles; it's in our emotional expressions, belief systems, and ancestral/cellular memory. Trauma is a preexisting condition to chronic illness and disease, because it attunes the nervous system to constantly be in a state of threat. This impacts our immune, digestive, and endocrine systems.

There are many forms of trauma. Throughout this book, we will focus on cultural trauma, which is trauma that we have inherited by existing within a culture founded on colonization, enslavement, and capitalism; historical trauma, which is multigenerational trauma experienced by a specific cultural, racial, or ethnic group; generational and ancestral trauma, which lives within our cellular memory and is passed on to us through our epigenetics; and racial trauma, which has been persistent since 1619 and is defined as stress related to racism. Racial trauma has been linked to hypertension, cardiovascular disease, diabetes, and infant mortality. From an African indigenous perspective, healing trauma is the process of becoming whole. It is the process of reclaiming and restoring our humanity.

THE NERVOUS SYSTEM includes the brain, spinal cord, and a complex network of nerves that help us identify if our body is in safety mode or threat mode. This system sends messages back and forth between the brain and the body. The brain is what controls all of the body's functions. The spinal cord runs from the brain down through the back.

EPIGENETICS, which is the study of genetics that are passed down from generation to generation, explores how our behaviors and environment can actually cause changes that affect the ways our genes work. There is research that has shown that the trauma our ancestors were subjected to has been epigenetically passed down. In other words, the ways we think, feel, and respond to our current environment is a reflection of the same trauma and survival patterns our ancestors experienced. Unlike genetic changes, epigenetic changes are reversible and do not alter your DNA sequence. However, epigenetic changes can be triggered by social determinants, such as age, race, response or sensitivity to pain, and socioeconomic status, which in return cause our bodies to respond differently based on how these factors are perceived in our environment. When we think about the legacy of colonialism, capitalism, and white supremacy on the Black body, there are direct links between how we show up inside ourselves presently and what we have inherited from those who came before us.

WHAT IT MEANS TO BE EMBODIED

The words "embodiment" and "disembodiment" will be especially important for you to understand as we travel down this road. Over the next few pages, we will explore why these two concepts are so essential to the work we will do together.

People in Western culture spend a lot of time focused on our physical being—our flesh, bones, muscles, and cells. But our ancestors believed that, long before we were born into our physical bodies, we existed as a soul and a spirit. Our souls are the part of us that exists into infinity. They hold the record and memory of every life journey we've ever been on since the beginning of time. I describe the spirit as our life force, the energy that is tied to a lineage we have inherited through our families, our ancestors, our wise or higher selves, and whoever we define as our higher power—whether that is God or some other divine essence.

In Western culture, both the soul and the spirit are treated as subconscious aspects of ourselves that we often explore only in faith-based practices, spiritual traditions, and religious systems. But those who came before us believed that true embodiment—or self-acceptance—requires us to acknowledge the connections between our physical body, our soul, and our spirit. Embodiment allows us to truly tap into the vastness of who we are and opens up more possibilities for healing.

Much of Western culture has cut itself off from the reality of the body-soul-spirit connection, because this recognition requires us to expand our perspectives outside of what is tangible and physically seen. We have been taught to fear and demonize the unknown and unfamiliar. In our Westernized, colonized society, it is not culturally acceptable to believe there is more to us than our physical presence on earth, that we could possibly exist in other spirit realms, or that it is possible to tap into different levels of consciousness beyond what we are experiencing in the present world.

This is just one example of what I like to refer to as our colonial conditioning: We are taught to accept a worldview that focuses solely on the individual. It is considered anathema to see ourselves connected to other worldly things such as plants, animals, universal elements and properties, and Mother Earth. This colonized point of view keeps us from reclaiming the indigenous one that is our birthright.

To break this down even further, let me share a few definitions found in the *Handbook of African American Psychology*, which compares European American–centered ideals to African-centered values. The European worldview focuses on individual achievement and a survival-of-the-fittest mentality. It emphasizes materialism, or the attainment of material goods. Controlling nature through science and development is revered, and objectivity is valued more than subjectivity.

An indigenous worldview like that of our ancestors, however, focuses on the collective. It is grounded in the belief that one cannot understand the individual if one doesn't understand the whole, the group, the tribe. The indigenous worldview emphasizes developing a spiritual connection with the Creator by finding harmony with nature. And in this belief system, the most important aspects of human existence are those things that are unseen, unobservable, and unquantifiable. To feel fully embodied, then, is to know that the physical cannot be separated from the soul and spirit. The body serves as the vessel that stores all of our physical sensations, emotions, thoughts, beliefs, desires, longings, behavioral patterns, and postures.

UNDERSTANDING OUR DISEMBODIMENT

As we've started to discuss, mainstream culture created a system where folks who have been historically and perpetually marginalized have had to take on patterns of disembodiment in order to survive trauma and systemic oppression. Silence and emotional suppression are the coping mechanisms Black folks have used for generations to address the trauma we've collectively experienced. We have been taught to downplay and discredit our emotional pain by saying "It wasn't so bad" or "Well, that person had it worse, and my pain wasn't as bad as theirs." Older generations may try to silence younger generations who are speaking out by saying "You think you have it bad—you don't know what I went through" or "What's the big deal—I had it worse and I got through it."

Many researchers and experts who study the mind-body connection have proposed that the legacy of white supremacy that has been passed down through many generations is ingrained so deeply in our lives that we don't even question it. These traumatic experiences will continue to be passed down until they find a body where they can be expressed. For many, the period we're currently in is the first time it has been okay to discuss and feel the weight of suppressed generational trauma. However, we still do not recognize how much it has infiltrated our culture, and how we may begin to unravel it.

We live in a society in which systems have both created and enforced the perfect conditions for disembodiment to grow, often
with devastating effects on Black people. Because we have become
desensitized to important cues within our bodies (facial expressions, sighs, bodily sensations) to describe what we are experiencing, our disembodiment continues. This adversely affects our
ability to comfortably exist in our bodies.

One of the more common examples of this involves suppression,
the instinct that we might have to push something down, forget
about it, and move on rather than allow ourselves to feel our emotions. Can you recall a time when something almost brought you to
tears or elicited an unexpected emotional response? Perhaps you
could have allowed yourself to let go, but something deep inside
you made you blink away the tears, swallow your emotions, and
shift uncomfortably in your body—or even completely change the
topic or run from the situation to get away from the discomfort of
the moment. This is a textbook example of disembodiment.

Far too many of us limit the expression of our emotions, especially those we've been taught to believe are bad, negative, or undesirable. Part of the reason for this response is rooted in our need
to feel safe through avoiding vulnerability, which we have been
taught makes us weak. The lack of safety we feel as Black people in
this society permeates every area of our lives, to the point where it
can be extremely difficult or uncomfortable to allow ourselves to
experience our authentic emotions, even when we are in an environment that is genuinely supportive of us.

We also have learned to repress the sensations our emotions
often activate within our bodies. How many times have we ignored
the signals our bodies send us that let us know that we've gone too
far or have had enough? Instead, we listen to the voice in our heads
that tells us to "keep pushing." When we make a conscious—or
subconscious—choice not to listen to our bodies, the resulting re-
pression can lead to injury and pain. Imagine the collective impact
of doing this for years and years. Now, imagine that behavior being

passed down from generation to generation, and it becomes easy to understand how, over time, we can adopt patterns of behavior that normalize our disembodied responses as "That's just the way it is." Meanwhile, our bodies continue to suffer under the weight of all that cannot be expressed.

Disembodiment can also lead us to develop a mentality that makes us feel like we are not enough, that we can never have enough, and that we can only exist in survival mode—a concept called "scarcity." Internalizing this belief system keeps us in a state of fear and helplessness. At its core, the scarcity mentality can be linked to our country's obsession with capitalism. Society's failure to distribute resources—namely money—in proportion to individuals' needs has created the social conditions for scarcity to exist. Only a few people at the top of the hierarchy, the one percenters, are able to thrive within these limited definitions of wealth, abundance, and prosperity.

In this man-made system, those who are at the bottom of the socioeconomic ladder will always have to fight to ensure that their basic needs are met, creating a culture where we either literally do not have enough to survive, or we *think* we don't have enough to survive, and are as a result constantly kicking down our neighbor to get ahead while telling ourselves that we will never have enough. Within these limited definitions, we have lost the village mentality, and are so deeply plugged into the system that we don't see the truths in front of us: that we *do* have enough—and that what we seek is already around and within us.

It's important to note that disembodiment isn't just about the things we don't allow ourselves to experience, or what we have inherited; it also affects our ability to discern what our bodies are communicating to us during times of distress. I've had many conversations with folks who may not verbally admit that they are experiencing some type of anxiety or intense feeling in response to distress, but who through nonverbal cues—such as how fast they speak, the inflection in their voice, the avoidance of eye contact, or the way their breath may get caught in their throat—enable me to detect what is really going on.

Sometimes when I am working with a client, I may notice my own heartbeat speed up, or my body temperature increase, or even feel a sensation of pressure in a specific part of my body. The connection can be so potent that I feel compelled to help the client to name what I am observing. I recognize this bodily response as one of my spiritual gifts and the way our nervous systems scan and operate as mirrors to one another. I may ask clients if they feel overwhelmed or share with them that I am noticing some pressure behind their words when they speak. Sometimes I notice that their breath seems to be shallow as they are talking about a certain topic.

Typically, I am spot-on in my assessment. Clients will usually pause and check in with themselves, eventually affirming that indeed they did feel overwhelmed, and that things may have been moving too fast for them. In these situations, I always invite the person I'm working with to slow down so that the emotion can be acknowledged and processed through their body, instead of being thwarted or becoming frozen with physical tension.

The work I have done to return back to my body has expanded my ability to pick up on what my clients are feeling. I'm able to recognize when an outside force or energy begins to pull me outside of my own bodily connection. In somatic therapy, which is a body-centered approach that examines the mind-body connection, we describe this process of reading and being impacted by another person's body as "co-regulation." African spiritual systems and quantum physics espouse the belief that because we are vibrational beings, it's only natural that we pick up on the vibes and energy of others. Did you know there are actually brain cells called "mirror neurons" that are designed to reflect back what we are experiencing when in the presence of others? When we are grounded, connected, and settled within our bodies, our feelings can be contagious. This is why it is nearly impossible to be in a room full of happy people and not be affected by their joy.

THE IMPACT OF PAST TRAUMA

When we fail to develop a keen awareness of what's going on in our bodies, it becomes that much harder to accurately read the cues our bodies are giving us. We may feel that something is off, but without the right tools we won't know how to process what we are feeling. We may even turn to past memories and interactions to help us interpret what we are experiencing. But if these past experiences and conditionings are centered in threats, fears, and oppression, we're more likely to draw erroneous conclusions about our current condition based on those old traumas.

This is how trauma keeps us stuck in the past, preventing us from understanding why we are responding and reacting to situations the way we do. When we begin the practice of listening to and learning from our body's language, we can begin to reprogram our responses from reactions based on past trauma to bodily responses that are more affirming. This is how we begin to shift our communities and culture.

True embodiment is, in part, liberation and healing. It is personal, cultural, energetic, and ancestral. It is being both in our physical bodies and in relationship with our bodies beyond our physical existence, while also recognizing that we are human beings with much to offer to ourselves, our communities, and the world.

Embodiment is about remembering and reclaiming parts of ourselves that have become fragmented through our trauma, so that we are able to break long-standing generational and cultural patterns and step into the salve—the wisdom—and inherit the gifts that are our birthright. Embodiment comes from finally dressing the wounds that show up through imbalance, chaos, and disorder with our eating. When we repair our relationship to nourishment, we create the conditions necessary to return to ourselves—while simultaneously allowing our inner healing and transformation to ripple into the collective. We deconstruct systems of oppression, while cultivating regenerative and balanced systems that affirm our wholeness and our right to exist, just as we are.

RECLAIMING
THE
BLACK BODY

· ONE ·

How Our Eating Became Imbalanced

"Eating disorders are a natural response to intergenerational wounds, gender violence, and racial trauma."

—GLORIA LUCAS, founder of Nalgona Positivity Pride

WHEN I THINK ABOUT how eating became imbalanced in my own family, I know that food scarcity—or our lack of access to food—deeply wounded us. Whenever my parents went grocery shopping to fill our pantry and refrigerator, my siblings and I were often scolded for how quickly we ate the food they bought because, as our parents told us, "Groceries are not cheap." I also grew up in a "clean your plate" household, meaning that during dinnertime we sat down, said our prayers of gratitude to God, and ate *all* of our food without complaining. If one of us did complain, or refused to eat what was being served, we were either punished or made to feel guilty with statements like "Children in X country are starving—you better eat that food." In this way, my siblings and I learned to ignore our bodies' desires, to dismiss our hunger and fullness cues. We learned that listening to our bodies could cause feelings of guilt or shame. As a child I did not know what to do with those emotions, I just knew they felt bad. Dinnertime with our family evoked feelings of anxiety and distress because the message was always "We don't have food to waste."

Looking back, I don't blame my parents for doing the best they could with the resources they had to support our family. They were only repeating the behaviors that were passed down to them from their parents, who in turn received them from their parents. Instead, I hold accountable the class disparities in this country, and how our capitalist system has made food and our ability to nourish ourselves a privilege rather than a human right. I grew up hearing stigmatizing and false messages about Black people receiving "handouts" from the government for food stamps. Even though at times we were qualified to receive them, my parents refused to accept them—choosing instead to work multiple jobs and put in extra hours to ensure that our family had only just enough.

I later learned that we were always riding the line between being too privileged for government assistance and too poor to actually afford the things my parents needed to support a family of five. We were struggling, but that struggle was preferable to the shame they felt for needing help in a system that had left us disadvantaged.

I carried the lessons of this upbringing with me into adulthood. In my early twenties, I would intentionally eat less because, even during periods when I was making enough money to afford a variety of foods to support my body's needs, I had learned to internalize the scarcity wound my family had experienced. I held the vestiges of my childhood within my body—I made a habit of rationing my meals because I believed that there might not be enough for me to eat, that I could not afford to eat more, even when I was in the financial position to do so.

Years later, as I began to delve deeper into my work with eating imbalances, I decided to take a closer look at my personal history with the hope of gaining a greater understanding of how *my* eating became imbalanced. Reflecting on the past, I began to realize that my Westernized Christian upbringing had a huge lasting influence on my thoughts around my body and food. As a young girl, I was raised to believe the creation story of Adam and Eve. Eve decides to eat an apple from the tree of forbidden fruit and, as the Bible story tells us, her lack of willpower and her human capacity to be deceived causes her to become disconnected from God. After consuming the forbidden fruit, Eve becomes ashamed of her body and is labeled as disobedient to God. I now realize that this famous story—one that many of us grew up hearing—is also a prime example of an imbalanced relationship with food and nourishment.

The story of Adam and Eve was a cornerstone of my conditioning around resisting "temptation," which included anything that could be deemed desirable: cravings, "guilty" pleasures, foods considered to be indulgences. Both the literal and figurative rigidity around the creation story began to fuel my eating patterns. I internalized the idea that the worst sin I could commit would be to fall into temptation around food I'd come to view as "forbidden." It was important to me that I force my body into obedience by controlling the way I ate. I followed what mainstream society told me was "healthy" and "unhealthy" to eat, and what diet culture said was the right or wrong amount of calories to ingest each day, or the specific kinds of foods I should be focusing on—eating only fruits, or vegetables, or proteins. By the standards of white-dominated culture, my Black body, with all its curves, was a disruption to the status quo. And so to conform, I followed the food rules that had been fed to me.

Although the story of Adam and Eve played a part in my childhood understanding of food regulation, as an adult who studied eating imbalances in graduate school and worked in the field with Black clients, I began to feel in my gut that the real origins of our community's eating challenges went much deeper. When I began my training as a therapist, I slowly came to realize that the mental health care system we're operating under—Westernized, white-centric, woefully bereft of diverse representation—was teaching me to pigeonhole eating disorders into rigid categories: anorexia nervosa, orthorexia, bulimia nervosa, binge-eating disorder, and more.

I found that this way of learning did not represent the experiences of diverse bodies, because the people I was working with did not fit neatly into those boxes. So I began to question my formal learning. My lived experiences, my evolution over the previous two years from the limiting title of "therapist" to the more expansive role of holistic embodied healer, and many ancestral rites of passage that I underwent all helped me understand that there are many levels to this biopsychosocial-spiritual illness—infinitely more than what we're taught in the classrooms of academia. I felt compelled to understand more about how our society's obsession with thin ideals, fatphobia, dieting, and the moralization of health have influenced the way Black communities think about eating imbalances.

As I began the journey of tracing back the roots of eating imbalances in our communities, I wanted to get to the core of how the condition was birthed into the human experience. I reached out to my ancestral healer and friend Ash Johns to seek guidance around how to go deeper. Ash encouraged me to engage in the process of discovery through ceremony and ritual, to spend some alone time meditating deeply on my family history and ancestral lineages' relationship with food. I soon realized that the pathway to understanding required me to address and come into relationship with feelings I had become used to avoiding and rejecting.

In Internal Family Systems therapy and Jungian therapy, there is a belief that to become whole as a human being, we must create a safe space to integrate the rejected, exiled, and shadow parts of ourselves—aka the parts of ourselves around which we experience shame. The eating patterns I had developed early in my youth had not only become my "personal shadow" (the unconscious aspects of our personality that drive behaviors we deem as negative or shameful), but also were part of a larger shadow that had been cast—and is still cast—on our ancestral and collective culture. In short, the shame that we feel has been passed down; those negative messages we've internalized over the generations impacts us globally, and on an ancestral level as well.

After years of deep diving, I now see more fully the way in which the legacy of ancestral trauma affected how Black women, including those in my family, felt about their bodies. Controlling the way we ate helped us to survive and adapt to a society committed to our annihilation. It forced us to accept the lack of freedom foisted upon us and the not-enoughness we were taught to believe about ourselves. The white supremacist patriarchal capitalist system had taught us that being in control was the only way to feel powerful. We never understood what it means to have a loving relationship with our bodies. We didn't know how to listen to our intuition, nor did we learn how to receive and use the ancestral medicines, gifts, and blessings that are our birthright. Instead, many of us found an outlet for our lack of freedom in patterns of imbalanced eating and in disconnection from our bodies.

WHEN FOOD IS CAST AS THE ENEMY

We know that food is a necessary source of nourishment and survival for all beings. From an evolutionary perspective, the relationship humans have had with food used to be rooted in animism, meaning that there was a collective orientation and understanding that animals, humans, and all living beings have a spirit, a soul, and a life force that show up in many different physical forms. No formation was considered insignificant. We had a consensual relationship to the earth, understanding that the process of eating and consuming food was a part of the reciprocity of the life cycle. We consumed nutrients from the earth to survive and the earth received us back when we left our physical bodies and returned to the spirit realm. Our reverence for an interconnectedness with all beings showed up through the intentionality we gave to planting and harvesting crops and through our sacred relationship to hunting and gathering as we offered blessings to the spirit of the animal for the sacrifice it made.

The energy of love that flowed through the process of preparing the food extended to the prayers of gratitude for the hands that prepared it, the earth that sustained it, and the Creator who provided it. We gave thanks for the natural elements of water, earth, air, and fire that allowed our food to be transformed to offer nourishment. Eating and food were threads bringing people together in a ritual that sustained us and connected us all through our shared experience of living and existing.

But nowadays, we often consume things without knowing the story of how they arrived on our plates. Our once harmonious relationship with eating, food, and our shared "beingness" became imbalanced through our natural, human response to food scarcity. This scarcity moved us out of a consensual relationship with the earth, and into one driven by overproduction—a by-product of colonialism and capitalism that exploits the land and its resources through forceful and violent methods and that eventually leads to ecocide.

This rupture in our relationship with the earth has had devastating consequences. Using the land as it originally existed is no longer sustainable. We do not nurture the earth in a way that encourages regeneration. Absent of that vital reverence for the interconnectedness of all beings, many of us no longer regard food as a *gift* of nourishment—and instead too often come to view it as a tool used to suppress and oppress. Food, in many ways, has falsely become the enemy. Only the process of accountability and repair can restore our collective relationship to nourishment and the land.

When we do not feel sheltered, nurtured, or sustained by Mother Earth through our food, our bodies can become uprooted and disrupted. It is what researcher and activist Sithandiwe Yeni describes as "a food crisis rooted in a vulnerable food system that has become socially, environmentally, and financially dysfunctional." Essentially, the decreasing number of small-scale farmers and the rise of industrial mass food production—which tends to rely on things like synthetic chemicals, pesticides, and genetic modification to create what we now consume—has altered our ecology in such a way that land that was once fruitful has become degraded, especially in poor communities.

I think it's important to note here that exploiting and overutilizing resources also means overworking marginalized people for a profit, while giving back only crumbs and calling it reparations—without any real investment back into our communities. This has always been a function of capitalism. Black farmland ownership, for example, peaked at 16 to 19 million acres in 1910. Today, it has decreased to less than 3 million acres, and Black farmers represent just over 1 percent of all U.S. farmers. What happened? Over time, Black farmers began to be forced off their own land as more "development" was brought to certain areas, raising costs and leaving Black folks with no option but to sell.

There's also the issue of heirs' property. The first generation of Black rural landowners had the ability to transfer ownership of their land to another family member after their death. But if the landowner died without a will or some other form of estate planning that would allow for the seamless transfer of ownership to another family member, that land became heirs' property. Without a will, the heirs of the deceased landowner had little way of proving the land was rightfully theirs, and no pathway for enlisting help from a biased white legal system. This issue led to many descendants of slave owners taking claim of land that did not technically belong to them in an effort to amass more wealth for them and their descendants.

Resolving land ownership can take years and cost thousands, and requires the help of a lawyer specializing in estate and heirs' property cases. Clearing a title requires tracing back the family tree, performing land surveys, and conducting exhaustive searches of many other documents. Organizations like the Federation of Southern Cooperatives work to fill that gap, but it can be an overwhelming undertaking. This is one more tool that has separated Black folks from the land and fragmented our relationship to growing our own food—changing, sometimes rapidly, our diets and how we're able to nourish ourselves.

At this point, some of you may be reading this and thinking, How does understanding past and present food ecology in this deeper, more expansive way relate to the way it shows up in our bodies, our families, and our communities? It all comes back to disconnection: how we became separated first from our homeland, then from the land we cultivated and harvested on the plantation, and yet again when our land was stolen and stripped from us after Emancipation. When there is limited access to food, and the land on which we rely for sustenance is controlled by massive industrial complexes that we do not own, it contributes to scarcity and deprivation.

The process of uncovering the seed of our eating imbalances is about moving away from the enmeshed relationship we have with its disordered energy—the energy that prevents us from receiving it with a sense of wholeness. Think of it like we are clearing out all the debris—layers and layers of it—that has been blocking our ability to create a pathway to return to ourselves. The goal of this process is to be able to have the freedom, the clear sight, to move back into alignment with the source of our nourishment.

WHY WE MUST ADDRESS OUR WOUNDS

Anything humans depend on for vitality has the potential to become imbalanced. In our complex relationship with food, we have pitted need and abundance against each other. Instead of seeing them both as necessary for our overall vitality, we demonize abundance. Yes, nourishment provides fuel for our bodies, but food also provides a pleasurable emotional connection that we all should enjoy.

When our eating is imbalanced, we cling to what external messages tell us our bodies need from us, instead of listening to our own instincts. We see these human expressions carried out through our cultural dynamics, and those dynamics begin to form systems. The two main systems that evolved from these cultural dynamics were colonialism and capitalism, which eventually birthed American chattel slavery, which enforced exploitation and overproduction.

The intention of these systems of domination was to eradicate our people—in mind, body, and soul—while also profiting from them. This capitalist structure is rooted in the energy of scarcity embodied in the colonizer.

The imbalance in eating behaviors that we are currently witnessing in our culture is a symptom of what I call "the original wound." This wound is an unaddressed trauma enforced upon our Black existence through colonialism, enslavement, and capitalism—as well as the roots of other socially oppressive systems like racism, patriarchy, and ableism that grew out of those systems. Imbalanced eating is a coping mechanism we've adapted in order to deal with this trauma. The wound is personal, cultural, and intergenerational—meaning that it has been passed down from our ancestors. It's also disruptive. It is *the* disturbance that interrupted our nourishing relationship with our bodies.

Think of it this way: When we have a wound on our bodies— from a scraped knee, a kitchen knife cut, or even a broken bone— that wound will never heal unless it is nurtured. Psychological wounds are even more complex to recover from. In order to heal them, we have to use a powerful salve that works on every single layer of disrepair. A Band-Aid won't do. There are stages to this kind of psychological recovery, yet mainstream society has told us not to heal, not to recover, but to just endure the pain.

The concept of psychological wounds has long been a part of the decolonized mental health space. Somatic abolitionist Karine Bell describes this type of wound as "the exposed crack or opening that threatens to expose the ways in which the environment contributes to the conditions for the trauma experience." Trauma is often described as a kind of stuck-ness related to an overwhelming experience that has happened to us. Bell encourages us to examine what it would take to heal from that trauma, to think about what might be holding us back from that healing, and to see what lessons can be gleaned from the trauma experience.

If we approach the wound from this perspective, then we know that whenever the symptom of the wound—i.e., imbalanced eating—is reactivated or triggered, it is also an opportunity to create a pathway back into the body. The wound calls out to us to pay attention, as it is the door into our healing, offering an opportunity to connect to our bodies the way we did before the disruption.

We live in a society, however, that thrives off our disembodied selves. Disembodiment does not allow us the necessary space to pause and listen, but rather reactivates our response to trauma with the familiar scripts we tell ourselves: "I shouldn't feel this way"; "I cannot trust what my body is telling me"; "I shouldn't listen to my body." This line of thinking encourages the behaviors we have inherited, rather than serving us in our present lives. The "disordered side" of our eating and food relationship uses our cultural and social conditioning, and our intergenerational wounds and trauma, to block out the inner knowing that calls us to slow down and listen to the wisdom of the wound.

In order to fully integrate this wisdom of the original wound, we must move beyond mainstream society's conventional, white-centric understanding of eating disorders, which barely scratches the surface, and beyond the limited diagnostic categories that are currently used in Westernized mental health practices. We must go deeper to discover the unseen energetic forces that are feeding the imbalance and to recognize the manifestations of that in our human experience. We must understand the origin of the roots to be able to move away from scarcity to a place of abundant connection in our relationship to food and to our bodies.

As I have expanded and deepened my own relationship with spirituality and energy, I have begun to see that energy can neither be created nor destroyed. Rather, I've learned that energy will fulfill itself, meaning that it will attract, replenish, and bring into completion experiences that are in alignment with its purpose. We can do the critical work of separating out the imbalance—the "shadow side"—in order to get to know it better, and then alchemize it. With honest self-reflection and deep therapeutic work, we can transform the imbalance and return it to its original state of abundance and regenerative nourishment.

Throughout this process, we must explore the ancestral parts of ourselves—the personal, intergenerational, and cultural energy from which the eating imbalance began to cast its shadow. We cannot change the past—the trauma that we have experienced on all of these levels has already occurred. But we can learn to metabolize and digest the trauma so that we can be more present in and connected to our lives now. The work that we are undertaking is a journey to integrate and embody the gifts, lessons, and wisdom of our bodies as we reclaim our relationship with food.

OUR PAST BECAME PROLOGUE

Along my personal journey, I have learned that my relationship with food began long before I was conceived in this body. It can be traced through all of my lineage to places throughout the continent of Africa and beyond, starting generations ago with the cultivation of rice in the land of my maternal lineage, now known as Sierra Leone, and continuing with the rich food practices of my paternal lineage in what is now known as Gabon. Many African Americans can trace back only three or four generations of our families, because records were not kept on our ancestors, or were destroyed or forgotten during migration. I am thankful for having been able to afford genetic testing, which resulted in the unearthing of some historical records that allowed me to retrace these steps, knowing that this is not an option for far too many of us. (One thing to note:

While Black people are indigenous to many continents throughout the globe, this book focuses mostly on the Black people whose ancestors were directly impacted by colonization in Africa and the transatlantic slave trade.)

My ancestors' relationship with food was disrupted by the treacherous voyage of the Middle Passage and transatlantic slave trade. Europeans took Africans from all over the continent and forced them into the bottom of ships. In these dark, confined spaces they could not sit up and were forced to lie near decaying corpses, feces, and other bodily fluids with no awareness of where they were going or if they would survive. While the horrid conditions made it impossible to properly digest food, the architects of slavery also disrupted our eating by providing the bare minimum of nutrition—nourishing our stolen African ancestors just enough so they could be sold as property to enslavers.

Many of those who were taken did not speak the same language or understand one another; however, they formed solidarity through nonverbal communication. Some Africans refused to eat, starving themselves as an act of resistance against oppression. The slavers even used a surgical instrument resembling a winged cork-screw, known as the speculum oris, to wrench open the locked jaws of those who shut their mouths against all sustenance, force-feeding them in order to not lose the money they'd invested.

The systems of colonialism and capitalism that birthed the enslavement of Africans in North America, and throughout the African diaspora, caused the disruption that disconnected Black communities from our motherland—and from the comfort and nourishment this land provided. Colonialism displaced African people from their families, from their indigenous land and languages (or mother tongues), from their worldviews, cultures, and tribal connections—and from their native foods. This disruption continues to fulfill itself today through the systems that oppress Black people.

While the intention of colonization and enslavement was to completely wipe out everything about our Blackness and being-ness, African people were persistent in resistance and in carrying forth our culture and spirit. There were remnants of our culture that were discreet and hidden in plain sight as our people fought to preserve themselves through dire circumstances. One example is the Kongo Cosmogram (Dikenga), a circular, cross-like symbol that was used by the BaKongo people as a sign of sacred prayer, depicting the four important phases of the eternal human life cycle based on the movement of the sun. The symbol represented the connection between the spiritual and physical worlds and was painted on praise houses designated for enslaved people who were not allowed to go to church with their white enslavers.

The Kongo Cosmogram was assumed to be the Christian cross, so to the uninitiated it appeared that the enslaved were practicing Christianity in their houses of worship. As white evangelical missionaries tried to convert our ancestors to Westernized Christianity, our people were able to use the Kongo Cosmogram and to continue to practice their indigenous spirituality, organizing and resisting oppression away from the white gaze, all the while masking it under the guise of Westernized Christianity. (I distinguish Westernized Christianity from Indigenous Christianity, the form of the religion that was practiced in Africa, particularly in Ethiopia, prior to colonization. It was not the same as the Roman-Catholic version that was brought to America and throughout the world by evangelical white missionaries.)

Many enslaved Africans were also crafty enough to bring over ingredients from the motherland, to carry forward a piece of what they were forced to leave behind into the new land. It has been documented that many Africans braided rice and seeds into their hair, and that after the Middle Passage they planted them in the new soil to represent the new roots that would grow from them. For African people and those of the diaspora, rice was the portal connecting their former homeland and life to the new life that would sprout from their survival. This food dynamic—this interplay between disruption and determination—represents both the light and the shadow sides of our eating patterns.

Land is often connected to nourishment, because it produces the food that we consume. Prior to enslavement, many of our African ancestors lived off the land and had a relationship with it in ways we'd now describe as in line with environmental justice and food sovereignty. But when pieces of Africa were stolen, arbitrary borders were formed, and lands were then renamed and reclassified by those who took part in the continent's colonization. The colonizers began to enforce a new relationship with the land, one based on exploitation and disconnection, which disrupted Black folks' relationship to it. The Middle Passage and transatlantic slave trade further drove this disconnection. And of course, it continued to deepen during three hundred–plus years of enslavement, after Emancipation during the Reconstruction period, and all the way through the Jim Crow era, when Black people were again forcibly removed from their land through redlining, followed by the gentrification we know today.

The multifaceted, multidimensional disconnection caused by centuries of colonization and enslavement has produced generations of Black people throughout the African diaspora whose relationship with food is complicated. We are told that Black communities have higher incidences of health issues and disease due to the food we eat. Many of us live in food-scarce environments. And we feel the shame and judgment that surrounds our relationship with food. The remnants of that collective trauma show up today in the ways Black people experience eating imbalances in the twenty-first century.

I believe that one of the reasons Black folks are dealing with eating imbalances today is that we feel the resistance of our ancestors in our blood, bones, and cells. We have absorbed the forceful nature of being fed the absolute bare minimum, of a nourishment provided solely with the intention of selling us off as chattel. Enslaved Africans were shipped primarily to North America, the Caribbean, and South America. Once they arrived, they experienced another traumatic disruption: the slave auction. They had to find new ways of surviving as they were sold across the Caribbean and the Americas, which caused further familial, cultural, and land separation and trauma. They were forced to work on new land as the property of enslavers, subjecting them to a lifetime of nonconsensual servitude and torture.

My own ancestors were forced to work in the rice, tobacco, and indigo fields of the Carolinas. Yet my people were eventually able to build a communal relationship with this new land, and after Emancipation became farmers. Both the maternal and paternal sides of my family were heavily into farming and gardening culture, and would often eat the food they grew; they also cultivated plants to use for herbal medicines well into my mother and father's generation. My grandmother talks about how food from the land never went to waste. Rather than food scraps being thrown away, they might be given to the hogs or chickens to eat, or repurposed and used as fertilizer.

Our enslaved African ancestors had been utilizing these practices for centuries. They used every part of the animal, because they were resourceful; this was the relationship they'd had to animals in their homeland. Food was a necessity, allowing us to survive the long days of enduring brutality and immense physical exertion. We also, of course, became accustomed to a pattern of being undernourished and of surviving on very little. This disruption of nourishment, as described by licensed clinical social worker Safiya McHale, was "a fracture of the mind, body, and spirit in Black communities." We cannot underestimate the impact systemic and intergenerational trauma and stress have had on our bodies over the centuries of internalized rage, shame, and deep-rooted grief that our ancestors experienced and continued to pass down through the generations.

STRESS, TRAUMA, AND OUR GENES

When it comes to how Black folks eat, we both experience and witness normalized patterns of undernourishment, wounds of scarcity, and disconnection from the individual and collective body. These issues have been exacerbated through widespread fatphobia, assimilation to Eurocentric standards of beauty, and societal obsessions with health and diet rooted in anti-Black racism. Most enslaved folks who experienced the impacts of colonization and enslavement were likely to also suffer from post-traumatic stress disorder (PTSD). PTSD is a mental health condition triggered by a terrifying event, either experiencing it or witnessing it. Symptoms may include flashbacks, nightmares, and severe anxiety, as well as uncontrollable thoughts about the event. Symptoms can worsen, and often did for enslaved folks and their descendants, lasting for months or even years and interfering with day-to-day functioning. Most people who go through traumatic events may have temporary difficulty adjusting and coping, but with time and good self-care, they often get better. But healthy healing tools were not available to the enslaved and their descendants.

It is imperative that we honor our long history of courageous resiliency and humanity in the face of madness.

The experience of PTSD and trauma can be transmitted generationally from parent to child through epigenetics, environment, and social conditioning, as the experiences of the trauma are stored at the cellular level of our DNA. Evidence suggests that genetics are a primary driver of eating imbalances, which are often seen throughout family lines. In addition to linking eating imbalances to genetics, researchers are exploring the interplay of genetics and the environment. Research shows that epigenetics is influenced by our environment, and we know that our current sociocultural-political environment promotes imbalanced eating behavior. In the face of certain stressors, it appears that some people who are genetically predisposed to the condition may develop the disorder.

Consider this: An unfertilized egg already shares the same cellular environment as your mother and grandmother. According to family trauma expert Mark Wolynn, by the time your grandmother was five months pregnant with your mother, the precursor cell of the egg you developed from was already present in your mother's ovaries. This means that before your mother was born, your mother, your grandmother, and the earliest traces of you were all in the same body—three generations sharing the same biological environment. In his book *It Didn't Start With You*, Wolynn writes: "It is within this shared environment that stress can cause changes to our DNA."

Scholar and researcher Dr. Bruce Lipton contributes to these studies, finding that signals from the environment can operate through the cell membrane, controlling the behavior and physiology of the cell. So, for example, a pregnant woman's emotional state, such as fear, anger, or love, can alter the genetic expression of her offspring. Even as a fetus, the body is preparing us for the world that we will soon have to navigate, and we are learning how to regulate our nervous systems to the environment we will be born into through our parent's womb.

In the unraveling process I undertook to understand my eating imbalance, I sat in meditation to seek out my ancestors to see if they had any wisdom or guidance to offer me. I closed my eyes and slowed down my body and mind so that I could fully listen to and digest what the ancestors would reveal to me. They offered me the knowledge that within our lineage, the women in our family were accustomed to taking care of everyone else, while neglecting ourselves in the process. We did not take our well-deserved seat at the table we prepared. We'd pour everything we had into the meal we served to others, then sit and wait and make our plate last. We might not even eat at all as we watched family members come back for seconds and thirds.

As I communed with my ancestors, more memories began to flood back from my childhood about how hard the matriarchs in my family worked to take care of and nurture everyone else—to the point of burnout. My child's mind began to associate nourishing others with burden, scarcity, and obligation. I came to see that the food relationships in our family were wrapped up in self-neglect and "mothering wounds," those practices that have been passed down to us from our mothers for generation after generation that seem to do us more harm than good.

When I was offered this wisdom I thought, *Well, that's just what Black women and femmes have always done.* We've always ensured that everyone else was taken care of no matter how exhausted we were—we were the givers and caretakers, but rarely the receivers of our own medicine. The way I was raised, the man (aka the traditional "breadwinner" of the house) sat at the head of the table and the woman (aka the traditional "homemaker" of the family) sat at the foot. The woman made the man's plate first, and then the children's, and then her own. Women of that time learned to put themselves last, to accept less, and to receive minimal support, because they did not think they were deserving of more. This remains the case even in present-day life.

My ancestors shared one more observation with me: that the devaluation of women over the years emerged as a consequence of our society's evolving out of collective tribal communities and into patriarchy. It became clear to me that healing my "mothering wounds" would require me to recenter myself in Black people's collective traditional practices and matriarchal wisdom. I needed to heal the ways I was nurturing and nourishing myself, taking up space in my life, and embodying my inner authority.

I have learned that in order to repair the disconnection within my own body, I need to continue to center myself in the belief that I am more than enough—and that the energy of scarcity does not belong to me. In my spiritual coaching, I have come to understand that I can take up space and be vast and expansive without withholding food to punish, numb, or suppress my feelings. I've learned that I don't have to feel shamed or burdened by the Western patriarchal teaching that tells me that as a Black woman I have to serve everyone else and then nourish and take care of myself last, or that I have to engage in self-neglect to benefit and please others. I have done the critical work to reclaim my rightful place at the table.

In Black communities where we are just now beginning to talk more about mental health, long-held coping strategies that we've adopted in order to avoid discussing difficult things may have provided short-term relief, but they have had long-term consequences. Researcher Dr. Arline T. Geronimus describes such consequences as the "weathering effect"—the idea that Black women and femmes literally age, or become "weathered," much earlier in adulthood than other populations because of all the social, cultural, and economic disadvantages we've had to endure. Repeated exposure to social adversities such as discrimination, microaggressions, and marginalization can slowly chip away at the physical health of Black women and femmes. That wear and tear on the body's adaptive mechanisms—and our tendency not to talk about or process what is bothering us—builds up over a long period of time. In other words, our failure to acknowledge what has happened to us has very real and quantifiable physiological effects.

When a person is exposed to immense trauma, the part of the brain responsible for language, reasoning, cognitive memory, and decision-making is not receiving messages from the body; instead, the oldest part of the brain, which is responsible for our emotional response to danger, is activated to keep us safe and alive. While trauma fragments our language system and disorganizes our memory of what happened to us, the experience is communicated through our body in our sensations, emotions, images, and body language. Essentially, within Black communities trauma has contributed to numbing out, shutting down, and disconnecting from the body, not necessarily by choice, but as a response to being cut off from the ability to fully process our history and its profound impact.

For the women in my own family, the legacy of that kind of trauma showed up when they suppressed their feelings, minimized and discredited their emotions, and instead simply pressed on. It was a practice I inherited too: I learned to suppress my truth and eat my words. Controlling how we ate was a way of subduing our pain, feeling less of the void that shame had created within our bodies. The pattern of taking up less space emotionally manifested outwardly in our eating habits and in our determination to control our body size, shape, weight, and eating behaviors to claim a sense of worthiness and desirability in society.

THE PATHWAY BACK TO OUR HEALING

Transformative healing in our relationship to our body does not look like a top-down approach—we cannot rely heavily on our rational thinking brain. Instead, metabolizing trauma requires us to think from the bottom up: We must allow the body to guide us *inward* to create a sanctuary, a space of refuge, a home within ourselves. In the words of Bessel van der Kolk, author of *The Body Keeps the Score,* "We are a hopeful species. Working with trauma is as much about remembering how we survived as it is about what is broken. The great challenge is finding ways to reset our physiology, so that the survival mechanisms stop working against us."

The pathway back into the body can be found by starting here: through awareness of the way we have become disembodied. As we've discussed, for Black folks, disembodiment occurred through colonialism and capitalism, which birthed the enslavement of African people, a system that was created to thrive and capitalize off our disembodied selves. These institutions continue to benefit from our being checked out from our bodies, our communities, our collective human experience, and our spiritual existence as inhabitants of the earth. The impact is intergenerational, passed down epigenetically through the way that trauma is stored in our cells and through our adaptations and social learning around the trauma.

When generational trauma is perpetually retriggered through anti-Black racism without adequate care, it can cause the symptom—the eating imbalance—to show up in response to the wound, or trauma. In order to meaningfully connect back to ourselves, we need to understand that the eating imbalance is the *symptom* of the trauma, but not the origin of it. Collectively, we in the Westernized mental health community have been treating the symptom and the behaviors of the eating imbalance, but not actually getting to the root of the illness.

Before we judge ourselves for the way we've been able—or unable—to process our collective trauma, remember: When we are disembodied, it is a sign that our bodies do not feel safe. When our nervous system feels dysregulated, it activates our threat response, also known as fight, flight, freeze, appease, collapse, and a variety of other survival patterns.

When we experience a threat in our fight reaction, we may be the first person to use our energy to fight back or intervene to outwardly defend ourselves or others. In the appease—aka people-please—reaction, we may fawn over or try to befriend or go along with the situation to keep ourselves safe. When we experience a threat in our flight reaction, we may be the person who moves away or leaves the situation to protect ourselves or others. The freeze reaction pops up when we feel stuck in place, as if we cannot move or do anything in that moment. We feel the intensity of the experience emotionally, yet we remain still, almost as if we are frozen, which also helps us to protect ourselves. When we experience a threat that causes us to internally collapse, we may completely shut down and feel immobile, as if we cannot do anything, similar to freeze mode. We see this pattern with animals who "play dead" to avoid being attacked.

When these survival patterns are activated, imbalanced eating behaviors come in as protectors and coping mechanisms for the discomfort we may experience within our disconnected and dysregulated bodies. And although these patterns are activated to protect, in this state of hyperarousal our bodies also find it difficult to rest or digest—further impacting our ability to nourish ourselves adequately.

No response is better than another; they are normal evolutionary adaptations to threats in our environment—and as I indicated above, they show up in both humans and animals. For example, a lion creeps, undetected, toward a grazing gazelle. Suddenly, the gazelle's head perks up—she hears something. The lion, not wanting to miss its chance, leaps forward and begins the chase. Although the gazelle has been caught off guard, it is quick to flee, all the quicker in its state of panic. We tend to shame our nervous system responses to situations—especially when there may have been violence or abuse—by saying things like "Why didn't I fight back?" or "Why didn't I run?" But it is important to know that our bodies determine the safest options before our brains have the time to think about it. If you touch a hot stove, you don't pause and contemplate, *Wow this is hot; what should I do now to protect myself?* No, most likely you will immediately pull your hand away before you have time to process that the stove is burning it. Your body immediately increases your adrenaline and responds to keep you safe in that moment.

Our thinking brain then places judgments and criticisms on our behaviors based on what we have been told are socially appropriate ways to respond to specific situations. But the gazelle does not judge itself for running. I can imagine that once it finds a place of

safety and begins to settle and regulate its body, it may just be relieved to have survived.

As we continue to delve deeper into our work together here, a
lot of us might begin to excavate internalized shame that has kept
us silent about our issues. Shame is a deeply painful and immobi-
lizing experience that causes us to feel flawed and unworthy of acceptance and belonging. We can feel trapped, powerless, and
isolated, as if we have to hide ourselves and are unlovable. Shame
is often an emotional experience underpinning trauma and contributes to relational issues, depression, anxiety, and suicidal ideation. It often metastasizes and begins to infect all aspects of our
lives, keeping us from experiencing safety, dignity, and belonging.

To heal shame, we have to be willing to be vulnerable and need
safe and affirming spaces and empathetic relationships where we
can speak to it, deconstruct it, and destigmatize it. We will begin by
working with our shadows and parts of ourselves that we have
learned to unconsciously block out because we deem them unworthy or undeserving. We will bring them to light and work through
the judgment, criticism, and chaos that have developed around
these parts of ourselves.

In my own embodiment journey, I have been tasked with the
assignment of de-accelerating to a pace I had previously not been
accustomed to operating at. This slower path has offered me the
opportunity to wake up and check with my body first and allow its
wisdom to guide me throughout the day. Thanks to this process, I
now recognize that my body was already communicating with me
through sensations and impulses behind my emotions, through the
energy of my soul and spiritual journey, and through my ancestors.
I had been conditioned to ignore and bypass all these messages,
because I was stuck in the cycle of over-performing and over-
giving, and treated the moments of life as a checklist, day in and
day out. My personal journey required me to lean into solitude,
embrace the offering of becoming undone, and step into the new

pathway toward the version of myself that fostered joy, abundance, and celebration.

The process of coming back home to our bodies is not a destination, but a journey of continuing to come back—over and over again—despite how many times society and other forces try to keep us disconnected from ourselves. It is not supposed to be perfect; there will be times when listening to your body or being connected to what you are feeling is the last thing you want to do, and those survival patterns will kick in. However, my hope is that we will collectively learn how to recognize them, and slow down enough to work with the body in order to meet those moments with more possibility around what we choose to do next in those moments.

The first step to healing trauma and returning back to the body is finding resources and support with things that help us feel safe, nurtured, and protected. They help us increase our capacity to handle distress and to explore the fragmented parts of ourselves that got stuck in the traumatic state. Resources and support help to create space for progress, versus being stuck with only fragmented experiences of ourselves.

Black people have historically been storytellers and have come from lineages with an oral tradition. But when we experience trauma, the language part of our brain shuts down, and the story becomes disjointed. To restore it, we must listen to the bodily sensations, images, and emotions within ourselves, and allow that language to lead us back into our body to reclaim our narratives.

GUIDED PRACTICE #1

I encourage you to acknowledge the awakenings you may have experienced thus far, without trying to intellectualize them or be in your head about all that we have uncovered. I invite you to join me in taking a pause. Perhaps grab a sip of water or a blanket, rest your eyes, or stretch your body. Now, take note of what you feel. How is

your body receiving this information? Notice if there are any sensations coming up in your body. Do you feel any constriction or
tension? Is your heart beating fast? Are you experiencing any
tingling sensations? Twitching or shakiness? Fatigue? What about
any feelings of openness, expansiveness, or anticipation? For those
who deal with chronic pain and illness, this may bring up some
discomfort, so I ask that you listen to your body around what feels
tolerable and what does not. If possible, try to locate spaces in your
body where you are experiencing less pain, and notice if you can
invite stillness to that space as you purposefully allow your attention to enter and awaken your inner presence. Just for a moment,
be with all that is present for you right now. You don't have to do
anything with it yet.

Now, I want you to notice the emotions that you are having
alongside these sensations—happiness, fear, relief, joy, panic, over-
whelm, confusion, sadness, grief, curiosity, doubt. (These sensations and emotions are valid—there's no need to judge or change
them! In my own journey of embodiment, I have felt the ebbs and
flows of *all* of this, so I am right there with you, holding space for
you to be present with your body.) Can you locate the space in your
body where you feel these emotions and sensations? Maybe it's
your chest, your spine, your jaw, belly, hips, legs, eyes, or neck. Just
take notice of the areas in your body that are holding the experience of this present moment. If you find that it is difficult to focus
on that, no worries, just return to your sensations and emotions if
they are still accessible for you.

I invite you to now place a hand over your heart, and if that is
not an option to bring your awareness into your heart space on the
right side of your body, behind your chest. This is an opportunity
to send some intentional breath into your body. Intentionally noticing our breathing and engaging in breaths has the power to
transform our internal experience and offer us more emotional
regulation and connection. Try taking in an inhale of air through
your nose, hold it for at least five seconds, and then release the air

back out through your mouth. Now let's allow for that exhale to settle. Pause and notice—with kindness—how your body receives this, and then take your next inhale.

As you move through this exercise, focus on the process of breathing and sending breath into your body, and into the spaces that so graciously hold the sensations and emotions. You can choose to lower your gaze or rest your eyes during this time. Take as many breaths as you like, and on your last breath extend a gentle offering of gratitude to your body. For example, you may feel, think, or say, "Thank you, breath, for bringing me presence."

Now what was that like for you? Did you experience a shift, perhaps an opening? Was it hard or unbearable? Did you notice something that you did not notice before checking in? What did you learn? For those of you who checked in with your body, I want to congratulate you for engaging in the process of *being*. That is enough; no need to judge it or critique it. For those of you who did not check in, offer gratitude to yourself for listening to what felt safe and affirming to your body. Again, there is no right or wrong; this is about receiving information and guidance from your body.

I want to make a note that even when we begin to listen and turn our awareness toward our bodies, we may notice that our bodies reject it at first. You may feel defensive or uncomfortable, but this does not mean that you are doing it wrong. In my own early experiences, I would often skip over any activity that required me to pause and focus on my body, because I thought it took up too much time and I didn't want to feel anything, I just wanted to learn and be more engaged with the intellectualizing of information. I realized that this was an inherited avoidance pattern and a way that I would dissociate when I had to slow down, because I was used to moving through uncomfortable feelings quickly, without holding space for myself.

There is also a myth that to engage in a mindful practice, we have to be able to quiet our minds. This is not true. We are living beings—our minds are *always* working. Mindfulness is not about having a blank mind, but about being able to connect with ourselves in the current moment. Many of us have spent generations upon generations being disconnected from our bodies, building up protective mechanisms to survive, which often involved ignoring what our bodies needed and were communicating to us. And so, this new way of being in connection with ourselves can be unfamiliar, and may even activate the body into that familiar survival mode because for so long it has often been unsafe to be in our bodies and heal. Notice this, and reassure your body that you are okay in the present moment.

This is a practice of relearning, and relearning takes time. So, I would encourage you to check in with your emotional capacity and listen to your body. If you need to stop or pause, give yourself permission to do so. It may be helpful if you have someone in your life whom you can practice these exercises with—a friend, a coach, a therapist, or a support group. We have been taught individualism through Western culture—that we should do it all on our own and "not be a burden"—but our ancestors always healed in community, and it can be a helpful way to hold shared compassion and accountability throughout this journey you've started on.

QUESTIONS FOR REFLECTION

I encourage you to take your time with this book, perhaps even put it down for a bit and go outside for some fresh air. At the end of each chapter, I have included some questions to ponder before you move on to the next one. Feel free to journal and reflect on how you feel in this moment. As we work together, you may notice that the way you think about this process in the beginning may shift by the time we arrive at the end of the book. So, as you answer these questions, know that your responses are based on what has been offered to you so far, and accept that those feelings may evolve.

Give yourself the grace of flexibility. And regardless of how and when you choose to answer the questions, know that I am here to guide you, page by page.

Whenever you are ready, settle in and journal/color/draw/create/reflect on these questions:

1. When you think about your relationship with food, what immediately comes to mind? Notice how your thoughts are registering in your body. What sensations do you feel?
2. How do you know when you feel safe in your body—what cues and signals does your body send? What indicators—anxiety, frustration, the need to escape, for example—pop up when you do not feel safe? Try not to judge yourself—there are no right or wrong answers.
3. Consider what it might mean to develop a different relationship with food. What are some ways you can offer gratitude to what you are consuming, in order to honor the process and energy of its having gotten to you?
4. Earlier in the book we discussed the idea of embodiment. What would embodiment look, taste, smell, sound, and intuitively feel like for you?

· TWO ·

Patriarchy and the
Indoctrination Process

"Patriarchy—a social system in which men hold power and non-male people are generally excluded from it—played a role in silencing divine feminine wisdom. In a society marked by gender hierarchy, it simply wouldn't do for god to be female or have feminine characteristics. It also wouldn't make women believe they had access to truth that was supposedly reserved for men."

—CHRISTENA CLEVELAND, Ph.D, author, *God Is a Black Woman*

LOOKING AT MY FAMILY from the outside in, you would probably think that I grew up in an idyllic environment. I had what many in America would deem the perfect family unit: a married, two-parent, devoutly Christian household. I am the eldest of three siblings—two girls and a boy. Our family went to church on Wednesdays and Sundays and never missed a service. But once I began to take a more purposeful look at my upbringing, I started to realize how much that devout, Westernized Christian upbringing typical of Southern culture had taught me to devalue myself as a Black woman. It may seem odd to think of my imbalanced eating and the patriarchy I experienced in the church as being connected, but I assure you they are. Let me explain how.

Western patriarchal conditioning molded my father into a very rigid and religiously traditional man who would use fear tactics, violence, and threats to be in control. He controlled everything—from what music we could listen to and what clothes we wore to how we could celebrate birthdays, whom we could talk to on the phone, what friends we could have, and whom we could or could not date (which was no one). I believe he worried that his children would fall in with the wrong crowd, or that his girls might wind up as pregnant teens. It didn't matter to him that his control over us was intense, dictating all of our choices in every aspect of our lives. Taking on a Father-God parenting style was my father's way of ensuring that we were safe and protected, and, quite honestly, it was the only method of parenting that he knew.

Patriarchal households such as the one I grew up in insisted that women present a united front with their husbands. It was the job of Southern women to manage and protect the emotions of their husbands in order to avoid provoking them in any way. To be fair, I do believe my mother would advocate for us in private, but my father was stubborn, and wasn't someone who was easy to budge or be convinced otherwise once he made up his mind. My mother allowed and permitted a lot of situations we experienced because, as the wife, she had to fall in line and not interfere with the man's authority. As the head of the household and the breadwinner, the husband had the final say. In rural Southern culture—typically associated with the Bible Belt—the men were in control. It wasn't unusual to hear a woman concede her power and insight in favor of a man's.

Most people in the church I attended believed that God intended for a man to be the head of the household, and for everyone else, including the wife, to be respectful and submissive. Christianity established the blueprint; the men-first hierarchy is ingrained in its origins. Respect, in this instance, often meant following a man's lead, without question, and being submissive to male authority. So, when it was time for dinner to be served, for example, the woman was expected to fix the man's plate before anyone else could eat.

In psychology we describe this kind of parenting style as "authoritarian." It is extremely strict and is characterized by the imposition of high expectations on children, with more focus put on obedience, discipline, and control than on nurturing. Mistakes tend to be punished harshly, and when feedback does occur, it's often negative. Yelling and corporal punishment are also common, as parents expect the child to obey them, to not make mistakes, and to rigidly follow rules. My gendered response was to be obedient, something that perhaps comes more easily to women because we are already socialized from a young age, both at home and at church, to obey men.

Authoritarian parenting has been normalized within many church cultures for generations. The persistent messages—"To be a good Christian thou shall obey your parents so that you can live a long life"; "God said spare the rod, spoil the child"—and biblical verses support this train of thought. Ecclesiastes 12:13–14 says: "Fear God [who is described as our father] and keep his commandments [rules for living], for this is the whole duty of man. For God will bring every deed into judgment, with every secret thing, whether good or evil." This insistence on hypervigilance, control, perfection, and punishment has had a chilling effect on our culture at large, permeating Western Christianity and creating rigid rules around how those of us who ascribe to this indoctrination conduct ourselves.

And that includes the ways we eat. For example, diet culture tells us that every calorie we intake is a price we have to pay. I have heard many people say that an eating imbalance has become their new religion, because it shares so many similarities to a lot of the rigidity and rules born out of religious indoctrination. They are focused on thoughts such as "I can't eat this, it's bad food" or "I must follow every rule of my diet, and if I make a mistake, I have to purge for my body to feel good again." Or "I must religiously fast and deny myself nutrition to express my devotion and purity to God."

Despite the Bible and Scripture being reinterpreted for countless generations by fallible men who had different understandings of The Word based on different languages, cultural worldviews, and history, it would have been considered an abomination to question or critique what we were learning about our Western-based religion. Everything in the Bible was interpreted for its literal translation, considered as the only universal truth, and applied to the way that a "good Christian" should live, lead, and raise their family. (The same can be said for the way medical doctrines around weight are regarded as universal truth; the penchant for seeing patriarchal beliefs as the one true North Star is quite similar.)

To be a good child in a household that was indoctrinated through Western Christianity was to be one who aligned closely to godliness, meaning that as an extension of you, your body had to be perfect, disciplined, and obedient. All mistakes or wrongdoing, therefore, needed to be punished and repented for. Adults who were raised in authoritarian households tend to experience low self-esteem; difficulty in social situations due to an inability to express themselves to others; issues with regulating their emotions, resulting in enacting violence onto others; self-harming behaviors or substance abuse; an inability to accept failure; a tendency to be harsh on themselves and experience negative self-talk; struggles with perfectionism and procrastination; and conformity to social pressure accompanied by anxiety and/or depression. While on the outside we may see a person who is functional in society, we do not see the impact that this conditioning can have both on our internal experience and in our relationships with other people.

Also built into the church culture is the notion of purity: As Black girls, women, and femmes, we were expected to comport ourselves with modesty and humility. For example, we always had to make sure we wore a slip and pantyhose to church, or at least used a prayer cloth if we wore a shorter skirt, so as not to "be disrespectful to God" or tempt any of the men in attendance by not being modest and pure. Hypervigilance around women's bodies, even at a young age, was part of what molded us. The church and its patriarchal teachings around purity put the onus on us as girls and women to present ourselves as being above reproach.

Patriarchy teaches women and non-men to make ourselves smaller. It enforces this lesson by using religious indoctrination to justify why we need to put limits and restraints on our lives—telling us that we are inherently out of control and should be tamed by men, as ordained by a higher power. Obsessing over what we eat and assigning value to the way we nourish our bodies are how we have been taught to keep our bodies—and by extension ourselves—in control. When we are constantly focused on eating "clean," being moral and pure, and modifying our bodies to conform to standards that were intended to limit us, our sense of who we are disappears. We are then bound and relegated to viewing the world through the limitations that have been offered to us.

For example, during the 2016 presidential election, many of the Black women whom I went to church with questioned whether a woman would be capable of being the president of the United States—"After all, wouldn't she be too emotional?" One common critique was that Hillary Clinton's politics regarding abortion were sinful and ungodly. The internalization of patriarchy aimed at politicizing and controlling "subordinate" bodies, coupled with religious dogma intended to demonize an individual's right to make her own reproductive choices, caused these women to vote against their best interests, which resulted—as we know—in policies and laws that enforced *more* limitations and offered *less* protection for the body autonomy of all women, especially Black women and femmes.

In writing this chapter, I began to question the patriarchal household I was raised in, and in doing more work on myself a number of patterns emerged for me. I did not learn how to deal with or regulate my emotions growing up; most of the modeling and learning that I received around this was through watching my parents, who would discipline by yelling, hitting, spanking, and lashing out in anger when things were difficult or overwhelming.

However, as a girl, I was not allowed to be angry or express that I was upset.

In the South, women still hold on to the remnants of suppressing our feelings, stifling our voices, being polite, making ourselves smaller, putting others' comfort above our own, and relinquishing our own inner authority when it comes to how we define respect and hospitality. Southern women have the unique experience of being conditioned into Southern etiquette and hospitality. We are taught and expected to be overly accommodating, nice, and pleasing. I hear it in our tone of voice and how we ask questions or word certain things. We are not as blunt or as straightforward as, let's say, someone from up North, because in the South that is considered rude and off-putting.

These things show up in the ways that we express ourselves to people who we perceive are in positions of power over us, and link back to patterns that our ancestors inherited and then passed down to us through "respectability politics"—from enslavement through Jim Crow and beyond. What I mean when I use the term "respectability politics" is that many of us have internalized messages about ourselves from an early age. There is an inner child within each of us that still uses our early social conditioning to dictate how we live our lives and what safety feels like. We have been told that our bodies are the problem, and that if we can control our food, weight, and eating we will be afforded safety, autonomy, dignity, and respect. We often suffer with feelings of shame, emptiness, isolation, and a disconnection from self because there are parts of ourselves that we have to disassociate from by suppressing or shutting down physically, emotionally, and/or spiritually in order to survive.

These things also define how Black people learned to survive in white spaces. However, Black people have continued to practice these survival behaviors even outside of the presence of whiteness; it has lost its original context, and particularly for Black folks in the South, it has become the cultural norm. Growing up, I learned that you never question an authority figure. You do what you are told with an outwardly positive attitude—and the only respectable re-sponse to an adult who is addressing you is "yes/no, ma'am" or "yes/no, sir." I learned to swallow my anger until it became so in-tense that the only way to let it out was to engage in self-destructive behavior. (More on this later.) From a young age I was taught that getting good grades was what would keep me out of trouble.

Such academic achievements also made me feel seen and ac-cepted. I learned to excel in school, and everyone would praise my parents for how smart, well-spoken, well-mannered, and well-behaved their kids were. I won't say that this was not true, but a lot of it was a performance we felt we had to put on to avoid getting in trouble. We had learned that getting bad grades would result in punishment, typically a spanking. The girls in the family learned that the only way to be seen as worthy of the acceptance we craved was to earn it by being perfect, agreeable, and overachieving. The value attached to productivity and perfection is a capitalist main-stay. Is it any wonder, then, that some of these same behaviors show up as characteristics of imbalanced eating?

WHEN VALIDATION BECOMES A NUMBERS GAME

In a Western-driven, patriarchal value system, measurements such as numbers, calories, miles, time exercising, or hours at the gym are used as physical proof of our worth. These are the ways we are taught to validate ourselves. Growing up, I was told that I had to be better than everyone around me. I understood that I should aim to bring home only A's in my schoolwork and that, especially coming from a low-income Black family, I had to work twice as hard as everyone else in order to make anything of myself.

I see the same perfectionist patterns in some of the low-income, first-generation college clients I have worked with around eating imbalances. On the outside they are high academic achievers, and society and their families view them as having it all together. But on the inside, the eating imbalance is what truly offers them a sense of mastery over their own bodies. It is a way to survive the pressure placed on them to be the face of Black excellence—and to be the first in the family to navigate the terrain of college and graduation. All this is expected while they hold down a job so that they can either lift the family out of their own situation or be the example of the one who made it. Their whole identity is tied to what they *do,* how hard they have worked, and what they have achieved, but they don't know who they are outside of these things.

The eating imbalance helps them fill the void of their loss of identity by allowing them the control they feel they are lacking because they cannot identify who they are. It allows them to control their bodies and gives them a purpose that the lack of identity has not. And it helps them fill the void of that perceived loss: In controlling their bodies, they can regain control of their identity.

I know this personally, as a first-generation college student myself. The paths and unfinished dreams of our families are often forced onto us from elementary school, and our path as the exceptional one is planned out for us, with little option to choose something different. It leaves us to perform as if we have it all together. As a result, we grow up too fast, and try to keep everything under control. The voice in our head says that we are never enough, or that we are not worthy or won't be accepted if we don't play the role perfectly.

In my own experience, being the first person in my family to go to college was about having to make sacrifices at a young age for financial reasons. Education was a strong family value. I grew up hearing "You can't do anything with your life if you don't get an education," and while I know now that this is not necessarily true, it put enough fear in me as a young person that I believed my only way out was to overwork academically. I didn't have a choice.

All through elementary and middle school, I earned mostly A's. When I did bring home the occasional B, I was often asked why it wasn't an A. "What could you have done differently?" my parents pressed. My parents were very open about the fact that they could not afford to put me and my siblings through college and that it was important for me to do anything I could to get ahead in life on my own. Over the years, I would hear their arguments and whispers about money. I knew that we were struggling, but my father would say, "We won't be like those people who take government assistance." He was caught up in the perception of not looking poor and appearing as if he was asking for handouts.

After middle school, I was accelerated into a five-year early-college program for low-income families who could not afford college; it was this program that allowed me to gain both my high school diploma and two years of college that resulted in an associate degree—a much less expensive option than pursuing a four-year degree at a university.

During high school and college, I also worked as a before and after schoolteacher and occasional substitute teacher at a preschool–eighth grade charter school to earn money and volunteer experience for college applications. I remember waking up around 6 o'clock every morning, getting ready, and being at the school to open it up by 7. I helped students settle in and get their morning snack, then headed to the cars for drop-off duty. Then I left for the day to go to my high school and college classes on campus, and after that, I headed back to the charter school to receive the students for after-care. I then left around 5:30 and came home to focus on my homework and chores before getting up and doing it all over again the next day.

I graduated with a 4.0 and went straight into college at the University of North Carolina at Greensboro afterward. "You've got two years," my parents told me—they wouldn't co-sign my loans past that point. And so, I graduated with my bachelor's degree in two years. While I had a balance of having fun and making friends, I didn't have time to join any extracurricular activities or organizations, because I was also working internships and paid jobs to get by.

While I was in college, I began heavily working out at the gym.

It was my way of building a tough exterior. I told myself that if I was strong, people wouldn't be able to take advantage of me and I wouldn't be vulnerable, the way I was when I was bullied in middle school, or when I'd receive physical punishment at home at the hands of adults who were a lot stronger than me. I would often lift two or three times the amount that I should have because I wanted to feel the heaviness and tension that it would cause in my body.

I found that I enjoyed the numbness brought on by ignoring the pain. It reinforced what I most desired—that even when dealing with emotional pain, I could be unfazed by it. The physical heaviness I felt during my daily workouts was a manifestation of the unaddressed heavy emotional burden that I had shouldered for years in my upbringing. I felt that in life I didn't have any option but to keep pressing on through the pain and pressure. I'd work out literally every day of the week, nonstop, without adequately nourishing my body. It was painful to carry my books because I was so sore. But I was equating my pain—how much I could endure and keep going—with how strong I felt I was becoming.

During my young adult years, I had developed quite a few maladaptive coping strategies—things that I used to numb out, to dissociate from and avoid my issues. They included emotionally absent men, alcohol, imbalanced eating, and excessive and dangerous exercise routines. I was an extrovert and people pleaser, so it was easy for me to put on a mask in order to be liked. I made a lot of friendships but didn't allow anyone to get too close, for fear of getting hurt.

The roots of these maladaptive coping strategies, including the imbalanced eating, went deep. They were born out of the emotional trauma I experienced within my family, and specifically the way that patriarchy and religion were used as ways to instill fear and enforce power. The wounds of my inner child were formed by the internalized anger I felt from being boxed in by patriarchal society. I put on a tough exterior because I didn't want to be seen as vulnerable and weak, especially as the eldest child, who had the responsibility to lead by example for my younger siblings.

I know now that those wounds were not just my wounds—they were passed down to me through my parents, who had wounds from their own parents, and so on, the cycle endlessly continuing. My family all had the same wound—wanting to be enough—but we only knew how to escape our bodies, how to shut down our needs and grasp for a sense of control. Even as I am writing this, I'm thinking about what my family members will say about what I'm disclosing here, as they have made tremendous sacrifices so that I could get to where I am now. They have always supported my success and been proud of my career and academic achievements, even when they didn't understand what I was doing. However, they were not conditioned to view the larger systems at play that were impacting us emotionally.

I don't share these things to shame, blame, or place judgment on my family or upbringing. I share them because as a mental health therapist in the process of my own healing, I recognize that we can't address, uproot, and heal what we don't talk about. My work has been about having the courage to talk about difficult things and being better because I leaned into that vulnerability—to name the skeletons in our closets, the things we are "not supposed to talk about" in Black families. I also understand and honor that people in our families have their own experiences of trauma to come to terms with, and they get to decide to heal if and when they choose to do so.

UNPACKING THE PATRIARCHAL PAIN

It took me years to recover from my patriarchal household. I had to deprogram myself from believing that men inherently should hold more power. As I grew up and out of this mentality, I ran in the opposite direction of the gendered beliefs I was raised on— becoming hyper-independent. I would deny my needs and over-work so that I did not need to accept money or rely on resources from men. I would be in relationships with men where I earned more money. This way, I believed, I could remain financially independent and in control.

I was also hypervigilant about how men in my life expressed their beliefs about women. I was once in a partnership with someone who had no concept of what it was like to live today as a woman. "As a woman in this era, when have you ever been oppressed?" he had the nerve to ask me once. His dismissiveness was too much to bear—this person who had never dealt with catcalling or sexual harassment while going about their day or been told that they should not walk alone at night. Who had never been judged for wearing "promiscuous" or "sexualizing" clothing or had someone not believe them when they reported an assault. Who can't relate to the experience of having their bodies tense up when walking past a group of men for fear of being sexually objectified or groped?

When someone believes that they can control everything that happens to them, and that it's their own fault if something terrible *does* happen to them, it unfairly places the accountability on the person who was harmed—even though issues like patriarchy, sexism, and misogyny are the real driving forces. It's our victim/ survivor–blaming culture that asks, "What did you do to deserve what happened to you?" Anytime I talked to a partner about something that was impacting me as a girl or a woman, he'd try to mansplain it away. It took years for me to understand that I did not deserve to be dismissed, invalidated, or brushed off as just "being dramatic." It took years for me to stop treating myself the same way—suppressing my voice, doubting myself, denying my needs, and repressing my emotions.

Abstract words like "systemic oppression" and "social construct," or systems like patriarchy or white supremacy, were not terms I was familiar with when I was growing up. In my rural town in North Carolina, most people were instructed to go to school simply to follow the money. When your main focus is on surviving, as it is for many Black/low-income folks, the conditions are designed so that you don't have time to intellectualize what you are going through or to think about how systems are impacting you. Because, at the end of the day, what can you do about it when you are just trying to keep a roof over your head, to put food on the table and clothes on your back? Most of the people I grew up around had blue-collar jobs and were barely scraping by. You might see things on the news or feel things in your body that you knew were not right, but you figured that's just the way it's always been, and that there was no way out.

So, when I describe Western patriarchy, it's not about women hating men. When I describe white supremacy, it's not about Black people hating white people, or white people being racists or bad people. Patriarchy has existed globally for millennia. I define Western patriarchy as a system that was parented by colonialism and has spread from the West across the globe through imperialism, with similar tenets of exerting control by force, violence, power over dynamics, and genocide. Patriarchy in the Western sense is a system of society or government in which men hold the power, wisdom, and hierarchy, and women and non-men have none, or are largely excluded from it. European versions of patriarchy forced women and non-men into subservient roles and normalized domestic violence, femicide, and child abuse. This rendition of patriarchy created misogyny—a dislike of, contempt for, or ingrained prejudice against women on the basis of sex.

We currently live in a society where we are not used to critiquing systems without it being received as a personalized attack, a summation of our existence. For example, when women critique patriarchy, we are often told that we are attacking men, or are demanding "men not be men." That is an oversimplification and an attempt to dismiss the critique. However, patriarchy is a system that harms women, non-men, *and* men; it keeps us all disconnected. As ancestor author bell hooks once wrote, "The first act of violence that patriarchy demands of males is *not* violence toward women. Instead, patriarchy demands of all males that they engage in acts of psychic self-mutilation, that they kill off the emotional parts of themselves. If an individual is not successful in emotionally crippling himself, he can count on patriarchal men to enact rituals of power that will assault his self-esteem."

Critiquing the system allows us to really examine patriarchy and identify precisely *who* is most empowered and disempowered by the system. It then encourages us to see the places within ourselves where we have internalized patriarchy and used it to keep people out or to concede our own power and agency, and helps us recognize and release the conditioning around what has not served us. I have heard from men that they are also tired of things like gender roles that were created out of patriarchy and that put pressure on them to be the sole provider or protector. These indoctrinations don't allow for the myriad ways that people, regardless of gender, show up in our human experience. When we do not conform to these gendered social expectations, we are often rejected—labeled as deviant or wrong, and culturally shamed. Instead, we must recognize the macro and the micro—the larger systems as well as our personal experiences—as working in tandem, while also becoming aware of the ways in which we might benefit from the same systems we are critiquing.

For example: I am college-educated *and* I think that we need reform in the education system. If someone says that we need to reform or dismantle the way that we administer education, I am not going to take that personally and ask them, "So are you saying that I am a terrible person because I am educated?" On the macro level, I recognize that our education system is flawed, that everyone does not have access to the same education and resources, and that we collectively would benefit from redefining what an education is. On the micro level, I recognize that even though I struggled to get an education, I have benefited from the education system by being able to obtain certain jobs and opportunities due to the level of education that I earned.

Now, with the privileged position that I have, I can help make the process a little easier for someone else, while also working in the community to envision and create nonhierarchical and inclusive learning environments. This is what it means to look at issues on a macro and micro level, without personalizing it and making it the summation of our identity. It moves us away from the reductive, polarizing line of thinking that people are either "good" or "bad" based on their circumstances and instead honors that we are complex and layered human beings.

We do the work by addressing structures designed to put certain people in power—namely wealthy white men—while marginalizing everyone who does not identify in this way by creating systems that are designed to keep out, punish, and disembody people. The goal is to keep people in survival mode, or as my grandfather would say: "making the Man rich at our expense." The more proximity to power people have based on social identities, the more they can use the system to oppress groups that do not have as much power.

Trauma is not confined to a specific space and time, but it can also keep us trapped in our bodily responses and behaviors. As somatic abolitionist Resmaa Menakem once shared, systemic trauma makes us think that it's our personality that is at fault when in fact it's something we learned a long time ago that has been passed down to us. Most of the time we don't even know that we are responding or reacting out of trauma, because we haven't been taught to examine it. As I stated earlier, when you are focused on surviving, you don't have the time to think about why you are doing the things you are doing. It is an input-and-output system that we have been opted into automatically. Many of us never stop to question if the systems align with our personal values. Nor do we consider who these systems historically have served. We go along to get along, identifying with and abiding by systems created to oppress us.

HOW OUR INDOCTRINATION SHOWS UP TODAY

Patriarchy keeps us focused on picking ourselves apart, or bonding over self-deprecating commentary. Have you ever noticed that men don't often gather to highlight their flaws and insecurities? Rather, they get together and talk about things that are happening in the world and their shared interests. They don't often meet and greet each other with notions of how they can take up less space, such as "Wow, you have lost weight" or "What diet plan are you on?" The message seems to be that women should not eat so much, that it's unladylike, as if undereating or not consuming everything on your plate makes you more of an ideal woman.

This belief that women should be undernourished is part of this patriarchal systemic oppression. It focuses on the vanity and desirability that are often forced onto women to determine our social acceptability and status. It discounts the fact that undernourishment and food scarcity are actual conditions that are systemic, and that impact Black communities at higher rates. Patriarchy ignores its dangers and continues to enforce the messages that food needs to be moralized as "good" or "bad," or that women need to monitor portion sizes, or that there is a "pure" or "clean" diet out there for them to subscribe to.

I once had a middle-aged client, a larger-sized Black woman, who came to me because she could not seem to break her restrictive-binge cycle of eating. As we worked together, I learned that her eating became imbalanced from an early age. Her mother was very critical of her body size, and food was the only thing she felt she could turn to for comfort. As a result, the client had experienced all forms of abuse at home and was bullied at school. She was dealing with severe depression and suicidal ideation, but it went unseen and ignored. She was young, but felt she had to take on the weight of the world while also dealing with her mental health and the negative comments made about her body. In time, she realized that her eating was connected to never feeling good enough, and not having a space to hold that emotion.

Most times when I get together with other Black women, there is commentary about how much "junk" they have been eating, or the fact that they are gaining weight and need to get back on the clean-eating track, or that they want to get back into the gym to get "snatched." We have become conditioned to come together and center our conversations around self-deprecation. We have become conditioned to bond with other women around our insecurities and perceived flaws. In fact, this behavior is considered a form of belonging. This, too, is the impact of patriarchal conditioning, keeping women focused on our appearance and altering our bodies for the male gaze, rather than focusing on ways we can dismantle the systems that are oppressing us.

When a woman doesn't conform to these narratives, we tend to label her as being too radical. I can speak about this from my own experience. One of the greatest forms of isolation I have experienced from my own community of Black women was when I began to push back and challenge fatphobia and diet culture and began to link other systems of oppression such as anti-Black racism with the eating imbalances. Even people in my own family could not understand why I no longer tolerated inappropriate comments about my body without consent; why when people would engage in self-deprecating talk about their body size and shape I would gently push back or disengage; or why I began speaking up for myself when men in our family would comment on my food choices.

This has been a hard-fought battle for me, one I did not arrive at easily. I promised you earlier that I would return to my own self-destructive behavior. Here is what happened—the culmination of years of patriarchal influence. Remember when I talked about how I used to exercise obsessively? Well, the obsessive behaviors only became worse with time.

I thought that I would be able to take a break after earning my bachelor's degree, but I was told by a mentor that in order to be a psychologist or counselor, I had to go to graduate school. I spent the next six months researching different programs and beefing up my curriculum vitae and resume. Navigating these systems with no support was challenging, but I continued to play the narrative in my head that I had to be the best, while also still engaging in eating imbalance behaviors as a way to cope with the pressure. I was achievement-focused, goal-driven, and ambitious. I wanted to be exemplary, and at the age of twenty-one was the youngest person to enter one of the top graduate programs in the nation for clinical mental health counseling. I managed to finish my program in two years while holding down a job, internships, and professional leadership positions. I secured a high-paying job right out of school. I had followed a trajectory that society deems successful.

I constantly felt I had to be doing something to get ahead, or that I didn't know enough. I began to feed off this perfectionist energy, always trying to get it right. Part of this pattern was financially driven; I was always preparing myself for a rainy day by living significantly below my means. This desire to be as frugal as possible was an inherited trauma response I had learned from my family. I felt guilty for spending money on myself and had the mentality that I had to "make up for what I spent" by overworking. This was an ancestral pattern I had to break; it was an endless cycle of holding everything in, restricting myself, then splurging or bingeing, and then feeling that I had to make up for it by working my body to the bone.

The impact of all of this caused me to ignore my body's cues: that I was, in fact, *exhausted.* Over time, I had to learn that perfection does not exist, and then do the work to heal. My inner child had to learn that I did not have to over-perform to prove that I was valuable and worthy of love. I had to tell her that she was no longer being punished or in trouble for not knowing something or not having the right grades, and that it was okay for her to just live without worrying about the survival of the family. My adult self had to finally accept that I had achieved success.

When I look back on my childhood, I also remember the good times, savor the family trips, and recognize the hard work and sacrifice that my parents were putting in to survive and be perfect themselves in a Southern, conservative environment. However, my body holds the stories of the wounds, the pain, the suffering. I have appreciation for my Southern roots; so much cultural progress has come from Black history and the civil rights movement in the South. And now, living in a larger city, I long for the freedom of the open road, the sounds of nature, the way that time seems to slow down, and the deeper ancestral stories that the South holds within the land and oceans that I still call home.

But I also recognize that my story is one that holds both trauma and triumph. Through my own healing I have learned to integrate the two, to see that it doesn't have to be a rigid "all or nothing." I am learning to accept the parts of myself that I had once learned to run from.

This work led me to the realization that I want to be a generational pattern breaker—and I'm already making headway. In addition to being the first person in my family to graduate from college, I am the first person to divest from the 9-to-5 job force and become an entrepreneur; the first to not have my financial and family security dependent on marriage or a man; the first to break away from the scarcity mindset. And I am the first in my family to say that I am healing *us* out of the inherited epigenetic trauma that has been passed down, that has made so many of my family members lay their bodies on the line for their jobs.

In my healing process, I once held a lot of anger and resentment, specifically toward my maternal ancestors, for the ways I've seen patriarchy influence our relationships, marriages, and mothering. And for how that patriarchy would dim our light and cause us to show up in ways that feel disempowering. But I also recognize and have offered compassion and grace to my people for moving the needle and doing the best that they could with the resources and capacity available to them at the time so that I could get to this place. I recognize that they picked up the baton and did what they had to do in their own way, and that now it's my turn to honor their legacy and do the same for my descendants.

We were born into a patriarchal system and culture that has taught women to subordinate themselves, digest self-limiting beliefs, and apologize for taking up space. At this moment, I invite all Black women and femmes to pause and begin to uproot this indoctrination that has not served us. It is important that we ground ourselves in nourishing practices. We need space to develop a critical consciousness around what we have been taught. In this way we begin to reclaim freedom of choice and self-autonomy around food and our bodies. Healing these inherited cultural wounds is a huge challenge, especially when we live in a society in which this indoctrination is still very much alive. I want us to get into the practice of checking in and being present with ourselves as we grow out of this indoctrination.

Through this book we are building up our capacity to stay in our bodies and remain present to our experiences as we deal with the hard stuff. This helps us expand our holistic capacity and experience an array of emotions. We cannot say that we are fighting and advocating for justice, healing, and liberation while treating our bodies in the same way that systems of oppression have treated them. I believe that my body, your body, our bodies have an innate ability to heal. We must slow down and turn toward ourselves with compassion and curiosity, while rebuilding self-trust in order to follow the guidance and wisdom our bodies are offering to us within every given moment.

GUIDED PRACTICE #2

The first step in breaking away from indoctrination is identifying resources, supports, and strengths that help you feel safe. These are things that you can keep coming back to in order to help you pause, center yourself in your body, and ground yourself when things start to feel too overwhelming. Pleasure, safety, and softness help heal trauma in the body. Here are some examples of healing exercises that have worked for me—but I would encourage you to write, draw, record, or engage in a way where you are able to document and identify how these things might manifest for you.

RESOURCES: My resources are essential oils in my diffuser (lavender, lemon balm, cedarwood), a blanket, a grounding crystal, a Bible, a candle, a stress ball, soft music, a glass of water, a cup of tea, sage, a sketch pad, stretching, body movement, nature, hiking, a peppermint, rest, taking time away, pausing, recalling a memory of a happy and/or calm space.

SUPPORT: My support system involves calling a good friend or family member, spending time with my dog Zora, nurturing my plants, engaging with my spiritual and/or religious beliefs, talking with my therapist, coach, teachers, support groups, or social media community. There are also mental health emergency numbers available, such as the twenty-four-hour 988 Suicide and Crisis Lifeline or the Warmline Directory, which is a state-specific crisis support line if you need someone to talk to. Even if you don't have anyone who feels supportive in your life, imagine someone, maybe a character on a TV show, whom you view as supportive.

STRENGTHS: Think about your personal strengths. I am a skilled listener, self-aware, open-minded, adaptable, dependable, loving, and determined. What might this list look like for you?

Once you have checked in with your body, I invite you to be with your breath or posture, allowing what comes up. Notice what happens in your body when you take in this statement: "All of who you are is welcome here." Take note of any sensations, thoughts, feelings, and defenses that come up, and notice your initial response. What is familiar to you about that response? Is there an additional response that comes after it?

QUESTIONS FOR REFLECTION

I want us to get into the practice of checking in with ourselves as a way to trust our inner wisdom and what it has to communicate to us. I am going to invite you into a brief five-point check-in as you digest this recent chapter. My only request is that you engage in this check-in without judgment. Just be aware of what is present at this moment.

1. What's on your mind? (Thoughts, concerns, questions)
2. How does your body feel? What does it want you to know? (Notice sensations, impulses, reactions)
3. What does your breath tell you about your current state? (Is it constricted, expansive, shallow, labored?)
4. What do your feelings need right now? (Notice associations you have with certain feelings)
5. What is the quality of your energy at this moment? (Are you fatigued, energized, anxious?)

When we check in with ourselves first, determine what boundaries and resources we need, and then communicate our capacity to others, we create a practice of living in our truth and power. Now, when you feel ready, reflect on these questions:

1. How has patriarchy impacted the way you show up in your body as a Black woman, femme, or non-man?
2. What has Westernized religion taught you about yourself as a Black woman, femme, or non-man?
3. What messages did you learn about what it means to desire and experience cravings, indulgences, or pleasure?
4. In what ways have these messages shaped your relationship to food? How do they influence the way that you exist in your body?

· THREE ·

Girlhood, Interrupted

"I began eating to change my body. Some boys had destroyed me, and I barely survived it. I knew I wouldn't be able to endure another such violation, and so I ate because I thought that if my body became repulsive, I could keep men away. Even at that young age, I understood that to be fat was to be undesirable to men, to be beneath their contempt, and I already knew too much about their contempt. This is what most girls are taught—that we should be slender and small. We should not take up space. We should be seen and not heard, and if we are seen, we should be pleasing to men, acceptable to society. And most women know this, that we are supposed to disappear, but it's something that needs to be said, loudly, over and over again, so that we can resist surrendering to what is expected of us."

—ROXANE GAY, from *Hunger: A Memoir of (My) Body*

ARE YOU FAMILIAR WITH the term "adultification bias"? It is a belief system often applied to Black girls that says they are less innocent and more hypersexualized than white girls. A 2017 study by the Georgetown Center on Poverty and Inequality found that adults tend to believe Black girls—even those as young as five—need less nurturing, protection, support, and comfort than white girls, and that our girls are more independent and know more about sex and adult topics than white girls do. What a heavy burden to put on our young ones. In my work, I've seen the ravages of this bias play out over and over again—and far too often with devastating consequences. The sexualization of Black girls impacts the ways they begin to feel safe and connected within their bodies and can contribute to the early onset of disembodiment patterns in response to this trauma.

The deprivation of innocence described in the Georgetown study has a deep-rooted history in Western culture. Hope Moses, a diversity columnist, explains it this way: "When Europeans traveled to Africa during the 15th century, the minimal amounts of clothing African women wore, appropriate for the hot climate there, and the seemingly suggestive tribal dances, led Europeans to believe African women were sexually lewd."

To her point, during the eighteenth century William Smith, an English colonist, wrote that African women were "hot constitution'd Ladies" who were "continually devising schemes for how to gain a lover." Writings such as these led to the stereotype of Black women as promiscuous. Swedish taxonomist Carl Linnaeus, known as the father of taxonomy, laid out his racist beliefs that questioned our moral and intellectual capacities. He described *Homo Afer,* or African people, as cunning, lazy, lustful, careless, and governed by their emotions. This "scientific" rhetoric by Linnaeus and other white men was used to both dehumanize and fetishize Black people. His beliefs were spread throughout the world and embraced by Europeans to justify African enslavement under the guise that Black people were scientifically inferior to whites.

With this kind of historical bias haunting us, it is no surprise that many of our young Black girls today are still feeling the aftershocks and have difficulty with accepting the bodies they currently inhabit.

DESPERATELY SEEKING ACCEPTANCE

Not long ago, I worked with a sixteen-year-old client—let's call her Dawn—who said she hated herself because she did not look like the thin white girls at her predominantly white and affluent school. She had recently moved to North Carolina and was having trouble making new friends. She constantly compared herself to others on social media. With the rise of TikTok and other platforms that use filters, it was not uncommon for young girls to beg their parents for surgery or injections so they can look like the filters—filters based on Eurocentric features and rarely associated with one's own culture. She believed that her weight was the only thing she could change. She was too young for a cosmetic procedure, so she began to use fitness apps to track her calories. Before long, apps became an obsession. She would use them to both exercise compulsively and restrict her diet.

At first, the apps gave Dawn the validation she wasn't getting in real life. She worked out three hours daily, and as her body began to get thinner people took notice. What Dawn didn't realize, however, was that her weight loss had become dangerous. She was eating only eight hundred calories a day, and eventually lost her period. She had constant headaches, no energy, and couldn't focus on school. Dawn became so severely underweight that she had to be hospitalized. I was assigned to work with her after she left the hospital, along with a dietitian to help address her eating disorder.

Once Dawn returned home from the hospital, her mother became hypervigilant, monitoring everything she ate in the hopes that her treatment would soon be over. She'd even FaceTime her daughter during meals to make sure that she was eating. It got to the point where Dawn wasn't sure if she could trust herself. In therapy, we worked on her areas of fear, such as eating "bad food," which she associated with her Black culture, or being afraid to eat after a certain time.

At first, she was just going along with the therapy to make her mother happy. She told me that she had no intention of recovering and that she wasn't sure she would ever be happy in life. What I had to remind her of is that her eating disorder—the terminology I was using at the time—was telling her things about herself that in reality were not true. When we worked together, I asked her to consider this question: "What is your eating disorder telling you today?" This was a way of externalizing her experience so that she could begin to repair her relationship with the disorder.

What Dawn was experiencing was the internalization of anti-Black beauty ideals reinforced by social media. Social media's influence is so insidious that it can be hard to pinpoint where our discomfort is coming from if we aren't paying careful attention. Dawn didn't have the language for what she was experiencing. Instead, she internalized the beliefs that she was not good enough, that her culture was not good enough, and that she was wrong about how she felt and needed to change. She also struggled with mood swings, which entail issues of "emotional dysregulation," a term used to describe an emotional response that is poorly managed due to a number of inciting factors.

With emotional dysregulation, it's hard for someone to understand what's happening within their body, or to listen to their body. Their thinking patterns are very black-and-white, and they often run a negative script on repeat in their heads. It isn't unusual for someone with emotional dysregulation to suffer from low self-esteem and anxiety and to have feelings of worthlessness and hopelessness. Dawn coped with these feelings by turning to restrictive eating as a way to control how she was feeling and punish herself for being "bad."

Dawn is by no means alone in her thinking. A 2012 study published in the National Library of Medicine tested the direct effect of watching children's television on body satisfaction in preadolescent girls ages six to eight. The girls watched three television clips in random order containing either (1) thin-ideal animated characters or (2) animated characters with no thin-ideal features or (3) "real" human actors with no thin-ideal features. The researchers, who measured the girls' body satisfaction after they watched the programming, found that girls with higher levels of thin-ideal internalization showed higher body satisfaction after exposure to the

thin-ideal characters than after exposure to animated or real characters featuring no thin-ideal features.

Another study conducted with teenagers and young women in
2012 by Larson and Gosain found that the thin ideal can lead to a
worse body image. This concern among young women results in
making different choices to obtain the desired image, including
surgery.

A LEGACY OF BODY-SHAMING

When I was about nine or ten and my siblings and I would stay
with my grandparents, we were always eating out. My grandparents would take us to fast-food restaurants and buffets—anywhere
that allowed them to feed three hungry children on a budget. I
remember once, after my grandparents and I had just gotten back
from our usual trip to Bojangles, I was excited to devour my two
blueberry biscuits, also known as Bo-Berry biscuits, drizzled in
icing. I walked past my grandmother and remembered her saying
something along the lines of "Watch out— you're going to get a big
ol' butt eating all of those Bo-berry biscuits like that" while laugh-
ing in a warning tone. At the time, I had a very small frame, but I
was just beginning to develop small curves, mostly in my stomach
and buttocks area, about which I already felt self-conscious because the boys at school were constantly making comments about
my body and trying to touch me without my consent.

My grandmother had a pattern of judging food choices and policing her own desires. She would say things like, "Are you going
back to get more food? Well, get me a second plate. I don't want to
look greedy going back up there myself." Or she would chastise
herself for indulging in foods she enjoyed, saying, "I really don't
need to be eating sweets, I'm already picking up weight."

So, when my grandmother projected her casual inner criticism
onto me, it caused me to be more aware of my food choices as well.
While it may seem like a harmless comment, the tone behind my

grandmother's warning was important to me, because she is someone I've always held in high regard. To have her make a comment
about my body felt like a personal rebuke to my developing body.
At that age, I thought I had done something wrong. I remember
feeling so self-conscious in that moment and feeling shameful
about the biscuits I was about to devour. That comment caused me
to stop eating Bo-Berry biscuits for years. I didn't want the "big ol'
butt" my grandmother warned me about—which, from her tone,
felt like the worst thing in the world.

Historically, Black women have been fetishized for the size and
shape of their bodies—from hips and thighs to butts. I'm thinking
specifically of Saartjie Baartman, known as "the Hottentot Venus,"
who was treated as a curiosity for her body shape, and was exhibited and examined as if she were some kind of circus freak. Baartman was of Khoikhoi descent, born in Cape Town, South Africa.
Around the turn of the nineteenth century, when she was twenty-
one years old, Baartman was trafficked from her homeland and
forced to put herself on display in London venues. White men
used her body to connect fatness with Blackness, and created fear
around the Black body. She was looked upon with lust and disgust
and was denigrated. Even after her death in 1815, her brain, skel-
eton, and sexual organs remained on display in a Paris museum
until 1974. Her remains weren't repatriated and buried until 2002.

The more time I spent around my grandmother, the more I
came to realize that she talked about everyone like she did to me—
from the women in the stores whose clothes didn't "fit their body
shape" to the hairstyles she didn't approve of. She projected all of
her learned insecurities onto everyone around her. This was the
first time I began to associate my food choices with the development of my body and the attention that it would receive.

As an adult, I now realize that my grandmother's comment was
rooted in a place of fear. She had dealt with internalized and societal fatphobia and weight stigma as a Black woman and did not
want me to experience that as well. She also had been socialized to

be fearful around my developing body and wanted to protect me from the sexualization Black girls are disproportionately subjected to. This pattern of degradation and attempting to make Black girls invisible to presumably protect them has been passed down for generations. It is a mentality we've inherited from slavery, when mothers would often degrade their daughters in front of their enslavers in an attempt to protect them from sexual violence.

These messages were compounded by the teachings I received growing up in a conservative Southern Black Christian household. I constantly received messages from the women in my family and my church community that, as a girl, I had to cover up my body, because a body that was exposed or that developed "too fast" could make me more susceptible to unwanted male attention. As Black women and girls, we'd been socialized to believe that we needed to move within our bodies in a certain way to avoid provoking the desires of grown men. I now understand that our elders were using the tools that were passed down to them by *their* elders as a way of trying to protect me. This was another coping strategy we had been taught to believe would keep us safe. It gave us a false sense of control within ourselves and caused us to police each other's bodies.

This sexualization "talk" is something that Black girls and nonmen typically receive, in ways that often instill shame and fear around existing in our bodies. This "talk" is as common as the other conversation that occurs in Black families about what to do when you're pulled over by a police officer. I was taught at an early age to be hypervigilant about how I carried myself, to take up less space in order not to arouse other bodies. I was taught to downplay and second-guess myself to make others comfortable. These talks are meant to help us survive, but often shift the blame and responsibility of violence onto us, rather than putting it where it belongs: on the systems and the people that carry out the violence.

The sexualization and sexual violence experienced by Black women and girls can be traced back to the transatlantic slave trade and was carried forth in the culture of the plantation. Reverend John Newton, author of the song "Amazing Grace," wrote in his personal account that "when women and girls are taken on board the ship, naked, trembling, terrified, they are often exposed to the wanton rudeness of white savages. The prey is divided upon the spot. Resistance or refusal would be utterly in vain." Children were enslaved in droves, with young girls ranging anywhere from nine years of age to their mid-teens.

While most of the narrative around slavery is focused on the actions of white men, white women were equally if not more invested in the brutality that enslaved girls and women endured. The girls were often given to white women as gifts from their husbands, and as wedding and Christmas presents. Whenever the wives were angry, they would lash out against these young Black girls in their households—often sexually exploiting them, using horsewhips to attempt to discipline and control them, and treating them in other terrible ways. Stephanie E. Jones-Rogers, author of *They Were Her Property: White Women as Slave Owners in the American South*, wrote, "White mothers treated enslaved women's bodies, their labor, and the products of their labor as goods, and in consequence were able to commit violence against these women, in their role as mothers, that slavery and the slave market made possible." In prioritizing their own infants' nutritional needs over those of their wet nurses' children, white mothers separated enslaved mothers from their children, often prevented enslaved women from forming maternal bonds with their infants, and distanced them from the communities and kinship networks that were integral to their children's survival.

The dehumanization of Black women and girls during the period of slavery, says Dr. Joy DeGruy, author of *Post Traumatic Slave Syndrome: America's Legacy of Enduring Injury and Healing*, extended to "rape laws" that said, "No white could ever rape a slave woman due to the regulation of law designed by the white race, sexual intercourse does not and cannot for obvious reasons, apply to slaves, their intercourse is promiscuous." The psychology of sexual abuse toward Black women and girls was not just economic; it was also used as a weapon of terror to reinforce white domination over them as human property and to stifle resistance. Sexual abuse of Black women and girls extended beyond the transatlantic trade ships and into the slave fields, where Black women were further sexually abused.

Black women were also labeled as "breeders," existing only to replenish the slave population. Many of the enslaved girls were forced into breeding as young as thirteen years of age and were often raped and impregnated by the enslavers. While white women were viewed as innocent victims who needed the protection of white men, enslavers organized and violently forced Black men to perform rape and assault on Black woman and girls in front of an audience of white men for the purpose of entertainment. Enslaved girls throughout the Southern and Northern colonies often endured heavy labor (as early as seven years of age), poor housing conditions, and an inadequate diet. They were worn out, barely sheltered, and starving, yet were still expected to engage in brutal work from sunup to sundown every day. And as a result, the average Black woman did not live past age forty. Plantations were the economic power structure of the South, and slave labor was its foundation.

The system of slavery not only tore families apart, but also drove a wedge between mothers and their young daughters as a by-product. Mothers were not encouraged to praise and uplift their daughters, especially not in front of slave owners, their families, and their white overseers. To do so would be to put one's child in harm's way—call too much attention to them and risk the wrath of the slave owner's wife, for example. Instead, it was more acceptable for mothers to treat their daughters with the same disdain and rejection levied by the slave owners and their progeny. Imagine the cruel mind game of having to deny love to your own flesh and blood in order to protect your child.

This constant state of denial and being deprived of anything close to a normal childhood has had devastating effects on us into the present day. Those tensions between mothers and daughters did not necessarily cease to exist in our communities over time, and in some families continue as a way of keeping young girls "in their place." The resulting pain has had to manifest itself somewhere, in some way, which leads us back to our bodies, where much of this pain has been stored.

Black women and femmes tend to experience higher rates of issues like endometriosis, fibroids, infertility, and other uterine and womb issues that can be manifestations of the historical legacy of the extensive sexual, verbal, and emotional abuse our ancestors endured. Perhaps our bodies are trying to protect us through cellular memory and protest by saying, "No more human bounty will come through this body." These are the wounds that we have to work with the body and with our ancestors to address.

In her book on Black men and masculinity, Black feminist author and beloved ancestor bell hooks said that for a lot of enslaved Africans, the sexual deviance of white men was foreign and their infatuation with the Black body was disturbing. Westernized Christianity was often forced onto enslaved Africans to separate and disconnect us from our indigenous spiritual practices and to enforce power and control.

Long after Emancipation, many Black folks continued the faith practice of Christianity, because it offered the idea that our bodies had the potential to be good, saved, sanctified, and delivered from all we had been through. This point of view also fed into "purity culture," which places a strong emphasis on abstinence from sexual intercourse before marriage. Dating is discouraged entirely in order to avoid premarital sex. Women and girls are told to cover up and dress modestly to avoid arousing sexual urges in men and boys. Purity culture also emphasizes traditional gender roles.

Even with a belief system such as this one, that both polices and controls women's bodies, we still must acknowledge that Christianity and the Black church served as one pathway for enslaved Africans and their descendants to initially protect themselves from the disturbing sexualizing and exploiting of our bodies by white people.

Some of this backward thinking has led to outdated stereotypes that still linger today. Take, for example, the Jezebel archetype. Sociology professor Dr. David Pilgrim put the archetype into perspective this way: "The portrayal of Black women as lascivious by nature is an enduring stereotype. The descriptive words associated with this stereotype are singular in their focus: seductive, alluring, worldly, beguiling, tempting, and lewd. With the rise of slavery, white women, as a group, were redefined as models of self-respect, self-control, and modesty—even sexual purity. But Black women were often portrayed as innately promiscuous, even predatory. This depiction of Black women is signified by the name Jezebel."

This narrative that Black women's bodies were not like white women's bodies and therefore needed to be controlled by any means necessary only reinforces the belief that Black women and girls are at fault for their objectification. The Jezebel archetype is the reason a lot of women and girls grow up being told we should not wear short skirts around men, or that we should wear modesty cloths at church if our dresses go above our knees so that we won't "tempt" the preacher or other men in the church.

THE IMPACT OF GIRLHOOD ON WOMANHOOD

Children are the most heavily impacted by a patriarchal society, as they are one of the most unprotected classes of citizens in the world. They are sentenced to powerlessness even in messages like "Stay in a child's place" or "A child is to be seen and not heard" that are often used to silence children and demand that they take up less space.

These messages imply that children are in service to adults or authority, but not actual living beings with their own needs, desires, and contributions to make. Within this culture, adults are placed at the top of the hierarchy, and children are placed at the lowest end as the subordinate. In Southern Black religious communities, it has been normalized to lash out, hit, silence, manipulate, and control children in the same way that the enslaver controlled the bodies of our Black ancestors. It is a pattern of instilling fear and control, under the guise of fostering respectability and obedience to God.

While this culture is changing, with more activism around respect for children as human beings and the incorporation of indigenous African practices, such as gentle or conscious parenting, I can remember a time where it was forbidden to say "no" to an adult or someone in a position of authority. If you did say no or try to advocate for yourself, you were labeled as disrespectful and were punished or violently harmed. This made it easy for adults in Southern Black religious communities to degrade and take advantage of children, particularly young girls, and get away with it. It allowed them to enact the wound of their own trauma onto the bodies of those most vulnerable.

Adults indoctrinated through this Southern Black religious culture did not have the skills to regulate their own emotions, and therapeutic healing outside of the church was stigmatized as being for "crazy people." Their inner child continued to be activated and triggered when they experienced children being free in ways that they were told to shut down, police, and shrink within themselves.

The women in my church had become accustomed to being self-critical and judgmental, enslaved to a lifetime of shame, fear, and guilt for simply existing. They continued to pass on this trauma wound that had been internalized through patriarchy and unquestionably upheld through Westernized Christianity, generation after generation.

Here is an example. I can remember the summer I came home from my first semester of college. I was enthused to see my friends from church, and to share my academic accomplishments. I had gained weight, but was not too focused on body changes at the time. The whispers from the grown women at church were "She must be at college being fast, because her hips are spreading; she's going to get pregnant and have to drop out one day."

Labeling young girls and teenagers who move freely within their bodies as "fast" is one way that women have learned to control and police the bodies of people who take up space. Being labeled as "fast" is another way we label someone as sexually deviant or hypersexual. It doesn't consider that even if a child is sexually active at a younger age, it is often the result of an adult's introducing the behavior to the child. Instead, the culture blames young people, but particularly young girls, for their sexual objectification. And it also often protects adults who are engaged in hypersexualization and abuse by placing the responsibility to shrink oneself onto the young developing bodies and minds of Black girls under the guise of modesty.

Meanwhile, college offered more access to food options than I was accustomed to, and I was coping with the challenges of adjusting to a new environment and dealing with depression and anxiety as a result of being away from family for the first time in my life. Naturally, my body changed, and I remember feeling self-conscious about it. The comments made at church certainly didn't help. Shortly after my visit home, my imbalanced eating patterns began to ramp up. It would also be the last time I attended a service at my home church. The visit reaffirmed what I had long been feeling: that the church culture did not align with the values of the faith. I was tired of feeling unsafe, self-conscious, and judged every time I attended.

The persistent low vibrational petty gossip from the women in my church toward young girls, women, and femmes was a manifestation of their low self-esteem and the healing they needed within themselves. They had been taught to uphold patriarchy and concede their power and authority to men. They were trained to overlook the sexual abuse and violence carried out by men in the community. Instead, they directed their energy toward other women, using one another as targets and emotional punching bags—masking a deeper, unarticulated anger and resentment toward a system they allowed themselves to be complicit in. For me, this energy and behavior tainted a religious institution that was supposed to be about love, liberation, and acceptance.

THE SEXUAL TRUTHS WE DON'T TALK ABOUT

Many Black women I have worked with around eating imbalances have also disclosed to me a history of sexual abuse and violence. They describe having their physical, emotional, and energetic boundaries and vulnerability dishonored repeatedly, which led to early experiences of body disconnection and unresolved trauma. These women shared that their eating imbalance developed as a coping mechanism in response to the sexual trauma they had experienced. The trauma disrupted both their ability to regulate their nervous system and their connection to their bodies. The eating imbalance, then, offered a perceived sense of control in response to the fear, loss of self, and internal chaos and dysregulation they were experiencing. However, it was also a trap door, leading them into further disconnection from their body. The numbing, suppressing, and dissociation that resulted was keeping them stuck in the unresolved pain of their past.

According to the National Center for Injury Prevention and Control and the Centers for Disease Control and Prevention, 35 percent of Black women experience some form of sexual violence during their lifetime. Studies show that one in four Black girls will be sexually abused before the age of eighteen. While the rates are alarming, Black girls often do not receive the support they need, either because they are not believed or because they've been taught to be silent around their abuse in order to avoid bringing shame on the family. Particularly in Black communities when the abuser is a cisgender-heterosexual (cis-het) Black man, Black girls and women are taught to feel guilty about speaking up or seeking help, because they are told that they are contributing to Black men's being incarcerated or being killed by the police.

This belief that Black girls are responsible for the actions of grown men, and not allowed to hold their abusers accountable without severe repercussions, causes an internalized shame that can then manifest as depression, numbness, and disconnection from the body. When young girls and women are forced into silence around their abuse, it allows the cycle to continue. It can cause them to shrink to be unseen or form a barrier of protection around their pain by altering their bodies. Engaging in imbalanced eating is one of the ways girls begin the process of taking up less space in the world, as a way to protect themselves. They turn their shame inward to lessen the pain and gain a sense of control over their bodies.

As I've grown in my skill set as a space holder for transformation, I have worked to create more emotional and energetic safety and support for clients in therapy, so that they might be able to expand their tolerance for simply being with their own trauma. When they feel safer with me and have developed the practices and skills to expand their emotional capacity, we are able to get into the ways their bodies have learned to hold the trauma. This part of the process often elicits emotions of sadness, grief, and anger as they are finally able to truly feel what they're experiencing— without being judged, overwhelmed, or re-traumatized.

My clients have described feeling hopeless because they believed they did not have any other choice but to engage in imbalanced eating behaviors with the aim of becoming the body ideal that society represents as worthy of protection. Other clients have shared that the eating imbalance had become a learned cycle of punishment and self-sabotage that they were carrying forward as they blamed themselves for what had happened to them.

One common sentiment they each disclosed was feeling isolated and alone within the imbalance. They often shared that they were in treatment programs that either ignored their racial identity and cultural background or that came from a space where the legacy of white supremacy and colonialism covertly dominated their treatment. Some were working with providers of color, but these providers did not have training in eating imbalances and were still operating out of discriminatory mindsets like fatphobia, anti-fat bias, and weight stigma. They also described not having access to community spaces outside of the short-term recovery facilities where they could engage in ongoing recovery with people who shared their social identities. And many shared that systemic issues that impact their communities regarding food scarcity, lack of access to diverse food options, and proximity to fresh produce limited their recovery.

They shared that being at the nexus of these realities with no healing in sight caused them to feel even more isolated, which led them to feel *more* ostracized and stuck in deep cycles of body shame. Many experienced recurrent hospitalizations and the need for ongoing inpatient treatment. These factors, which were never addressed in predominantly white spaces, were described as the core issues connected to their survival that were driving the eating imbalance.

The women I met with talked about their bodies being sexually objectified while simultaneously being resistant to taking agency over their sexuality due to fear around being harmed. They talked about their bodies being viewed as offensive or disruptive in childhood based on how they dressed or how their bodies naturally evolved and developed. They felt othered from the concept of "femininity," softness, and gentleness—and felt this even more if they were larger and had experienced fatphobia, weight stigma, or anti-fat bias. They talked about existing in a world where they were both invisible in their pain and visible when it came to backlash around their bodies. Some shared that they never felt as if they were enough, simply by existing. The mental gymnastics they were navigating led to their not being able to be present in their bodies; they had never learned or been socialized to accept their bodies. The shadow of the eating imbalance sold them the broken promise that changing their bodies through their eating pattern was the only way to lessen the pain, when in fact it just fueled further disconnection, dysregulation, fear, rigidity, and feelings of unworthiness.

My clients' lived experiences were valid and based on toxic messages that women and girls receive from society that tell us we should cover up our bodies so as not to arouse mostly male attention. Eating imbalances become a part of the disembodiment as a coping strategy to escape the fragmented parts of ourselves that developed from the trauma. These parts show up in our sensations, emotions, and our body, and we hold them through bracing patterns, tension, and knots in the body that manifest in our physical postures. The most common posture that I have seen with clients dealing with imbalanced eating is a collapsed-inward position, as many come into my office, grab a pillow, and place it in front of their belly. They then lower their gaze and often curl into themselves, almost as if they are making themselves into a little ball trying to disappear. Others have disclosed that their binge eating, and in some instances subsequent weight gain, was created to build a barrier around their bodies and protect themselves from sexual abuse and violence.

THE VIOLENCE WE HAVE INTERNALIZED

Allow me to share one more example with you. My client Erica was a twenty-two-year-old college student, and self-identified as a larger-sized, lighter-skinned Black woman. I remember that she giggled when I asked her in our initial assessment about imbalanced eating behaviors. Her response, after a longish pause, was "No, I don't eat a lot." As we talked, I soon learned that she was eating only once a day. When I offered her language and examples describing how undereating and undernourishment can show up as anorexia or restrictive eating, tears welled in her eyes. She shared that she did not know that someone who looked like her could have a restrictive eating pattern, mainly because those with eating imbalances had been portrayed as thin white women. She shared that she mostly heard of the stereotype of binge eating—or as she described it, "comfort eating"—as being common in larger women. She also shared that because she didn't eat a lot, she never thought that she had an imbalance.

As we talked more, Erica shared that she desired to lose weight for aesthetic reasons. She had trained her body to ignore her hunger cues, because she had a pattern of suppressing and dissociating, typically through substance use. As we continued to work together, Erica eventually shared that during her childhood she had experienced sexual abuse from a family friend. She said she had been sexualized and had received many comments on the "thickness" of her body from men in her family throughout her childhood and adolescence. She shared that she began to feel self-conscious, and turned her disgust and grief into her body and no longer trusted herself. She recalled her mother constantly telling her, "Don't wear shorts—your uncle is coming over." She also recounted that one time she got a whooping for dancing too freely, her mother telling her that her body was jiggling and shaking too much. She was labeled as "fast" and told that she was being "too grown."

Erica said that she began to feel insecure in her body, and uncomfortable and unsafe around her family. Over time, she began to wear oversized clothes, silence her voice, and internalize the shame that she experienced about her body by punishing herself and refusing to eat. She continued this pattern throughout her teen years, and now, as a young adult, she was still using restrictive eating habits and numbing substances to address her core wounds: inner separation due to sexualization and abuse in girlhood, and her mother's internalized patriarchy and trauma.

As her therapist, I worked to create safety and help Erica set boundaries and explore what a yes, maybe, and no felt like in her body. A "yes" meant anything her body was clearly in alignment with—thoughts, ideas, activities that elicited joy and pleasure. A "no," conversely, meant anything the body felt uncomfortable with. This might show up as a sense of dread when certain thoughts arose—feeling tired or tense, or perhaps noticing the body closing inward.

A "maybe" is a mixture of the two. In these instances, perhaps the physical body is demonstrating a "yes"—nodding, verbal agreement, an open posture—but the *internal* self is reflecting "no" through tension, anxiety, and so on. Sometimes the "maybe" resolves itself into a "yes" or a "no" eventually, and at other times it stays firmly in the emotional middle, and that's okay. The most important thing Erica and I worked on was learning how to recognize her own boundaries and trust her body to feel its way into a response that was best for her.

Over time she became comfortable with the sensations and emotions that were behind her trauma responses. We then worked together to metabolize those trauma responses by holding space for us to explore her patterns of suppressing her feelings and substance use, during which time we both became more aware of when she would dissociate. For example, she would often zone out and ask me to repeat what we were talking about, or I'd notice that it was difficult for her to maintain her thought process. We went into her body to heal the younger girl inside of her who felt helpless and disempowered due to the trauma. We both listened and allowed the little girl to feel safe, and eventually released the knots and tension around her throat and womb space that had been holding the trauma for her throughout the years.

I often get the question of how this approach is supportive of women and femmes who are still in the situation where the eating imbalance is "adaptive," as we say. By this, I mean that our eating imbalances can be a response to a culture dominated by colonialism, capitalism, and white supremacy. I use a harm-reduction approach, one that was popularized to address substance use. But health care professionals are also using it to work with eating imbalances.

Harm reduction is a set of practical strategies and ideas aimed at reducing negative consequences associated with substance use—and it is also a movement for social justice, built on a belief in, and respect for, the rights of people who use substances. In the eating disorder field, there is a mainstream perspective around being either "recovered" or "sick"; however, more folks like me are saying that this binary view is limiting and discouraging and have aligned more with a harm-reduction perspective, which instead asks how we can minimize the harm of the eating imbalance while living in a culture that consistently inflames the behavior.

In my work with Erica, I encouraged her to offer compassion to the self-sabotaging patterns and fragmented parts of her that had assumed the driver's seat, keeping her from embodying the healing that she deserved. Instead of not eating all day and ignoring her body, we practiced setting a timer that would remind her to check in with her body every four hours to see if she was hungry or not. This was an introductory step into beginning to check in with her body, because without the timer she would choose not to or forget to eat.

As we worked around memory, her trauma responses to those memories, and learning how to listen to her body to guide us into healing the trauma, Erica shared that she began to trust herself more and feel safer in her body. She decided that she needed to pull back from the substance use. We also began to unpack cultural conditioning around labeling food as "good" or "bad," her beliefs that she needed to be slim and thick, and the way her internalization of toxic cultural and societal messages had manifested in her eating patterns. And, together, we were able to support her in coming into a restorative and nourishing relationship with food.

Erica began to work with a weight-neutral dietitian to provide nutritional support. We continued to work through her depression, anxiety, fear, confusion, and disembodiment as they came up in our work together. We focused on the process of recovery, forgoing the traditional binary eating disorder treatment that labels patients and clients as simply recovered or sick. Eventually, she began to sit straighter, and she shared that she was able to find more expansiveness in her body.

Erica eventually graduated college, and my journey with her came to an end. But before she left, she shared that she felt safer in her body and was better able to recognize when she would become disembodied. She used our work together as a pathway back into her body. Erica had become comfortable rebuilding her foundation, intentionally slowing down and pausing to listen to her body to guide her to the spaces that were holding her trauma. She began to get to know the fragmented and shadow parts of herself, and ultimately was able to integrate the healing, resulting in a greater capacity for safety, joy, and connection.

WHERE DO WE GO FROM HERE? START WITH YOUR INNER VOICES

As young girls, we develop eating imbalances as a way to cope with negative beliefs that have told us we are unlovable, not good enough, or deeply flawed. At this point I'd like to share with you a therapy modality I mentioned earlier, Internal Family Systems (IFS), that works with those parts of ourselves that have become fragmented. These parts are labeled as "the Managers," "the Firefighters," and "the Exiles/Rejected." Each of them exists on a continuum and shows up as our inner voice, often manifesting as a negative thinking pattern or core belief about ourselves.

The Managers are typically abusive, critical, judgmental, rigid, punitive, angry, and pessimistic. They say things like, "You are a terrible person for gaining weight; you will never be good enough." The Firefighters are rebellious, defiant, and pessimistic; they act out, numb, and procrastinate, are often apathetic and distracting, and say things like, "Screw it, I might as well go on a binge or do something destructive or self-sabotaging—nothing matters anyway." The Exiles/Rejected parts are often anxious, fearful, sad, and grieving; they feel worthless, ashamed, and full of self-doubt. I have found that it has been helpful to empathetically work with each part in tandem to restore balance and put the self back into the driver's seat.

The goal is not to get rid of the Managers, Firefighters, and Exiles/Rejected parts of ourselves, but to understand what *purpose* they are serving, hold space to honor what they are attempting to do for us, and create safety and space for them to move along the continuum. IFS therapist Amy Yandel Grabowski has described the process as helping the parts get unstuck, in balance, harmonious, and cooperative with each other. She shares that on the more integrated end of the spectrum, the Manager becomes the Mentor who motivates, organizes, solves problems, and plans, which can be highly effective for managing an eating imbalance and making sure that our bodies are adequately nourished. The Firefighter becomes the advocate who exudes "spunk," energy, assertiveness, protection, self-care, and balance, which can be helpful for setting boundaries and honoring our body's capacities. The Exile/Rejected part becomes the kid who is playful, fun, in awe, humorous, content, and feels worthy, which helps us be happy, easeful, and at peace within our bodies.

The self is described as who we are, who is in charge of our parts, and who leads us through life. When our self is unregulated, it becomes empty, hollow, lost, without identity, directionless, disconnected, and alone. When we have healed the parts that we had to suppress, shut down, and cut off to survive trauma, the self can reemerge and be compassionate, wise, stable, centered, calm, confident, clearheaded, creative, curious, and have a capacity for connection.

As you read through these descriptions, you may have noticed different parts of yourself emerging in response to being noticed. Listen to them. Hold space for them. And if any of this resonates, I would recommend working with a licensed mental health therapist who has experience working within Internal Family Systems.

A Love Note Before Our Guided Practice
I feel deep empathy and compassion toward any woman or femme who resonates with the stories or examples offered throughout this chapter. When we begin to unpack and show compassion and grace toward others, it often involves looking inward at the places where we were not allowed to have compassion and grace toward ourselves. We hold those patterns of being critical, judgmental, and insecure from a young age and carry those core feelings into adulthood, which impacts how we relate and interact with one another. Unlearning these patterns involves taking the responsibility off your inner child that believes "If I'd behaved better, he wouldn't have hit me," or "I caused it to happen—if only I hadn't worn X," or "I deserved it; I was a bad girl."

Understanding where these beliefs come from can be difficult to sit with, but is necessary if you want to unburden yourself. You may never receive an apology or an attempt at repair from the people who forced these belief systems onto you, but I encourage you to forgive yourself for what you did not know, be accountable to your growth, and repair the relationship you have with your own body.

It can be hard to question your indoctrination when it is all you have ever known. For some it may require an investigation into the question of "Who am I outside of all of these layers?" While this discovery can be both freeing and invigorating, it can also contribute to grief and sorrow as you consider the ways the trauma wound showed up in the adults around you and how they did not have the tools to protect you. If this is your story, I encourage you to take your time and be gentle with yourself.

As we begin to outgrow oppressive conditioning, we are often ostracized and rejected by people we love. They fear our wholeness, because they have been taught to fear wholeness within themselves. Remember that they are entitled to their process and journey; however, you may need to set boundaries so that you are not held back by their fears. Healing can be a lonely journey; it requires faith and surrender to the process of becoming undone and unraveled so that you can be fully transformed. You must stumble through the muck to get to liberation. You may get stuck, or regress out of comfort and familiarity and into fear of the unknown—hold space for that, while also recognizing the fact that, as an adult, you are responsible for your own healing now.

My hope is that you will lean into courage and continue to move forward. Moving out of denial around the impact of what happened to you is not easy, but it is necessary if you are to become free, and to begin to create generations of free Black people. My hope is that opening up these conversations will serve as a space for Black women and femmes to begin to heal and restore the relationship and trust that we have within ourselves and toward one another as a community.

GUIDED PRACTICE #3

Before we begin, let's first take a moment to pause. Discussions about the impact of sexualization and how it connects to our food and relationship to nourishment can bring up a variety of emotions, sensations, and bodily responses. Stay with it, and know that what you are feeling is valid.

Now, when you feel ready, I invite you to write a letter to your younger self. As we focus on the younger part of ourselves, other parts may emerge, and that is okay; continue to offer yourself some grace. As we support this inner child in writing a new story, I ask that you envision the younger you. Allow the vision to fully arrive: What do you look like? How do you feel in your body? If it is difficult to envision yourself as a younger child, perhaps you have an old photo of yourself; or, if that feels too intense, perhaps you can imagine you are speaking with a young child. For those who may have visual impairments, I recommend sensing into the spirit of a child. Ask the inner child if you can speak to them. What pronouns do they use? How would they like to be addressed by you? For this journaling practice, I will use the pronouns "she/her" to guide you through the connection.

If you can envision your younger self, take a moment and just notice where she exists in your body. Maybe you feel some activation in your chest, or in your belly. Maybe there's some tingling in your legs. Just notice what comes alive for you as you envision this younger version of yourself. If you are using a visual of another young person, notice where you feel activated in your body when her image comes to mind; perhaps this is an indication of where your inner child exists as well.

Allow your mind to drift into the space where you are feeling the activation. Allow yourself to really feel into the space in your body. What sensations and emotions are most present? Follow those sensations and emotions through your body as if they are a road map and see where they take you. Sometimes there is a deeper area that is storing the pain. Listen and be with what is present for you, while also knowing that if it gets too overwhelming or emotionally flooded, or if you notice that you are starting to dissociate, this is also an opportunity to pause the activity and listen to what your body is telling you it has the capacity for right now.

Once you have identified the space in your body where the inner child resides, I invite you to send your breath into that space. Allow for an intentional inhale through your nose and, to your body's capacity, hold the breath with a pause. Then offer a long exhale out through your mouth to release. Perhaps repeat this a few times, following the pattern of consciously inhaling, holding, and then releasing. Once your body feels a bit more settled, I ask that you come back into the place where you are sitting, lying, standing, or resting and offer yourself another pause.

Now we're ready to grab a piece of paper or something to record your words, to begin writing or recording a letter to the inner child self. Write about what she needed to hear at the time of the trauma and offer her the wisdom that you now have. Write to your heart's desire and allow whatever surfaces to come out. Once you finish writing, read back over your letter to yourself. How do your mind, body, and spirit feel as you receive this message?

QUESTIONS FOR REFLECTION

As we begin the process of reclaiming our Black bodies and turning away from white consumption and the white and/or male gaze, it is important to have a safe space to unpack shame and guilt. These damaging beliefs belong to a system that thrives on our being disconnected from our bodies, sexuality, pleasure, and sensuality; creating safety to come back into those places within us is the pathway to healing our relationship with our bodies. The pathway back into our body starts with recognizing the ways that we are being taught or have experienced separation from our bodies through violence, abuse, or any of the other multiple ways that our boundaries have been violated. As you take some time to go through the questions, create a space of safety and allow yourself to be resourced with some of the things we discussed in the last chapter—a soft blanket, a support person, or a mental image of a safe place. Allow yourself to use your breath to guide you inward, and if you are too overwhelmed with emotions, please stop. Maybe you will decide to come back to this page or chapter, or maybe you will skip forward. Above all else, listen to your body.

1. When you think back on your childhood, how much of your sense of self was impacted by the way others saw and treated you? In what ways did this show up in your life?
2. What beliefs were you taught as a young girl about Black women and femmes and how they should view their sexuality, sensuality, and pleasures?
3. Were you ever exposed to beliefs that categorized Black women and femmes as cunning, lustful, and promiscuous? How have you internalized these injected beliefs?
4. Have you ever yourself experienced or known of anyone who has experienced any form of violence as a young child (physical, sexual, emotional, etc.)? What belief systems did you/ she form around this experience? For example, some people are told that it is their fault that the abuse happened, which is always a lie. Or, sometimes to protect ourselves we form beliefs like "I can't trust anyone."
5. What role did eating play in the way that you/she learned to cope with this trauma?
6. What measures, if any, have you taken to disrupt the negative thinking patterns trauma can cause us in order to reclaim your self-esteem and feel more empowered?

Once you have explored and sat with these questions, I want you to affirm to yourself: "I am not what happened to me. I did not cause what happened to me. What happened to me was not justified." Perhaps say this a few times to yourself and see if there are places in your body where it resonates. If not, just notice the emotions and sensations of your body. Your body responses offer information, and we always want to approach these responses with curiosity and consent. Remember that your response and reaction to the trauma are not your fault; our bodies are wired to keep us safe through these responses. However, these responses, which were once helpful and normalized, no longer serve us.

Some folks may be reading this and thinking, *What if I am still in the trauma?* I totally understand that. If this is the case, ask yourself the questions above and continue to affirm yourself with the messages provided. If you are still in the experience of the trauma, can you identify at least one way that you can move to a space of more presence? You can even do this through naming the energy of fear, loss of self, chaos, or dysregulation that might be behind the trauma you're experiencing.

FOUR

What's Internalized Misogynoir Got to Do with It?

"I am a Black Feminist. I recognize that my power as well as my primary oppressions come as a result of my blackness as well as my womaness, and therefore my struggles on both of these fronts are inseparable."

—AUDRE LORDE

IN 2022, WELL BEFORE the controversy around performing artist Lizzo erupted, I came across an article about a TikTok Dance Challenge that she had launched in honor of her weight gain. The article applauded Lizzo for loving and celebrating her body. As I watched the accompanying video, I excitedly screamed into my cell phone, "Yass, sis!" And then, I scrolled down to the comments section. While I'd hoped to see other Black women celebrating with Lizzo in her joy, confidence, and embodiment, I instead read comments that were rooted in fatphobia and misogyny, specifically directed toward Black women and femmes—a concept known as "misogynoir." Coined in 2010 by queer Black feminist Moya Bailey, the phrase encapsulates both race and gender. Bailey describes it as the point "where racism and sexism meet." It's a concept grounded in the theory of intersectionality, which analyzes how various social identities such as race, gender, class, and sexual orientation interrelate in systems of oppression.

"Intersectionality" is an analytical framework for understanding how aspects of a person's social and political identities combine or interconnect to create different modes of discrimination and privilege. The term, created by Kimberlé Crenshaw in 1989, identifies multiple factors of social advantages and disadvantages. Racial justice and gender equality activist Amara Ochefu explains it this way: "Before the idea of intersectionality was widely known, most people assumed Black women experienced the culmination of racism (based on the experiences of Black men) and sexism (based on the experiences of White women). They did not acknowledge that Black women's experiences can be completely distinct from either group."

Misogynoir aligns with an intersectional perspective by looking at the ways that Black women are impacted by the system of patriarchy that birthed sexism, and the system of white supremacy that birthed anti-Black racism. It also looks at the ways other social and political identities—such as being a Black queer woman, or a Black trans woman, or a Black fat woman, or a Black disabled woman— also intersect and create compounding forms of oppression based on marginalization and privilege.

And here lies the real crux of the discussion that we'll be having throughout this chapter, an additional layer of destructive power: Misogynoir becomes internalized when we absorb messages from society rooted in sexism and anti-Black racism. These messages are intended to put limitations on Black women and femmes by placing us in narrow boxes that tell us who we can be and how we should show up in the world. The reactions to Lizzo's story that I read were clearly influenced by these internalized messages. A number of Black women and femmes dropped toxic comments like, "This is disgusting," or "One minute she is crying and the next minute she is celebrating herself. She's bipolar." Someone wrote, "She is going to regret posting this and have a tantrum again," while others said things like, "She is promoting obesity," or "She will be like other celebrities like Mo'Nique and eventually realize that she needs to lose the weight," or "Her knees will feel that weight gain later." There were also a few backhanded compliments like, "Good that she feels confident, but she is not healthy."

The vitriol these Black women were spewing was sickening, angering, and saddening. Yet in all of it, I saw evidence of our underlying trauma—the hate we have internalized due to society's expectations, causing us to believe the worst about fat Black bodies.

Black women often act out toward other Black women in ways that are emotionally and verbally abusive as a means of controlling and policing others' embodied choices of self-expression. Social media has only emboldened this behavior, allowing folks to see someone living an expansive, liberated life and to immediately critique it. To be triggered, or emotionally activated, is to have an intense emotional or physical reaction, such as a panic attack, or an intense visceral reaction that jolts our nervous system. This knee-jerk reflex to pass negative judgment is brought on by the lack of freedom and expansiveness folks may feel in their own lives, and the internalization of the oppression we have received.

As I continued to read through the comments, I allowed myself to pause and feel all that was coming up in my own body. I took a couple of deep breaths, put my phone down, and grabbed my journal. I wrote about the fear I recognized in all those women's responses, how they were triggered by a woman celebrating herself in her body and felt the need to lash out; how they felt the need to "keep her in her place," extinguish her joy, minimize her confidence—and ultimately, demand that she take up less space as a fat Black woman.

You may be thinking, as so many in our society do, that this kind of criticism and negativity comes with the territory of celebrity, that it's an inevitable by-product of being a public figure, something those in the limelight must just accept. But the reality is that this ideology is based on dehumanizing people, often to cover up one's own hurts.

All of the comments I read were based on things these commenters likely had heard about themselves or other Black women and femmes, and they were repeating them without exploring the societal conditioning behind what they were expressing. This conditioning, I repeat, is what keeps us from seeing, connecting with, and trusting one another as Black women. We—even those of us who claim to support women's rights and Black women's liberation—have internalized the oppressor's mentality as a result of living in this society, and it requires intentional unpacking and practice to undo.

I've also seen misogynoir show up within my own sister circles. A simple brunch outing with Black women can ignite a noticeable energy shift, especially when it comes time to survey the menu and order food. I can sense the fear, hesitation, and silence around what choice each woman will make, and what that choice will mean or say about them. Nowadays it is almost noble to publicly announce that you are vegan, vegetarian, or on some other food or dietary restriction. It serves as a representation of what it means to be a "good Black woman," and is used to separate us from the culture that raised us, because we, unlike people who eat "unhealthy Black food," are supposedly more refined, and it shows in our diet and food choices.

To be clear, I am not saying that there is anything wrong with being vegan or vegetarian or having dietary restrictions due to allergies, preferences of taste, or mindfulness around illness. However, most of the energy of fear, separation, and disembodiment that occurs at the time the menu arrives is related to the messages we have received, the whispers that tell us that in order to be desirable or attractive, we need to lose weight or watch our figures— because, ultimately, we believe the myth that as Black women our desirability, health, and worth are based on how much we can alter our size to fit into the box that society deems attractive and worthy.

This energy of hesitancy hovers over the meal like a shadow, and even dictates our table etiquette. Some may worry about choosing an item that is "too Black," like fried chicken, or other foods that have been associated as "bad" Black cultural foods—a reaction rooted in internalized anti-Blackness. Others may not eat "too much" because we don't want to be perceived as greedy or unlady-like, a notion rooted in internalized sexism. Boys and men rarely grow up receiving messages that eating more makes them less of a man, in the way that girls, women, and femmes do. These behaviors are often exhibited throughout the meal as we monitor each other's plates in silence to see who is eating and how much, with the unspoken goal of being the one who eats the least, thereby proving we've mastered self-discipline. Sometimes the shadow takes a seat at the table, as folks constantly talk about what they don't need to eat because it's "soooo bad" or label what they are eating as a "guilty pleasure."

Rather than cultivating the energy and ease of celebration that food and our relationship to nourishment are intended to have, this dynamic creates more disconnection from the body. At its most extreme, misogynoir can lead us to put ourselves and our bodies in harm's way just to fit into society's Westernized standards.

THE TROPES THAT HAVE TRAPPED US

Dig deeper and you will find that at the core of misogynoir is our tortured collective history. The fact that we were stolen and brought over to America has conditioned many of us to believe that we do not belong to ourselves, and that the primary role we have is to be in service to someone else. The intention of enslavement was not to have us survive and live freely within our bodies but rather to have us exist in invisible and subservient roles. Our bodies also had to fit into the archetypes white society created for us: the Jezebel, the Sapphire, and the ultimate model of selflessness and servitude, the Mammy. Ferris State University's Jim Crow Museum of Racist Imagery describes the mammy as an "obese, coarse, maternal figure. She had great love for her white 'family,' but often treated her own family with disdain. Although she had children, sometimes many, she was completely desexualized. She 'belonged' to the white family, though it was rarely stated. She was a faithful worker. She had no black friends; the white family was her entire world."

The mammy trope is usually characterized by a fat, dark-skinned woman whose legacy is to eagerly put everyone above herself, to nourish and feed others while never offering those same necessities to herself. Aunt Jemima, for example, came from nineteenth-century minstrel shows during the Jim Crow era and was portrayed by white men in blackface who would sing the song "Aunt Jemima." This racist trope was created to benefit the narrative that white America wanted to create around Black women. The mammy caricature implied that Black women were only fit to be domestic workers; thus, the stereotype became a rationalization for economic discrimination. It literally boxed us into the role of being a household staple for white families—a product, a box of pancake mix and syrup that conveyed the message that we existed to nourish and labor for white folks, rather than to prioritize ourselves and nourish our own.

Which brings me back to Lizzo. The haters in the comments section believed that as a fat Black woman, Lizzo should be in service to someone else, that she was "too sensitive," and being too sexual by reclaiming her birthright to her own body. These beliefs reinforce the mammy trope that says that fat Black women should be our caretakers, in servitude to others, and should want to participate in that role with a smile on their face. But Lizzo consistently rejects the mammy trope and instead is in service to herself. While I don't know the depths of her inner life, in many of her public interviews she has shared the importance that she places on self-care and self-love.

I would be remiss, however, if I did not acknowledge the controversy I mentioned at the beginning of this chapter. In August 2023, three former Lizzo dancers and a costume designer filed lawsuits alleging that the performer fostered hostile working conditions and engaged in sexual harassment. As this book goes to print, the lawsuits are still in progress, and Lizzo is countersuing. But as I have outlined, *no one* is immune from internalizing the systems of patriarchal violence, misogynoir, and other forms of oppression—even those most impacted by these systems, and even folks who outwardly project the opposite. This is why it is imperative that we work to simultaneously deconstruct these systems and generate realities that are safe and affirming for ALL bodies.

This kind of misogynoir is proof positive that we have internalized the same survival responses as our ancestors—the need to be subservient to others in order to stay protected, alive, and under the radar. We strengthen these remnants every time we speak to ourselves and other Black women and femmes in a way that reinforces misogynoir. When we do this, we are taking these external systems of misogynoir, bringing them into our internal worlds, and allowing them to dictate how we live our lives. This is what I like to call internal policing: We no longer need the system of slavery to hold us in bondage or chains. We have internalized the bondage, to the point that we are enacting our own mental enslavement, restricting ourselves to self-limiting ways of existing.

How many of us grew up hearing women make a mistake and say, "I'm so stupid," conflating our human proclivity to mess up sometimes with our inherent sense of intelligence? I have engaged in this kind of negative self-talk often, and found that I'm harsh and critical of myself even for small things. Black women deserve more kindness. We need to allow ourselves the compassion we surely don't receive enough of from the outside world. Why not allow our bodies to be a home where we neither talk down to ourselves nor constantly beat ourselves up?

Shawna Murray-Browne, a licensed clinical social worker and award-winning community healer, speaker, and mind-body medicine practitioner and friend, offers a different approach to these ideas. Instead of saying we have internalized systems of oppression, she believes it is more accurate for us to look at the history and contend with the fact that we did not actively *choose* to take part in the internalization. The oppression that we are experiencing was often projected onto us through colonialism, capitalism, and white supremacy, and became normalized within our communities. I tend to view the internalization and projected beliefs as a form of spiritual wounding, meaning the beliefs have become so ingrained in us that they are felt in our spirits and souls. These beliefs dictate how safe and connected we feel within ourselves. If we say we want freedom, liberation, and healing in our communities, we must first start with ourselves and the ways that we have both internalized and been force-fed narratives that limit us.

Black women especially often feel like we need to armor ourselves against vulnerability—projecting an image of being unbreakable, immovable, totally immune from the psychological impact of hardship. This strong Black woman trope is an extension of the mammy trope. The strong Black woman archetype is always working and never letting anyone see her sweat. She holds the world on her shoulders and is boxed into limiting beliefs that say the only way she can be strong is to neglect her own emotional needs and desires. The strong Black woman is always taking on more, and society treats her as if she is its mule. She works so hard that she forgets to eat and sleep. The capitalist system has made her into a machine that is constantly putting out while rarely giving back to herself or receiving anything in return.

If we are allowed only to be strong, then we don't get to be gentle, tender, and at ease—and the world doesn't have to treat us with softness, either. These are the things that are important to our existence as human beings, that honor our divine feminine energy and help us to return to our bodies. We are not intended to carry everyone else's burden. So, when we internalize projected beliefs that we must always hold it together, we keep ourselves tightly bound in our unexpressed emotions and fears. When we embrace the idea that we always have to be perfect, we dehumanize ourselves and each other. We are saying we are not worthy enough to have normal human reactions and emotions.

The work that we must do to disavow all that has been ingrained in us is imperative. I've seen its damaging effects on this current generation of Black women and femmes. We are moving up and getting positions as the heads of companies, taking on more leadership and representation in entrepreneurship, perhaps even making more money than anyone else in our family. Society looks at us and says, "Wow, you all have arrived: You got the job, the house, the partner, the money. What else could you possibly want?" Successful Black women and femmes reached their great heights by learning the system, prioritizing the mind over the heart, and, importantly, being in competition with others—relying on fear, scarcity, and overworking to get us through.

For a long time, the strong Black woman archetype resonated with me a lot. I had been told from a young age that I needed to work twice as hard as my white peers to make it in society. I learned to never let anyone see me sweat or shed tears, because white people would use my vulnerabilities as an excuse to undermine and undervalue me, and I would not be offered empathy or compassion. I couldn't just be a Black girl, I had to be Black and exceptional. I couldn't just be great, I had to be perfect, because otherwise I would be defined by my shortcomings. If I made a mistake, the world would never let me forget it, and that one mistake would reflect badly on the whole community—and could undo all my hard work. So, I worked intensely. I put on the strong Black woman cape, shut down my emotional needs, pushed through adversity, and kept it all together, all while feeling like I had to carry the community's representation of success on my shoulders—quite literally.

A somatic teacher once shared that the emotional impact of racial trauma is stored deep in our bodies, in our very tissues. In my mid-twenties, I noticed that I was experiencing pain and limited mobility in my shoulders and neck, which I came to realize were manifestations of stress and anxiety. I knew that if trauma was stored inside our muscles and tendons, then our bodies could form postures around our various pains and emotions. For example, shame usually takes on a body posture of collapse: Our head is often cast downward, our eyes are averted, our breathing is constricted, and our spine is bent inward. In order to release the emotions associated with shame from our body, we have to create a sense of safety, one that allows us to sit upright in a posture of dignity. This is impossible to do when we are steeped in emotions of shame. It is amazing that we literally wear our emotions through our body postures.

In my own personal mental health therapy, I realized that I regularly lifted my shoulders toward my ears when anything became overwhelming for me. In one of my therapy sessions, after guiding me into my body, my therapist gently asked, "What are your shoulders holding up for you right now?" I felt my body slightly soften with the acknowledgment. Physically I was carrying around the heaviness of stress and anxiety, and on an even deeper level, emotionally I was desperately holding on to what I would later define as "the emotional superwoman cape." I was storing the emotional and energetic burden from cultural conditioning that I had inherited around being a strong Black woman.

I have learned that the difference between other forms of trauma and racial trauma is that when we live in a society governed by race dynamics—the kinds of dynamics that create hierarchy, harm, and disadvantage—racial trauma is consistent and ongoing. Therefore, while I have done body healing and liberation work to free myself from the strong Black woman archetype, this archetype is still culturally prevalent and I am also still in the process of healing, because racial trauma is continually being uprooted, investigated, felt through my body, and released.

THE DAMAGE OF DISTRUST

So much of our worth and value is tied to external validation. This external validation is almost always associated with proximity to whiteness and maleness. Patriarchy created a white male–dominated society that moved us away from our inherited knowledge and intuition and forced us to accept the notion based on white male beliefs that the mind and body are distinct from each other. When we are constantly taught that we need to concede our self-autonomy, it contributes to learned helplessness. This happens when people repeatedly experience a stressful event. They come to believe that they are unable to control or change the situation, so they don't try—even when the opportunities for change become available. This type of thinking, rooted in Westernized colonialism, keeps us stuck in our heads and out of our bodies. It also contradicts everything we instinctively know about how to heal trauma and return to embodiment.

As I'll continue to emphasize during our work together in these pages, we have been taught to disconnect from our inner knowing: our lived experiences, ancestral wisdom, otherworldly intelligence, and intuitions that don't always have "logical explanations." Our inner knowing honors the fact that multiple things can be true at the same time, and that those truths are dependent on our individual lived experiences and cultural worldviews. So, when we uphold colonial standards that say there is only "one" truth, based in Western ideology, we deny ourselves a much more expansive human experience. The cost of denying ourselves an expansive human experience shows up as a lack of self-trust.

This learned lack of trust can manifest as impostor syndrome, where we feel as if we do not belong or have anything of value to contribute—this, despite all the ancestral wisdom we hold within us through our cellular memory. Lack of self-trust feels like ignoring our bodies and our intuition by automatically assuming that we are wrong or distrusting our heart or emotions for fear of being seen as too "touchy-feely" or "too emotional." This belief has been used to divide us internally by pitting logic and intuition against each other. As a result, we're forced to value one over the other, preventing us from reaching a natural balance. Lack of self-trust causes us to downplay our lived experiences, emotions, and sensations because we feel as if there is not enough "evidence" to explain why we feel the way that we feel.

Misogynoir often plays an active and aggressive role when it comes to distrust. It rears its ugly head when we say things like, "I can't be friends with other Black women because they're hard to get along with" or because "they're too much drama" or "can't be trusted." Black women have been socialized to smile and remain composed in the face of oppression so as not to be seen as angry, aggressive, or disruptive. We suppress our authentic reactions in the moment, which often leads to internalizing our raw emotions, which we then release by venting our frustrations to one another.

Venting in and of itself is not a bad thing, and can cultivate emotional safety. However, misogynoir comes into play when the venting we do is self-deprecating, critical, judgmental, divisive, harmful, and unfruitful. Yes, I'm talking about gossip. Gossip is a learned bonding and belonging behavior that is often the magic ingredient for the creation of drama. While drama is a part of the human experience, gossip is intended to cause harm. It only provides temporary relief, when what we are really looking for is resolution and connection. Black women need spaces to vocalize and be transparent about our feelings and boundaries without being shut down or ostracized.

We have been taught to be silent around our pain for fear of coming across as the Angry Black Woman. It's this kind of dangerous trope that leads to our greatest form of suppression. It comes out of the Sapphire caricature that portrays Black women as rude, loud, malicious, stubborn, sassy, bitter, irrational, hard to get along with, and overbearing. This perspective typically comes from a patriarchal place that negates Black women and femmes who hold firm boundaries, or who decide not to go along to get along. And we, other Black women, demonstrate that we buy into this belief when we call each other "bitches," or label someone rude for setting firm boundaries and speaking her mind. Or when we reinforce the notion that we must always be pleasant, pleasing, accommodating, and agreeable—perfect and infallible—even when it goes against our values.

Growing up, I witnessed these beliefs playing out all the time in the way the Black women in my community spoke to each other. I saw it whenever an upset young girl was told, "No one feels sorry for you. Stop crying." Or whenever I heard phrases directed at other women like, "Your needs come last." These messages play into white society's intentions to suppress and ignore us, in order to make us feel as if we are an inconvenience or a burden to others for asking for our needs to be met. And they reinforce the belief that we should settle for less, because we have been conditioned to believe that what we really want is not obtainable or should be put on hold. This kind of misogynoir has led many women and femmes to be silent around the issues that impact us most. It has made us feel uncomfortable speaking up during disagreements, and causes us to struggle to engage in direct communication with people who have more social power than we do in order to avoid being labeled aggressive, hostile, or irrational.

As we begin the process of redirecting ourselves back home and unpacking our internalized misogynoir, we must first become aware of the ways it shows up within our own bodies. As we do this, we will recognize that misogynoir keeps us disconnected from our sisterhood, siblinghood, and community, and most important, from ourselves. When we are experiencing misogynoir, we are often being triggered by both sexism and racism. This trigger brings us back into the disembodied state of the previous trauma. In imbalanced eating, the trigger manifests in Black women as a lack of self-trust, disembodiment, fear of taking up space, feeling as if we are not good enough, policing and moralizing our cultural and ancestral food choices into binary categories, fear of fatness and negative biases and associations with fatness, a striving for the Eurocentric thin ideal, and self-limiting beliefs around how Black women and femmes should move or be in our bodies.

We can recognize that we are triggered when we express extreme emotions of anger or irritability, when we experience unexplained or unexpected mood changes, when our minds disconnect from our physical bodies, or when anxiety is present—which is often associated with self-limiting thinking patterns and a perceived loss of control.

When triggers are activated in your own life, remember that the wound is a portal to healing. Achieving a fulfilling connection with our bodies and our food relationship requires a mind-body shift where we notice and acknowledge when we have been triggered. Instead of immediately going into hypercritical judgment mode, we can offer ourselves a pause and reflect. We can ask ourselves questions like, "What emotions are being stirred up as I survey this video, or this image, or this food menu? What is coming up right now for me in my body? What are these sensations asking me to explore or be present with at this given moment?"

Once we have answers we can ask where this belief, feeling, thought, or sensation originated. Maybe it was passed down in our family, injected into our culture, evangelized by our friends—or maybe it is just ours. We can question whose narrative it ultimately serves, and on the flip side, whose it oppresses. And we can ask ourselves whether this narrative, belief, or idea functions in alignment with our healing and liberation. As we go through this mental process, we should offer ourselves compassion and grace around our social conditioning, knowing that we do not get anything out of trying to control and police our self-expression.

We neither have to conform nor contort ourselves to accept the toxic thinking patterns we have been injected with and internalized in this society. We can begin to metabolize and move beyond the trauma rooted in survival and beyond the messages and stories that were passed down to us and went unquestioned. Here and now, we get to experience the empowerment of writing a new story that acknowledges the oppression behind the trauma and frees us to honor the greater power of who we are.

GUIDED PRACTICE #4

Take some time to get settled into your body, and together let's do an envisioning practice. The only requirement for this practice is to find a quiet space in which to get still and daydream.

I want you to first imagine all the messages you have received around what it means to be a Black woman/femme. Allow all those thoughts, emotions, and sensations to come to mind. Be with them, look at them with curiosity, perhaps validate the experience of them. What does it feel like for you to be with these thoughts, emotions, and sensations in your body?

Now I want you to sit with this reflection: If today we were able to completely liberate society from misogynoir, what would you do differently? What would you look like? How would you dress yourself? How would you exist? How would you talk to yourself? How would you talk to others? When we say that we want to transform or abolish systems of oppression, we are in large part imagining what change would look and feel like for us. Once you have envisioned a life filled with all the things you want and would be doing easefully, ask yourself, what is at least one thing from my free and liberated world that I can embody within me *right now*?

If it is difficult to answer that question, try this: Ask yourself what you don't like about misogynoir. Start there, and follow where it leads you. Feel free to journal about what comes up for you, and maybe even tap into your creative energy through your envisioning practice and let your imagination run free.

QUESTIONS FOR REFLECTION

1. What message have you internalized around being "less than" or unacceptable based on your identity as a woman and/or femme? For example, maybe you learned that our moon cycle, or menstruation, was gross, or that body hair was manly, or that wearing short skirts meant that you were immodest.
2. Who benefits from your believing these things about yourself?
3. What messages have you internalized around being "less than" or unacceptable based on your racial identity? For example, maybe you learned that you had to be strong and keep it together. Or perhaps you learned that self-care is selfish.
4. Where did you learn these beliefs? Do they serve you?
5. Can we rewrite a new story together? What would you like your new relationship with your body to look like when it comes to nourishment? This is how we begin to uproot the misogynoir and transmute the energy of imbalance into eating and nourishment.

· FIVE ·

Fatphobia and the Black Community

"We must investigate the story more than the symptom . . .
because if we focus on the symptom, we are going to miss the
root. Why is the symptom there in the first place? Can we look
at the roots of our stressors and pain?"

—GABES TORRES, cofounder, the Heritage Workshop

CONTENT WARNING: This chapter will discuss examples of fatphobia, anti-fat sentiments, and weight stigma. While I intend to describe these terms and experiences to offer more context and aim to discuss these things in an honest and responsible way, I understand that this topic may be triggering or activating for those who are fat or in larger bodies and for those who live with eating imbalances.

IN WRITING THIS CHAPTER I acknowledge that I can speak only from my own experiences—experiences that have been privileged in society based on my body size, weight, and shape. I have interviewed clients and with their consent incorporated into this book their stories about how they have been impacted by fatphobia. My hope is that the narratives in this chapter amplify the voices of those most impacted, and that they offer validity into our unpacking and divorcing from the fatphobia that began with the dehumanization of the Black body and has been internalized and upheld in Black communities ever since.

Before we move further on in our discussion, I want to be sure the terms I am using are clear to you. So here is a brief guide:

OBESE/OBESITY: Terms used by the medical field to stigmatize and pathologize fatness and to discriminate against those in larger bodies. These terms were developed from the Body Mass Index (BMI), which was never intended to be a measure of health.

FATPHOBIA: The vilification of or discrimination against fat people. Fatphobia is based on fear and dislike of obese people and/or obesity, and also includes the fear or obsessive avoidance of consuming fat. Fatphobia can be experienced by those of all body shapes and sizes, and pervades industries, institutions, and individuals. In recent years, some have begun to use the term "fatmisia" as an alternative to fatphobia, arguing, as fat activist Aubrey Gordon does, that "oppressive behavior isn't the same as a phobia."

INTERNALIZED FATPHOBIA: Beliefs, attitudes, thinking patterns, and narratives about fat people that have been absorbed by those in larger bodies.

ANTI-FAT BIAS: The social stigma of fat/fatness broadly defined as bias or discriminatory behaviors targeting larger-bodied people because of their weight. Such social stigmas can span one's entire life, starting from a young age and lasting into adulthood. It can show up as fat shaming.

WEIGHT STIGMA: Used interchangeably with weight bias or weight discrimination, it refers to ideologies used to describe discrimination or stereotyping targeted at individuals' weight and size. It can also show up as internalized weight shame.

DIET: At its core, to diet is to restrict oneself to small amounts or specific kinds of food to lose weight. Over time it has evolved into the language of a "lifestyle change" or "health journey," but the deeper roots are altering food preferences for the purpose of weight loss. People who do not have access to food may also experience a limited diet and restrictions. Those who have allergies and intolerances and conditions triggered by certain foods may also experience restriction or a limited diet. The takeaway here is not to pathologize all dieting behaviors and modifications, but to acknowledge that dieting for the sole purpose of weight loss, where one puts one's body at risk for the pursuit of thinness, is normalized in our culture and was created out of body oppression.

DIET CULTURE: This type of culture is rooted in colonialism and white supremacy as a way of policing Black bodies. It idealizes white supremacy beauty standards and promotes weight loss at all costs. It demonizes food and oppresses people who do not match up to the thin ideal.

ABLEISM: The discrimination and social prejudice against people with disabilities based on the belief that typical abilities are superior. At its heart, ableism is rooted in the assumption that disabled people require "fixing" and defines people by their disability. The term "able-bodied" is used to describe those who are labeled by society as "fit, strong, and healthy."

OBSESSED WITH SIZE

I come from a long line of Black women who exist in rounder bodies, ones that are both soft and sturdy. These are bodies that pushed forth life, and those new lives then grew up and became our lineage. These are also bodies that have survived many challenges while embracing and experiencing so much joy. Yet, these were not the initial messages I received from the women in my family about their bodies. They all tended to focus on a long-gone past, when they were a smaller size. They shared this information with both nostalgia and grief, as if their formerly slender selves were better than how they existed currently. These messages were usually coupled with complaints about health and about "bad health" breaking down the body. For example, if someone had joint issues or high blood pressure or was diabetic, their condition was always blamed on what they were eating.

The women in my family saw their body sizes and shapes as barriers to movement. I was able to stretch and practice flexibility, and was told that I was capable of doing these things only because of my smaller body size. As I was growing up, the women in my family were constantly complimenting me on my physique, all the while offering warnings and advice such as, "Stay small—you don't want to be like me" or "Keep your figure so that you can get a husband."

By the time I reached middle school, I knew that being in a larger or bigger body was considered socially undesirable. Thinness, it seemed, was the golden ticket to security and acceptance as a Black person, and especially as a Black woman. We were told that if we worked hard enough to achieve and maintain thinness, we could obtain social power, financial success, love, safety, dignity, belonging, and autonomy. I now know this is simply not true. If it were, all thin Black people in society would have these survival needs met and no longer experience the impacts of systemic and institutional oppression. However, at that time I did not have this critical awareness. I was being inundated with and internalizing messages that were quite the opposite.

The constant barrage of messaging came from everywhere—my family, kids at school, church, TV shows, and movies. As a result, I grew up with way too much fear that my body would change, particularly that I'd gain weight and it would eventually resemble the bodies that I was told were undesirable. At the time, I was underweight according to the BMI chart when compared with the "average" numbers for my age, weight, and height. I would go to school and be critiqued for not fitting into the more common beauty ideals then popular in Black communities. Being curvy or thicker in all the "right places" or having the "right look" was being celebrated in hip-hop lyrics; the idea that we should have lighter skin, long hair, a thin waist, curvy hips, and more developed breasts—the "slim-thick" ideal—was pushed heavily throughout Black culture.

I've heard similar sentiments repeated by my clients. Many of them shared that they were afraid to gain weight because they felt their body size would be a deterrent to finding potential partners. This fear was so present for some that they contemplated removing themselves from the dating pool altogether. In our work together, I validated the emotional experience of their concerns and fears—a fear that ran deep in my own life for many years. I often had to remind them that our bodies *will* shift and change throughout the course of life, and that this is completely normal. And I explained that even if they were to lose weight to attract a particular partner, there would still be the question of whether a person who values them solely based on their current body shape and size is really someone worthy of their time and energy.

When I first learned about eating disorders, I found myself in the restrict-binge cycle, a cycle that begins after a period of restriction, deprivation, or starvation. Our bodies do not have the awareness that "I am going on a diet to achieve a certain body ideal." Instead, dieting and restriction signals to our body that it is going into a state of starvation or famine, which causes it stress. Even thinking about going on a diet can send our body into survival mode, because our thoughts communicate that our body needs to prepare to work harder to maintain equilibrium.

While we may initially lose weight, over time we often gain it back, as our bodies begin to store more fat for energy when we finally do have access to food. When we are dieting, our brain and body are constantly seeking to nourish and rebalance themselves. Which is why when people go on diets, they begin to think more about food and may even label themselves "food-obsessed." This is a biological response to communicate that we need to nourish ourselves.

Our bodies are wise, and in this part of the cycle we may consume more to "make up" for what the body didn't receive when it was dieting. This can contribute to weight gain, as our bodies increase their biological-weight set point to make sure that we have enough if we ever were to go into a food famine again. During this binge cycle, some folks may notice that they consume more food than intended or eat until they are uncomfortably full. This restrict-binge cycle can also contribute to weight cycling and metabolic issues. It is evolutionary; we see this pattern in other species that gather and store food for hibernation seasons, when there will not be enough food for them to survive.

These survival patterns show up in other iterations of eating imbalances as well. For example, with bulimia and purging disorder, the body is often not adequately processing nutrients from the foods that are being consumed. This creates imbalances in the minerals and vitamins in the body, which impacts how the organs function. Many folks notice teeth deterioration, fragile hair and nails, and dry skin, as the body puts in more work to fuel the heart, respiratory system, and other essential organs to keep us alive. With any eating imbalance, despite our best efforts or "willpower," the body is designed to seek equilibrium and to support us in surviving. Dieting behaviors are not sustainable, and most folks find that they have to take more extreme measures over time. This is why the majority of diets fail.

Way back when—before my years of training and self-reflection—in my desperation to achieve the "slim-thick" ideal, I pushed my body to unhealthy extremes. I'd go through phases of restriction, which would then fuel a carb-and-sugar-dense binge so that my brain and body would have enough energy to get through the day. It didn't matter that my genetic composition would never allow my body to reach such an unattainable "slim-thick" goal. It was my desire to fit into the limited box of what it meant at that time to be a desirable Black girl. I constantly heard messages from family and saw representation in magazines, movies, and TV shows that if I wanted to be deemed attractive and desirable, I shouldn't "let myself go." In other words, don't gain too much, I was warned. Don't become too fat.

THE BMI MYTH

Black people have historically experienced the brunt of tools meant to exclude people—case in point: the Body Mass Index (BMI) assessment. This outdated measure of health has been adopted by the health care system, the military system, and life insurance companies, among other institutions. Its creation has been widely credited to a nineteenth-century mathematician named Lambert Adolphe Jacques Quetelet, his intention being to define the "ideal" male body type. Quetelet hypothesized that this could be measured by determining a man's weight-to-height ratio. In 1985, the National Institutes of Health began to implement BMI to define "obesity" in the United States—even though Quetelet himself once said that it was never intended to be used as an indicator of health. The height-to-weight ratio is simply a physical characteristic; it would be equivalent to looking at someone's finger length ratio or noting that someone has freckles or red hair. It is simply a characteristic that was then given a meaning by society during a specific time.

Terms like "obesity" and "overweight" changed in 1998 due to a shift in medical standards, categorizing thousands of people as "overweight" and increasing their insurance premiums despite their individual health status having gone through no known changes. Black bodies do not experience shorter life expectancies and issues such as high blood pressure, diabetes, and stroke because our bodies are inherently "bad" or our food is inherently "unhealthy." When we interpret the data in the way that it is truly intended to be, and look at the studies without overgeneralizing, health has very little to do with food and more to do with the social determinants of health, which we will talk about more in a future chapter.

The disparities we see in Black communities are symptoms of four hundred–plus years of unaddressed body terrorism under a system of white supremacy. It is the legacy of trying to survive in a

colonial society that has succeeded in exacerbating the social determinants of health. I don't think that as a collective we have ever
had a time in history to address the impacts of the racial trauma
and intergenerational trauma, and the lasting impacts of inherited
and learned trauma stemming from human enslavement—the
trauma that has been stored in our bodies for generations and that
has physically manifested as illness, disease, and chronic conditions in our communities.

What I am identifying is not new: Many fat liberation activists,
researchers, and body oppression deconstructionists have shared
that we grouped people into "normal" and "abnormal" categories.
We assigned them a BMI range. And then we set about *proving*
why abnormal people were "bad" and normal folks were "good."
Ironically, recent studies show that a BMI of 25-30 is "healthiest,"
so what has been taught to us is that "abnormal" is actually more
sustainable than "normal." Individuals in the "overweight" category also have the lowest mortality rates, according to a 2005 study
by Daniel McGee.

In their work, fat liberation activists have also proposed that
when folks are prescribed calorie deficits to combat "obesity" or
encouraged to strive to fit into BMI categories, this restriction and
calorie deficit is not sustainable in the long term, because the body
compensates by lowering its basal metabolic rate, or metabolism.
The brain will respond by increasing hunger signals, and after that
point, weight cycling is inevitable. In other words, we will gain back
weight, often becoming heavier than we were before, as our bodies
detect a need for an increase in weight to regulate and sustain itself.

These are the workings of our evolutionary biology, which is
hardwired to help keep us alive. No study, exercise, diet, or surgery
has *ever* demonstrated long-term maintenance of weight loss for
any but a small few. In one study, participants in structured weight
loss regimens regained most of their weight loss after five years. Despite the widely held belief that a higher body mass index causes

poor health, empirical research does not support this. Studies show that one in four dieters will develop an eating disorder. Weight cycling and losing and gaining weight is directly related to compromised health.

Even with the awareness of the scams and the checkered history of diet culture, its impact continues to affect folks' access to life-affirming care. For example, many folks deal with high insurance premiums due to a classification created by BMI, are denied life-saving surgeries and procedures, and are encouraged to engage in harmful and extreme restrictions by their medical providers before they can get the care they need. These subpar health care practices are based in fatphobia and anti-fat bias, further proof that there is little interest in investing in the resources that would be the most supportive to fat people, thus reinforcing the pathologizing and dehumanization of them.

BMI has also been used to deny people life insurance. Even the military structure employs BMI to determine if someone meets the necessary qualifications for being physically fit enough to serve. This practice targets and often impacts low-income and Black and Brown people, who tend to enlist in the military at higher rates. This can result in healthy people going on restrictive diets and putting their bodies under extreme pressure to conform, eventually leading to poor health outcomes and imbalanced eating patterns.

Let me share with you my own experience working with an agent to get a life insurance policy. My insurance agent reached out to me to offer me a monthly quote, which was a high rate, and to also confirm my height and weight. Their records indicated that I was five-foot-two—but I am in fact five-foot-five, which I shared. There was a brief pause before the agent said that the height difference would significantly bring down my monthly premium, considering my height-to-weight ratio. I was floored that such basic characteristics could determine how much I would have to pay; it was a difference of almost $30 per month in my case, but can be higher based on where someone falls on the BMI ratio.

I spoke with a friend who has also worked with folks with eating imbalances—advocating for them to receive life insurance when outdated BMI standards become a barrier to accessing or qualifying for insurance—and she told me that she's spoken with a life insurance agent who admitted that BMI is used on purpose to discriminate against larger-bodied people and keep them from being a "burden on the system." The agent she spoke with also shared that size discrimination is completely legal in the U.S., and that I had been lucky to even have been offered a premium rate, because most people who do not fit into the standard BMI requirements are denied access to life insurance entirely.

I thought about how many people are pushed out of or can't afford to buy life insurance, and how this leaves the burden of taking care of their debts when they die to their loved ones to figure out. Those left behind have to sort out who will pay for the funeral costs, mortgage, tuition, student loans, and other debts the deceased may have incurred. I thought, too, of course, about how being denied life insurance based on one's body size and height could likely trigger eating imbalance patterns.

WHEN BMI IS USED AS A WEAPON

The unchecked power of BMI goes beyond insurance companies that stand to gain by oppressing folks in larger bodies. Within the medical field it is an undisputed standard, a benchmark, and providers have been trained to treat it this way. Many health care and medical providers are ill-informed and will neither deviate from nor push back against what they were taught in their educational training and residency programs. They have been trained to heavily rely on misguided practices, which have largely gone undisputed because our society lifts up medical professionals and the medical field as the "unquestionable all-knowing experts," even when their practice does harm to the people they claim to be supporting.

In rural, low-income Black culture, we do not challenge or push back against the medical system or our health care providers. We have been taught that these science- and fact-based professionals are the experts and the authorities of not only the medical field, but of our bodies. It is considered deviant and/or disrespectful to challenge that notion. We are also, as we have discussed, inundated with messages that blame the health issues we have in Black communities on our individual behaviors, which are centered on what we eat and how much we move our bodies.

Articles and news outlets tell our stories something like this: "Obesity is on the rise in America, with most African Americans experiencing high blood pressure and other diseases that lead to mortality." These sorts of statements are often associated with negative and fearful connotations that Black people routinely internalize around our health, wellness, and bodies.

And of course, those in low-income communities, often without access to the various food options in their surroundings, are impacted the most. A 2020 study by Carolyn Becker and colleagues titled "Food Insecurity and Eating Disorders: A Review of Emerging Evidence" found that there are cross-sectional associations between food insecurity and eating disorder pathology, particularly for bulimic-spectrum eating disorders among adults.

Studies have shown that those who deal with food insecurity or poverty internalize weight stigma and discrimination associated with their bodies and demonize foods associated with culture and with what they can afford or access. On top of these factors, someone who does not have a research background may not be accustomed to interpreting research and reviewing factors like statistical techniques or ethical practices to offer a critique of a particular study. The culmination of these factors has contributed to our acceptance that as Black people our eating and mobility need to be constantly critiqued, policed, and be fixed through the lens of the white Western system. We have adopted the myth that if we follow all the rules we will be "healthy" and save ourselves. We never stop and think that it is the standards themselves that need to be investigated and critiqued.

In fact, I did not know how to challenge notions around weight stigma and discrimination or Body Mass Index until graduate school, where I saw that my white colleagues seemed to feel comfortable with regularly self-advocating and presenting research to challenge their health care providers. Once at an eating disorder conference, a presenter handed out a fact sheet about the prevalence of eating disorders associated with weight stigma. We were told to show the fact sheet to our health care providers as a way of educating them about eating disorders. It was assumed that providers would take the paper, review it, and immediately change how they were treating us.

My white colleagues seemed to have access to clinical language and scientific studies, and from birth they were taught that they are entitled to advocate for themselves. They received minimal push-back from their health care providers, and were respected or at the very least tolerated, particularly those with thin, privileged body sizes. When my Black colleagues, clients, and I tried to advocate for ourselves within the same health care system, we received harsh treatment, were often ignored, and, as time went on, were systematically pushed out of our workplaces through toxic tactics such as micromanagement and wrongful termination.

When Black people speak up for ourselves, we are often made to feel like we cannot speak our truth without being labeled noncompliant. Health care providers often play the "know-it-all" card, where we are patronized and treated as ignorant or uppity, or they play the white fragility card, where we are labeled as aggressive and argumentative. While explaining my medication in a visit with my endocrinologist, I was asked "What's your background?"; my provider seemed intimidated that I knew so much about my condition and treatment. When I shared that I was a mental health therapist, she smirked and said, "So you know when it's time for the patient to be quiet, and when it's time for the doctor to talk."

It does not matter how well we adjust our tone, monitor our facial expressions, dress professionally for the visit, contort our bodies, calculate our words, and try to come across as cool and collected—the response to self-advocacy is the same. I have heard stories of security being called if a provider felt that a (non-white) patient was being aggressive instead of recognizing that the patient was simply being direct or disagreeing with or questioning the treatment a provider was offering.

Even when I gained this awareness of how to interpret research and stopped holding the medical community up as the Holy Grail, I was met with pushback not only from the system but from members of my own community, who said I was trying to force my beliefs into "hard science" and facts to fit my own narrative. It was exhausting, frustrating, and lonely being in a position where I did not have the privilege to show up in the way that my white colleagues did, while also not being able to find a safe space in my community to challenge the medical and health care system when their biases and training negatively impacted us.

In communities with low incomes or lack of access to education, the health care provider is the gatekeeper to information about health and wellness. We have been taught to trust Westernized expertise because we live in a system where we are collectively disconnected from our indigenous and ancestral medicinal wisdom. People in these communities often don't have time to debunk the research, and may not even be able to access academic journals. Many are simply working to make sure that their basic needs are met, and may only have the capacity to take in the information that they receive from the health care professional and do their best to adjust to it with the meager resources that they have.

With this understanding, I encourage clients to be strategic and mindful about self-advocacy. More than a few of my patients have admitted that it is easier to speak up for themselves when they are working with a provider who shares their racial identity. But even this approach has its flaws. When health care providers of any race are indoctrinated in Eurocentric teachings, they may lack the additional training necessary to understand, unpack, challenge, and liberate themselves from that practice and training.

I cannot reiterate this point enough: While it has not been widely accepted by the medical community, modern studies have shown that BMI is *not* an accurate predictor of a person's life expectancy or overall health. BMI is just another tool used to marginalize folks. Not only does it perpetuate fatphobia and anti-fat bias, but it also ignores more accurate social determinants of health, such as family medical history, pollution, clean water, access to quality health care, food insecurity, generational trauma, and chronic stress. And it certainly does not account for different shapes and sizes: BMI does not consider fat distribution, bone density, or muscle versus fat. Research shows that we have been told that our weight is determined by food, exercise, and willpower. Actually, health is determined by socioeconomic status, the systemic impacts of discrimination based on race/ethnicity, gut microbiome, imbalanced eating, sleep, stress, food, exercise, infection, trauma, medications, weight cycling, and genetics.

For all of these reasons, I conclude that the obesity epidemic is the summation of lazy medicine and of practitioners and researchers struggling to differentiate between causation and correlation. I challenge the medical community to adopt studies that have been done on the impact of weight stigma and to use that research to inform their practices when working with patients and clients. BMI, which was implemented to target, shame, and demonize fat and larger bodies, should be abolished and replaced with more accurate measures of health and well-being.

ANTI-FATNESS IS ANTI-BLACKNESS

I've come to realize how, in order to appear desirable to others, I've upheld fatphobia in my own life and, in turn, supported anti-fatness. Da'Shaun L. Harrison, author of *Belly of the Beast: The Politics of Anti-Fatness as Anti-Blackness*, unpacks this even further, likening anti-fatness to anti-Blackness. In an anti-fatness world, desirability is determined by who the majority/mainstream deems to be attractive and alluring. That determination, it has been shown, largely leaves out any of the attributes ascribed to the Black community. In essence, we are told to conform to a belief system in which we have no place, no currency. However, devaluing fatness is devaluing oneself, Harrison asserts, creating a vicious, self-perpetuating cycle. This bias isn't an easy thing for most of us to admit, because it means unlearning a litany of beliefs around fatness that have been drummed into our psyches for ages—beliefs that tell us that fat is bad, ugly, and disgusting.

Through Da'Shaun L. Harrison's scholarship and lived experience, I understand fatphobia in Black communities to be twofold: There is pressure to conform to beauty, desirability, and attractiveness standards, as well as the pressure to survive and get one's needs met by attempting to alleviate racialized oppression. These systems—anti-Blackness and anti-fatness—are intrinsically interwoven, so to divest oneself from one is to also let go of the other. To invest in one is to participate in your own oppression in the other. Unpacking and liberation are interdependent on each other. We are now at a crossroads, with imperative decisions and choices to make.

I spent my high school years teetering between overeating with the hopes of developing curves and engaging in patterns of restriction for long periods that I sometimes masked under the guise of religious fasting. My hope was that the places where I did have fat, such as in my stomach, would disappear and that one day I would wake up and have a body similar to those of the women I saw in music videos and magazines. I began most mornings eating a can of fruit—and I would do that only after I'd finished the latest exercises for getting the "perfect abs" as featured in *Seventeen* magazine.

At the time I didn't realize that the subconscious fears that were driving my behaviors were rooted in the deeper systems of anti-Blackness and anti-fatness. The pursuit of and obsession with thinness was so ingrained and standardized in society that I wasn't aware that I was dealing with values, beliefs, and ideals rooted in my own oppression. I just knew that I wanted to experience acceptance and safety within a white-dominated world that led me to believe that I was the problem, and that my body needed to be altered to fit in.

These systems of anti-Blackness and anti-fatness keep us so self-obsessed with fitting into desirability ideals, developed out of the culture of white supremacy, that we are unconscious of or apathetic toward how they are designed to annihilate fat Black people in our communities. We uphold rhetoric that proposes that we should continually strive to eradicate or reject parts of ourselves, by labeling our bodies as deviant. We then reinforce this with our cultural obsession around weight loss and health, without thinking about how the system does not serve *any* of us. But those who are most severely impacted are also the ones who cannot—or choose not to—contort themselves into white supremacy standards. Their fat or larger-sized Black bodies are going into battle with every system, every day, to fight for the right to exist without conditional or moralized expectations around their humanity.

The imbalanced relationship I had with food and my body was exacerbated by the fact that my family didn't have access to what dietitians would describe as "nutrient dense" food, which is the opposite of the processed, microwavable products we were often eating. My parents would occasionally cook family meals when they came home from working multiple jobs, but the fast, processed foods we typically consumed made up the bulk of our diet.

Toward the end of my teen years, companies began to promote more mobile apps that were often aimed at weight loss, and workouts based on body shape. I became obsessed, often working out before eating breakfast. The family members who regularly praised me for being small had no idea that I was engaging in extremely restrictive eating. I didn't have access to a therapist at the time, but if I did, I am sure that by clinical standards I would have been diagnosed with an eating disorder.

But my health care providers never acknowledged my having any issues and would often praise me for my size. Most of the doctors I encountered in my hometown were white and thin, and would often enforce their personal fatphobia during interactions with patients. In my case, because I met the "standardized growth curve," which is comparable to BMI for babies and kids, I was automatically deemed as a compliant and healthy patient. No one ever assessed whether or not I had an eating disorder.

Black people who deal with eating imbalances, especially those in larger bodies, are often praised if their behavior results in subsequent weight loss. The people who effectively condone imbalanced behavior often have no regard for the harm that these "well-intentioned compliments" have on the bodies and well-being of others. They are consumed by diet indoctrination, a food religion that constantly promises that the next diet will be the one that works, if you only follow all of its commandments. Diet culture tells us that with consistent discipline and controlled consumption, we will earn what society deems a worthy and acceptable body—which translates to thin, able-bodied, and of course, white.

INTERNALIZED FATPHOBIA

Back in high school and during my college years, I didn't have the language for what we now describe as "fatphobia" or "anti-fat bias." But I was certainly drinking the Kool-Aid. The messages I internalized were that thinness is desirable to men and white culture, and that I would be considered more attractive and receive more praise if I conformed.

In previous chapters we have discussed the road map that got me to that point: Through my patriarchal conditioning as a young girl, I had learned that it was "unladylike" for a woman not to leave some food behind on her plate. Through my religious indoctrination, I had been taught that being "greedy," "gluttonous," or "indulgent" was a sign of immorality. And through the health-obsessed culture I was immersed in, I learned that certain foods were "good" or "bad," and that I should avoid all "bad" food.

At the time, it all seemed to make sense. In both my mostly white-dominated early-college high school program and my part-time job as a local charter school teacher, I noticed that thinner people were treated better. I also observed that in white environments the conversation among most white women teachers was around the subject of weight loss. They were always talking about shrinking their bodies through dieting, or talking about what they could or could not eat during their free time. This, combined with the way the women in my family blamed their health concerns and range of mobility on their body sizes, caused me to equate being in a bigger body with "unhealthiness"—and something that limited what someone would be able to do in their body.

This reductive teaching impacted the way that I viewed my own body, and it was reinforced through the moralization and polarization of body size in the media, something we've examined in other parts of the book. Beyond the magazines and apps that I increasingly spent time poring over, in almost every TV show and movie I watched I could see that the thin actors played the roles of the protagonists, or "the good ones," while the antagonists, the "bad ones," were in larger bodies. This subtle conditioning starts early on, even in Disney movies like *The Little Mermaid*. The beautiful Ariel existed in a smaller body, while Ursula, the evil witch of the sea, was in a larger, rounder body. These are the kinds of narratives that colored my childhood and continued to haunt me throughout my adolescence and young adulthood.

I learned the lie that fatness was undesirable, ugly, unhealthy, and a pathway to mortality and disease. Later on, watching shows like *My 600-Lb. Life,* which regularly played in my household, I was further conditioned to fear being connected to a larger body size. I saw fatness as something that was controllable and could be changed if someone just worked hard enough. I was taught that people who were in larger bodies deserved to be treated poorly and violently and should constantly be in the process of trying to lose weight by any means necessary. I watched as participants of the show described being humanized for the first time after losing weight. They shared that they were respected, loved, and finally listened to once they had lost an exorbitant amount of weight. Many of them said that it was the first time that they felt they could advocate for themselves as the experts of their own body, even if it was conditional.

Shows like *My 600-Lb. Life* and *The Biggest Loser* rendered their subjects as less than—as oddities to be gawked at and insulted—rather than considering them as living, breathing, feeling human beings. In the case of *The Biggest Loser,* we never saw the long-term impact on those who were involved in the show. What were the metabolic consequences of losing weight so rapidly? How did restriction contribute to stress in their bodies, which is a precursor to health conditions? How did the trauma of weight stigma, bullying, and fatphobia manifest in their bodies?

This treatment of fat bodies and fatness in general has paved the way for how society has conditioned folks to treat fat Black bodies very specifically. In a lot of Black communities, we don't even realize that our conditioned ideas around fat people and fatness have also colored our beliefs about things we believe to be true about ourselves. And there are systems in place to encourage us to continue to hold these negative attitudes, beliefs, and fears. "It's not the thin ideal that pushes most of us to shrink and contain our bodies. It is a society that tells us that our abundance needs to be restrained," notes Jessica Wilson, author of *It's Always Been Ours: Rewriting the Stories of Black Women's Bodies*. This restraint, Wilson says, is a coping mechanism we employ in the hopes of not being seen as threatening or unsafe, but rather as respectable. It is our way of seeking shelter.

If we don't use this lens when thinking critically about diet culture, then we fail to acknowledge the larger issues of white supremacy that contributed to promoting certain diets as the standard while stigmatizing others. We fail to address the way that diet culture was birthed out of body oppression. The fact is, we still have a medical industry that promotes dieting, despite evidence that shows diets are 95 percent *in*effective and often lead to weight *gain*, long-term health issues, and for many, eating disorders.

Let's contend with that for a second. If a provider prescribed a medication that was 95 percent ineffective—with all of those harmful "side effects"—most people would refuse to take it. However, when it comes to dieting, our society continues to take its chances on the 5 percent hope that it will work. The diets and medications prescribed by medical providers to "curb the appetite" serve to disconnect us from our bodies' communication, dialing down our hunger signals and leaving us to distrust our body, while also stigmatizing our desires and need for pleasure.

For example, let's take a hard look at the current trend of using drugs meant for other purposes, like Ozempic and Wegovy, to lose weight. Besides the fact that using these drugs creates a shortage and unavailability for those for whom the drug was originally intended, manufacturers fail to mention that there is a strong likelihood that the weight will come back. And no one knows the long-term effects on the body of taking a drug that was never intended for weight loss in the first place. Still, a 2023 report by data analytics firm Trilliant Health shows that quarterly prescriptions for Ozempic quadrupled between 2020 and the end of 2022. The study also found that a little more than half of the patients taking Ozempic or a similar drug have a history of diabetes, an indication that many others are mainly using the drug for weight loss.

Both my grandmother and my mother were dieters; they each tried whatever variety of programs and restrictive eating plans were currently on the market, such as SlimFast and WeightWatchers. And I remember my grandmother's house being inundated with SlimFast magazines and VCR workout videos. They both considered themselves to be overweight, but if we look at them from the outside in, their internalized fatphobia did not reflect their reality. The spectrum of descriptors used in fat activism communities range from small fat, mid fat, large fat, super fat/infinifat to death fat. These terms are not intended to be applied rigidly, and within these communities there are no negative connotations associated with these names. My grandmother and mother would have fallen into the small fat range, meaning that they were below a U.S. women's size 18, or a 1X–2X.

According to fat activist and blogger Linda G., those who exist in the small fat end of the spectrum can straddle the line between "fat" and "straight size," meaning sizes small through large for women, or sizes 0–14. They likely face medical discrimination and poor interpersonal treatment but are generally able to participate in public life with few restrictions based on size. Linda describes the mid fat spectrum as folks who are likely able to shop less frequently at plus-size stores with brick-and-mortar options, and says that large fat is the end point for most plus-size clothing. It sits along the middle of the size bell curve. Most folks in this category experience more size discrimination in health care and at work and may have trouble fitting into seats and other public spaces. Further along the bell curve there is "super fat," also used interchangeably with "infinifat," which refers to a body size larger than a women's size 32. People in this range experience a lack of access due to their weight on a regular, daily basis. They experience discrimination in health care, the workplace, public spaces, and are excluded from many areas of public life.

Plus-size retailers often do not have options for people who identify as super fat, and there are generally no brick-and-mortar clothing stores that serve them. The term "infinifat," created by Ash, host of The Fat Lip podcast—and creator of Infinifirsts, a once-monthly Instagram project honoring super fats and infinifats— describes people who face significant barriers due to institutionalized sizeism on a daily basis. According to Ash, "infinifat" refers to anyone who is a size 34 or above and/or size 6x. People in these communities are so neglected that many may not know their actual clothing size, because plus-size retailers do not include them at all. They may have to have clothing made custom. People in this size range are excluded from participating in many areas of public life, face intense discrimination and mistreatment in health care, and are the most underserved of all members of the fat community.

This spectrum is meant for folks to use to self-identify, so it does not explicitly look at shape, which takes the bust-to-hip-to-waist ratio into consideration. Some folks cannot relate to the fat spectrum, but I have found it to be a reality check for myself as a straight-sized person. While I have received negative comments, have had doctors label me as "obese" according to the BMI chart, and have experienced societal pressures around never being "thin enough," I still can navigate the world in a privileged body. Because of that, it is important for me to work to dismantle the system of fatphobia and make it safer for folks across body variations to navigate the world more easily, as well as to amplify those voices of folks across the spectrum who have the lived experience of being systematically oppressed by fatphobia.

Prior to having children, both my grandmother and mother spent the majority of their lives in what are socially considered to be straight-sized bodies. They did not require plus-size clothing, and body size was not a barrier for them in their daily lives. But societal expectations about "snapping back" into their prepreg-nancy bodies, navigating aging bodies, and dealing with the inter-sections of being in both a Black and a small fat body caused them to experience layered oppression, including dealing with weight stigma in the medical system. I watched them spend years trying to get back to their pre-childbirth bodies by yo-yo dieting (another term for weight cycling)—gaining weight and dieting in response, then regaining that weight.

Modern research shows that it is *not* one's weight that impacts health issues, but the experiences of weight stigma, or weight dis-crimination, stereotyping based on a person's size. For people with larger bodies, this kind of wrongheaded treatment can lead to long-term health concerns. When larger-bodied people, for in-stance, visit their health care provider and are immediately pre-scribed a diet or a weight loss drug, or are recommended for weight loss surgery, without any regard for their concerns or any clinical assessments, they might be labeled "noncompliant" if they don't follow their doctor's recommendations, or do comply but don't lose the weight. The health care provider might even assume that the patient "wants" to be "unhealthy" and might carry around a bias that the health issue is actually the patient's fault for being medi-cally disobedient.

This label follows patients throughout their lifetime in the health care system, and often impacts the type of treatment they will re-ceive from future providers. It is assumed that providers can just look at someone and gather everything they need to know about the person's health simply based on body size and weight. This lack of assessment became widespread with the rise of the obesity epi-demic in 1976 through the 1980s, also known as the "war on obe-sity."

Because I didn't understand the many layers of body oppression at the time, I thought that dieting and being preoccupied with weight was simply something that all Black women do. I have even heard folks suggest that their own young children pursue weight loss, or that they would volunteer to pay for weight loss surgeries for their child's developing body if they'd agree to a restrictive diet or meal plan. In fact, in 2023 the American Academy of Pediatrics released guidelines that children as young as two years old could be put on diets, and that adolescents and teens could qualify for weight loss drugs and surgery. The Academy used photos of Black children in their marketing of this statement, pathologizing and problematizing the bodies of our youth.

There is no evidence to show that pushing diets on children, regularly weighing them, or labeling their food choices as "good" or "bad" is beneficial to their health. There is evidence, however, that weighing children damages their health by increasing their risk of developing eating imbalances, poor mental health, and weight cycling. These are the risk factors that contribute to higher morbidity and mortality in the long term. It is entirely developmentally appropriate for children to gain weight prior to and during adolescence and throughout their lives. Weight loss should never be a decision made on behalf of children without considering how they feel in their bodies, or the long-term implications of choosing to do weight loss surgery before their bodies are even fully developed.

I saw the impact of these harmful practices play out time and time again in my clients' stories. I am reminded of Kayla, a larger-bodied client of mine who came to me to explore her feelings around fatness. Growing up, she was always what the medical field describes as "overweight," and from the time she was ten years old her doctor recommended that she be put on a diet. Kayla's mother, who was also in a larger body, consistently made comments about her daughter's size by saying things like, "You're too fat for cheerleading" or "You need to lose weight—let's get on a program." Looking back, Kayla realized that she internalized those negative beliefs, believing that her mother despised her. She committed to doing everything she could to lose weight and be a "good daughter."

Kayla lost a lot of weight in her teen years but then, in her early twenties, her mother passed away unexpectedly. Kayla told me she felt completely lost and out of control and began to binge-eat, followed by purging. This cycle continued, and by her late twenties her weight had fluctuated so often that she constantly felt that she was in a vacuum and could not focus on anything but her body size. She explained that during this time she lost many friendships and relationships because her developing eating imbalance was all-consuming.

Once she began to gain weight, every doctor's visit seemed to be accompanied by a note in her chart that she was "morbidly obese." In fact, the last time that she had gone to her doctor, he'd told her that she would benefit from weight loss surgery. Kayla remembered that in that moment tears welled in her eyes; the rest of the visit was a blur. She rushed home and binged. In those moments, she shared, she began to experience herself outside of her body, watching herself on the couch, numbly eating. And then, she thought, *I don't deserve to live, I'm a failure.* After that last doctor's visit, she stopped going to any doctors for years, and continued to struggle with the eating imbalance until her mid-forties.

One day, Kayla woke up surrounded by a medical team after collapsing while working out at the gym. She couldn't remember the last time she'd eaten, and shared that she would rather have died that day than go to a doctor. The anxiety she had developed after a lifetime of dealing with weight stigma alongside the isolation, deprivation, and constant war with her body had contributed to her poor physical health. Kayla shared that she was treated like less than a person and that her doctor refused to even look her in the eyes at her appointments—in fact, she said that they rarely wanted to touch her, and that when they did it was forceful.

Kayla was failed by a medical system that ignored important symptoms and blamed the issues she experienced on her weight. She suffered from the trauma of fatphobia, anti-fat bias, and weight stigma, which led to her avoiding her feelings and disconnecting from her body as a protective mechanism. Kayla also experienced delayed treatment for the actual unchecked conditions that she was describing to her doctors, but that consistently went ignored.

In our work together, we would check in often as she unpacked and processed her experience. We also worked on her developing a different relationship with the anxiety she felt and held in her body. We got to a place where we could honor what her anxiety was trying to do for her—protecting her, through avoidance. We worked through the difficult, unresolved feelings she had toward her mother, and she was able to grieve and feel safe to release stored trauma from her body. Together we were able to reduce her binge-purging patterns significantly. One day when we were at the midpoint of our work she came to a session and exclaimed, "Alishia, things haven't been easy, but I haven't binge-purged in two months."

Kayla eventually found a movement practice that was affirming for her body and began nourishing herself more adequately. She also connected with a doctor who approached treatment from a body-affirming, anti-diet framework. Her Black dietitian and psychiatrist consistently affirmed that her body was worthy of care, and that they were not going to focus on her weight. Toward the end of our work together she shared, "I wish I would have had this years ago. I wasted so much of my life being at war with myself, hating who I was, and wishing I wasn't alive . . . I have hope now."

OUR TWISTED HISTORY WITH FATNESS

The way that we understand fat or fatness has not always been so contentious. Fat is a necessity for our bodies; it is the most energy-efficient form of food. Throughout human evolution, having higher fat percentages in our bodies has allowed us to regulate our body temperature and ensure our survival. During times of food scarcity, it was dangerous to be in a body with low fat, particularly in environments with colder conditions, where it could lead to death.

Many hunter-gathering cultures were conscientious about both having enough food and consuming enough to sustain nourishment throughout the different seasons.

When we look at how this shows up for people assigned female at birth, our bodies' ability to hold on to more fat in our hips, abdomen, butt, and thigh region is often connected to our adaptive hormones to support birthing. Water weight and bloat also show up in our bodies in alignment with our menstrual cycles to cleanse and protect the body. The processes that occur in our bodies on a micro level also occur within the cycles of the seasons and represent the regenerative nature of Mother Earth.

However, there are so many products marketed nowadays to "reduce bloat," labeling it as inflammation and convincing us that our hormones are messed up, or unregulated, when it is often our body seeking homeostasis through its intuitive monthly cycle. Our culture reinforces ideas around patriarchy that the bodies of those who are assigned female at birth need to function in the same way as those assigned male at birth. But gender is not so binary, and our bodily functions do not all fit into standardized boxes. While some bodies do experience irregularities, it is important to consider how often symptoms are mislabeled as irregularities, followed by products being pushed on us to keep our bodies from exhibiting any form of fatness or change.

When we look at the history of fatness prior to the transatlantic slave trade, such as during the Renaissance era, we see paintings and sculptures of folks with larger bodies and know that their body sizes were representations of their access to wealth, beauty, and power. Renaissance art often glorified the sensuality and sexuality of larger bodies through art, which portrayed white bodies as softer and rounder. Class distinctions were made clear—that those who were in larger bodies were wealthier and those who were in thinner bodies were poorer because of their lack of access to food.

Going back even further in time, the image of the Venus of Willendorf, which has gone viral on social media over the last few years, shows us that our human ancestors lauded curvaceous figures from perhaps our earliest days. This carved woman figure is estimated to have been created some thirty thousand years ago. Many researchers presume that the figurine represents a deity— a goddess. There are many more stone figures and sculptures throughout the world and throughout the ages that depict body sizes and shapes of roundness, curviness, and fatness—and in all those representations, images of fat bodies were highly regarded.

To justify slavery, however, Europeans and other groups began to develop racial classifications. These classifications aimed to prove that Black people were inhuman and deserved to be enslaved. When folks in Black bodies were subjugated and brought from Africa in chains, there was a need for further racial stratification. Europeans justified their beliefs through racist eugenics and errant scientific, religious, and political theories. Creating separation through color, shape, features, size, and hair texture was a way to create solidarity among Europeans. Partially in an effort to distance themselves from Black bodies, they convinced themselves to willingly engage in starvation and scarcity through dieting and the adoption of a thin body ideal denoting health, desirability, and worth. Our genetics play an important role in body size and shape.

There are more than one hundred genes identified so far that impact weight. Fat has been protective, and most certainly benefited Africans, who were already surviving with so little in making the transatlantic crossing. Those who survived had certain genes— sometimes referred to as survivor genes—that helped them to store and hold on to fat in order to survive.

Black American bodies are a legacy of that resilience. Just think of what our ancestors endured, and how they continue to thrive *in spite of that*. I am convinced fat has something to do with that. I'm also convinced that this is another reason why white people are constantly trying to get Black people to lose weight, by associating our body size and Blackness with something to be feared, threatened by, eradicated, or avoided.

When white Americans see a Black auntie going to church in her heels and fancy hat—big, strong, wise, and full of spunk—they correctly assume she's a force to be reckoned with. But they also fear her power and audacity to take up space and exist assertively in her Black body. She belongs to *herself*. She is in service to *herself*. And that autonomy is what scares white-dominant culture. To colonize the Black body, white culture has made continuous efforts to crush our spirits, and souls, and physical selves, all while othering Blackness and fatness.

Racist scientific literature in the eighteenth century claimed that fatness was "savage" and "black." Fatphobia and the desire for slimness began as a way of instituting what French sociologist Pierre Bourdieu described as "social distinctions." That is, the elites of society have used the denial of food—along with social censorship, which forbade coarseness and fatness in favor of slimness—to prove the superiority of those who sit at the top of the social hierarchy. Bourdieu's assessment shows how, historically, diet and weight evolved as evidence of high-class or low-class standing.

Eating imbalances were only declared a public health crisis once they significantly impacted—and threatened—white populations around the early to mid-1980s. Because many were eating nutrient-deficient foods, white women with eating imbalances experienced a loss of menstrual cycles and a rise of fertility issues, which became heavily associated with low childbirth rates and even fatality. The "white race" was literally dying. Simultaneously, diet culture had created a profitable industry for the rich and wealthy, who postulate that the ability to achieve and maintain thinness confers superiority. This has kept white people in a cycle of spending their money and running back to their medical providers and other distinguished "experts" to achieve thinness, which in turn has made the top 1 percent within the diet industry and health care insurance system wealthy.

THE FATNESS FALLACY

Fatness is not a determinant of health. We do not owe anyone health; everyone does not have the capacity to just "be healthy" by our limited definitions. Think about those with chronic illness, trauma, or severe mental health concerns, among other issues. Fatphobia has often led to the fear of immobility, which is rooted in ableism. People who exist with physical disabilities may experience limited movement, but that should not be something to be shamed for or told to fix. It is also important to note that our bodies change over time, a biological reality that diet culture continues to ignore. It is easier to blame our body shapes and sizes on what we have been eating, and to point accusingly at health-compromised individuals or racialized communities with higher rates of certain health issues, than it is to look at the ways that fatphobia has been used as a tool to systematically oppress us and our communities, leading to poorer health outcomes.

Fatness is also not a feeling. I have been in many spaces with friends who will eat food, then say, "I feel so fat," or "I am so fat for eating this." This kind of talk is offensive, because it continues the narrative that associates our food choices and food intake with weight. It also dismisses the systemic and cultural implications associated with fat by demonizing fatness and labeling it as a costume, or an experience we can pick up and put on if we choose to do so.

A society that aims to erase and eradicate fat folks is a society that has been constructed to exclude, dismiss, abuse, and ignore Black bodies. We see this in every existing system. Think about the fact that most public places do not have seating options that are affirming to bodies above a certain size or weight. Airplane seats are often not accessible to folks in larger bodies unless they pay an additional cost for the seat next to them and a seat belt extender. This, in turn, can inhibit one's travel and freedom to move around. Public bathrooms are also designed to support smaller-bodied folks. Most stores may not carry items for those of certain body sizes. Health care offices often do not have appropriately sized blood pressure cuffs for those in larger bodies.

How many times have we pushed back or questioned the clinical relevance of being weighed at our doctors' offices? How often have we looked around our office spaces and thought about whether the furniture is affirming and comforting to folks of all body sizes? And how many times have we been able to go out in public to eat a meal without being concerned about being chastised, berated, or judged for nourishing our own bodies? None of these examples are outliers. Society has created structures to prevent larger-bodied folks from moving in ways that would foster a sense of freedom, belonging, safety, body autonomy, and dignity. All these instances impact the way larger-bodied folks show up in certain spaces, because they already know that their behaviors are being monitored and policed by society.

There are countless stories I can share with you that prove my point. One that comes to mind is the story of Brittany, a thirty-six-year-old Southern Black woman who resides in Mississippi. Brittany is a body liberation educator who creates curriculums around fatphobia and anti-fat bias. In her work, she aims to help others understand that diet culture is not only unhealthy, but oppressive. She describes herself as super fat, being brown all over, being fat all over, and not having the type of "well-proportioned" body that gets one noticed in our communities.

Growing up, Brittany was very aware of the differences between what thinness and fatness could yield you, in terms of attention, desirability, and value. She told me that back then, even shopping for clothes was insufferable, because there were not many stores for plus sizes. And although plus-size stores did eventually become more prevalent, they always seemed to have sizes only for those they defined as having the "appropriate" level of fatness.

Brittany shared with me some of the anti-fat sentiments she has experienced, which have ranged from people saying things like, "If you wanted to lose the fat you would," to folks telling her, "Fat people are lazy and deserve the way they are treated." She related how people stare at her when she is out and about, how she's been treated in everyday interactions with others—these incidents all factor into the macro- and microaggressions that she experiences.

When Brittany was pregnant with her son twelve years ago, her doctor assumed she had gestational diabetes because of her size. That was not so. He made her take a test for it, which came back negative. He did not trust the results, so he made her take it again. That doctor's biased beliefs were embedded in his treatment plan for her, and, eventually she decided to advocate for herself and stopped seeing him. These are the types of fatphobic aggressions and anti-fat biases Brittany has had to deal with—daily.

The reality is that fatphobia is embedded in practically every system we encounter. Just consider the diet industry: a seventy-five-billion-dollar business that includes programs such as Weight-Watchers and Jenny Craig, mobile apps like Noom, and fads like the Keto Challenge. The industry is designed to convince folks that if they just try hard enough and invest in the next big thing, they will be worthy of thinness—which is why we see diets continue to reinvent themselves to make people feel as if it is a personal failing that they are not thin.

Along similar lines, the adjacent health and wellness industry conspires to make us pay—literally—for our supposed defective habits, from flat belly teas and weight loss pills to workouts that promise "body goals." Some licensed dietitians who are not weight-neutral may even prescribe a meal plan without tailoring it to the individual person, as if one plan can work for everybody—which it can't. It's not unusual to see a lot of women-focused marketing that promotes losing weight in order to fit into a certain pant size, or to hear women who are getting married say things like, "I need to stop eating for months and get a gym membership so I can lose weight before the wedding."

Then there's the actual health care system, which nurtures its own stigmatized beliefs and biases by relying on BMI and weight classifications to determine if someone is healthy or not. There are documented stories of medical providers who have ignored diagnoses like cancer by blaming patients' symptoms on their weight, instead of offering an accurate assessment and listening to and respecting their patients. It's also common practice to refuse to perform life-affirming procedures such as knee surgeries until a patient loses weight for fear that it may be unsafe—despite there being no conclusive evidence to suggest this. Yet health care providers will recommend to those same patients that they are totally fine to undergo weight loss surgery.

And we've already noted how the fashion industry excludes most bodies. Consider brands that promote fatphobia like Abercrombie & Fitch, whose CEO in 2013 shared that they do not stock XL or XXL sizes in women's clothing because "they don't want overweight women wearing their brand." They are after the "cool kids"—and they don't consider plus-sized women to be a part of that group. The fashion industry also charges more for clothing that comes in bigger sizes. Even plus-sized and "body inclusive" brands will go up only to a size 5X, then call it body-affirming even though it still excludes people. It never occurs to us to speak up and disrupt the industry by not shopping at stores that won't even pay for enough fabric to make clothes that fit a diverse range of body shapes and sizes. Our worth should not be based on clothing numbers or letters.

Let's also not ignore how the fashion and clothing industry uses arbitrary sizes based on the manufacturers they choose to go into business with. For example, how is it that someone can wear three different sizes depending on the store where they are shopping? Many clothing brands will label their clothes larger than how they actually fit. For example, someone may pick up a size XL, but when they try it on, it actually fits like a size medium. This is another way that the industry focuses on making people fit into fabric, versus having fabric fit comfortably on people without all the smoke and mirrors. We hear the frustration and anxiety in the fitting rooms, as there is always that one person loudly proclaiming that they need to lose weight, or making negative comments about their bodies or the bodies of their children. I am grateful to stores that have a practice of putting positive affirmations on the mirrors in the fitting room. This is a small way to help mitigate disparaging comments and views regarding body image.

This inconsistency in clothing sizes has been a source of anxiety and stress for many of my clients. Some eating disorder treatment groups offer structured trips to go shopping for clothing to help reduce anxiety, especially with seasonal changes and the need to update their wardrobe with clothes that better affirm their bodies. Many clients have shared that group experiences like this help them feel less alone in their frustrations. These groups provide a space that is affirming to process what they are experiencing, and makes them feel less activated into eating disorder behaviors once they return home.

Finally, the media is one of the most harmful actors of them all. As long as the entertainment industry continues to cast actors with larger bodies in stereotypical roles—the sidekick, the person who is less intelligent than everyone else, or the fat person who is consumed with their weight—it will leave little room for more truthful, textured portrayals. Without those, we will continue to live in a society governed by false perceptions when it comes to the many varied bodies that populate this earth, all of which deserve care, respect, visibility, and nourishment of the deepest, most life-affirming kind.

ACCOUNTABILITY AND ACCEPTANCE CAN COEXIST

When Black women and femmes combine the internal pressures to change our bodies with the external messages we've received from family, culture, and society about how we should show up in our bodies, eating imbalances in our communities rise in number, as they have. But as we begin to seek healing and divorce ourselves from fatphobia and anti-fat bias, we also start to unravel the shame and guilt we have internalized around how we exist in our bodies. The role we play in all of this—taking accountability and seeking to understand all the ways we ourselves have been complicit in allowing fatphobia and anti-fat bias to thrive—is also key. This work involves unpacking the ways that society has conditioned us to believe thinness and slenderness are the ideal and the norm. We can then go deeper by developing self-awareness around the ways that we have internalized patriarchy—which has been used, as we've discussed, to control and force our bodies into submission through dieting and food restriction.

What are the ways that we are currently trying to alter our diets and ourselves to fit into molds and ideals that were not designed for our bodies? What are the deeper motivations behind wanting to alter our body size, shape, or weight? This process may involve examining personal biases and asking yourself what you've been taught about body size, shape, or weight in connection with race and culture. How do those teachings and beliefs show up in your day-to-day interactions with your body?

The healing and uprooting work can also look like examining the places where we have internalized religious messages around what it means to have a pure, moral, godly, and abstinence-based diet. This is not to say that fasting for religious purposes is necessarily a "bad" thing, but it does create space for more complexity around how fasting is impacting our bodies, what messages we have internalized, and how different bodies respond to the practice. We also want to be careful, of course, not to reinforce the colonial systems that we are attempting to leave behind by shaming people for engaging in practices that are indigenous and healing for them. Some bodies can engage in practices like fasting with minimal impact to their bodies; let's stay inquisitive and open-minded when discussing this topic with ourselves and others.

While we are gaining awareness and unpacking the systems within our bodies, we can also address the systemic issues that contribute to dieting and fatphobia in the professional spaces where we do hold power. For example, people who are financially secure may get involved in working to eradicate hunger by increasing access to food in communities with limited options. People who are responsible for determining what type of furniture will be in their workplace can be intentional about choosing options that are affirming to a variety of body sizes. People with power in the medical institution can begin to push back in meetings and advocate for conclusive and expansive research training and practices that address weight stigma. It is my belief that once we transform the systems within ourselves, we can then bring the change we have cultivated within into the areas where we hold power and influence in order to begin to shift and change cultures and communities.

We have been conditioned to look at others' bodies and make judgments and assumptions about their worth and lifestyle. What if, instead, we greeted others by asking how connected they are to their emotions, sensations, impulses, and the way their body communicates to them? The end game isn't about *always* feeling good in our bodies; it's more about the relationship we have with it. It's the dance of being *connected* to one's body, both in those times when it feels easeful and in those times when we might be experiencing pain and difficulty.

WHY WE MUST DO THE CRITICAL WORK

It is important to note that we cannot love or heal ourselves out of systemic oppression. Embracing our own body does not mean that this will in turn create an indelible immunity to the very real issues we face connected to our quality of life and the threats that come from external systems. I encourage us to continue to abolish, disrupt, and dismantle the systems that impact the way we see our bodies and how we experience safety, belonging, and dignity. But I also acknowledge that systems are cultural, collective, and personal. If we don't engage in our personal work to abolish, disrupt, and dismantle the systems within ourselves, we will continue to replicate those same systems outside of ourselves, even as we work to create something new.

We are both affected by and affect the systems that we live in. While systemic change and movement work often take a long time before we see the physical manifestations, the internal and personal ways we can show up within ourselves are in our wheelhouse to work through. The work that we are doing throughout this book is not just about acknowledging what we have internalized. It's also about knowing that we can change our minds or learn something new that may change our thinking patterns. But this work must begin at the body level; otherwise we won't achieve the substantial healing and change we desire. Working from the body level gets to the seeds, which then stem to roots and extend throughout our bodies.

Over time, our awareness and embodiment practices, coupled with feeling safe enough to open the spaces where we are storing the trauma in our bodies, will allow us to begin to build a reservoir of consciousness around how our body works. This consciousness facilitates how we manage our emotions, guides decision-making, and enhances the relationship that we have with ourselves. It also strengthens empathy and self-compassion and informs the tools we use to resolve trauma. The more we become attuned to our bodies, sensations, and feelings, the more we can begin to work through the trauma our bodies are holding on to. Getting to the root of the stories we have been conditioned to believe about fatness is one way to start.

GUIDED PRACTICE #5

All emotions are energy, and so I'm going to invite you into a guided movement activity to move the emotional energy through your body and foster more support within. Now that we have named and unpacked some core beliefs around what contributes to fatphobia in Black communities, we must listen to these anti-fat thoughts when they come up—and they will—and listen with compassion. While practicing this thought exercise, don't forget to bring in the truth that fatness and Blackness are descriptors that have been personified and politicized. They are ours to reclaim and ours to redefine. They are parts of ourselves that we get to liberate from the distortion of white supremacy. Offer yourself grace as you begin to uncouple negative connotations from fatness and Blackness. As we do this, we are replacing the lie with the truth, and even if we don't see it or believe it now, the practice of affirming that truth over the lie will eventually become rooted in the way we feel about ourselves.

I gently ask you to allow yourself to be supported by something that affirms your body right now. This supportive thing could be a chair, a hammock, the floor, or the ground or earth beneath you. Once you sit, lie down, or stand, I ask that you slowly notice what is holding you. Notice if it truly feels supportive and offers a sense of being held. Pause to see how your body is responding to this object or space that is holding you. If your body does not find it affirming, I would suggest finding a different position and posture that helps your body feel more supported.

Turn your awareness to your breath: Is it constricted and tight? Deep and expansive? Labored and shallow? Full and abundant? Just notice what is already present for you. Be with your breath without judging or changing it for just a moment. Now bring your awareness back to what is supporting you and allow your body to gently sink in and fall deeper into what is holding you—the back of your body, your thighs, hips, and legs. How is that for you?

Lean closer into your support system, allowing the chair, pillow, blanket, floor, earth, hammock—whatever it may be—to gently cradle your spine. Honor the capacity and access that your body has at this moment. Allow your head to roll back if that feels supportive for you. Notice your breath: Is it the same, or has it shifted? Offer awareness as you allow your body to experience gravity by taking pressure off the front of your body and sending it to support the back.

In my somatic training, I learned from regenerative somatics theorist Staci Haines that the back body holds history—of the ancestors and all the teachers who came before us. So often we are conditioned to come out of the back of our bodies and instead rely on the front of our bodies, which does not allow us much room for regulation and centeredness. Think about how often we are on our computers, phones, or leaning forward. How does it feel to be in your back body?

The practice of centering and grounding into the back of our bodies and allowing it to guide us to our center is a tool that can be used when we need to set boundaries or advocate for ourselves, particularly in settings such as going to a health care provider. I have found that when there is already a fear of going to a doctor's appointment, without being grounded we do not have a buffer against what we're experiencing. Many times, our bodies perceive the emotional threat of showing up, taking up space, and advocating for ourselves as too overwhelming, and trigger or activate us back into our trauma responses for protection. This can make it harder to advocate for ourselves, or to be in tune with what our bodies need.

Centering ourselves into the back of our body is an activity that we can do before going into the doctor's office or while in the waiting room. When you envision that all of your support people are behind you and have your back in those times when you are advocating for yourself, it can help you feel less alone and more in your power.

Some clients have shared with me that they feel they don't have people who love and support them in their lives, and that it can be very difficult to find love and support. I want to validate that experience here. If this is your truth, I encourage you to envision something that feels loving and supportive—a pet, a plant, a place. Love and support are not limited to just human interaction.

QUESTIONS FOR REFLECTION

Fatphobia is a system of oppression. When we are directly impacted by systems of oppression that do not allow us access to our humanity and that create unnecessary barriers and psychological turmoil, it can result in trauma. The questions below are less about writing or reflecting on specific events in a detail-oriented way and more about recalling an experience, then using the embodiment skills delineated in previous chapters to notice what happens in your body on a sensation and feeling level.

1. When you think about an experience of fatphobia or anti-fat bias, or about witnessing someone experience fatphobia or anti-fat bias, what happens in your body? (For example, does your heart rate increase, or does your breathing become shallow? Do you want to shut down or turn away?) Be patient with this step; it can take time to increase your awareness. Once you're able to identify the impact on your body, think about whether these sensations help or harm you.

2. What are three boundaries that you can set for yourself over the next few days, week(s), month(s), or year(s) connected to how you treat your own body in response to fatphobia, anti-fat bias, and weight stigma?

3. In the first question, we explored somatic awareness of sensations and emotions in response to fatphobia, anti-fat bias, and weight stigma. You may have noticed, for example, that your chest tightened. You may have felt heat radiating from your chest and belly area, and your body curl inward around that sensation and feeling. In the past, these kinds of patterns of making yourself smaller may have served you in response to a threat. Recalling them now, have these patterns outgrown their usefulness?

If the answer is yes, then we can create an opening around a particular pattern so that we can begin to let it go. This can happen by first offering gratitude and appreciation for the pattern, because it developed at some point in your life to help you. Meditate on this through journaling, drawing, music, or dance. The idea is to help the pattern feel supportive and safe. We can then ask our body what it needs to release this pattern. If there is an initial response to the trauma of shutting down, disconnecting, or dissociating happening in the body, it can be helpful to acknowledge what that response is doing for you, and to very slowly move the body so that the pattern can be released.

Put on some music and start slowly by shaking, dancing, or moving to your own capacity as you reflect on the situation. Notice what happens to the sensations and feelings in your body. If you notice that movement is not helping you, listen to your body and stop the practice. Instead, ask your body if there is something else that would be more affirming—an activity like humming can be a helpful tool if you do not feel like moving. (But also remember that it can be helpful to note what that resistant response is doing for you if that's what you initially experienced. Listen to this, too.)

Slow down and use your breath to create long inhales, holding the breath for a moment and offering longer and audible exhales to release. Journaling can also be helpful. Notice what happens to the sensations and feelings in your body as you practice these techniques.

· SIX ·

Black Food and Healthism

"Food is a spiritual practice. Eating is a spiritual practice. Cooking is a spiritual practice. Farming is a spiritual practice. Gardening is a spiritual practice. Do you see how important food is to us as a diaspora?"

—LYVONNE BRIGGS, award-winning author, speaker, and podcaster

IN MANY SOUTHERN BLACK families, the kitchen is the epicenter of our homes. I can remember helping my grandma make collard greens seasoned with pig meat or "neck bones" with a little vinegar and skillet corn and molasses bread—always served with a glass of sweet tea or Kool-Aid on the side. As we gathered around the kitchen table, it wasn't uncommon for my grandparents on both my maternal and paternal sides to share stories about raising farm animals, and how they had to engage in the process of preparing the animal to be killed and eaten. Of course, by the time I was born, most people were going to the Piggly Wiggly or Food Lion for their food shopping. But family scenes like this were often just a regular part of life growing up in the country.

My paternal grandparents, the McCulloughs, had a kitchen that was more of a small room that opened to a smaller backyard area with a squeaky screen door. Everything in my grandparents' house had that old-timey feeling. I can still feel the steam that came from their old wood-burning stove as I sat on top of an unfolded newspaper used to protect the floor from getting wet from the freshly washed greens. It was my job to pick apart the collard green leaves from the stem so my grandmother could put them in the pot to cook along with the meat. If I did the job well, I'd get a pack of nabs—peanut butter crackers—as a reward for my efforts. Droplets of sweat would form on my forehead, and the only relief was that backyard door that let in a few pesky flies and a humid summer breeze. The breeze would engulf me with the heavy smell of sweet molasses and warm golden biscuits, which I could also enjoy after I helped my grandmother prepare dinner.

My grandmother would sit in front of me in her wicker chair, her curls slightly drenched and her attention steady, as she reminded me, "Baby, make sure to take all the leaves off that stock of collards, throw the stems away, and put the collards in the pot, ya hear?" My nine-year-old brain viewed this process of pulling apart collard greens from the stems to be very tedious, especially because my grandmother would buy at least five bundles of collards for the two of us to separate together. During these moments we would not do much talking outside of her providing me with instructions, although she occasionally would hum a gospel hymn. We mostly both sat in that small room intently focused on what we were creating, as the thickness of the summer heat enveloped us and we enjoyed the sights and smells of both what had already been prepared and what was to come.

Today those memories feel like glimpses into another world, but they remind me of the amount of presence my grandmother embodied around the entire process of nourishment. She may not have had a cookbook, but she was still able to tell you what to do in the kitchen as if reciting it from old wisdom. After all of the prep work and cooking was done, my family would enjoy a rich meal. By that point the sun would have set, and the evening chirps of crickets, grasshoppers, and other insects would surround us. This was life for me growing up, where days moved slowly and you could see a sky full of stars at night. We were connected to the outside, using all of our senses. And dinnertime with family was one of our most important traditions.

In her contribution to the Bryant Terry anthology *Black Food*, JUSTUS Kitchen founder and cooking activist Jocelyn Jackson wrote, "Black food isn't just ingredients and recipes and stories. It is also the spiritual practice and sacred spaces created when cooking and gathering together around these foods. It is the permission and invitation to feel welcome. It is the opportunity to honor our ancestors and our Afro futures. For me, food is a prayer. It is a sacred practice inherited from all my peoples. The stories of our food inspire empathy and connection. Food is about relationships and survival and creating the world we wish to see."

The sentiments Jackson expressed were certainly true on the McCullough side of the family. Eating out and getting fast food was simply unheard of when my father was growing up. It was always expected that his mother and sisters would provide food for the family. I imagine that the kitchen sometimes felt like a restrictive environment, because cooking for a family of twelve children was a full-time, unpaid job. But I also imagine that, in some ways, the kitchen was my grandmother's place of peaceful solitude, allowing her time to talk with God.

Born in 1924, my grandmother was a strongly built, dark-skinned woman with a soft, slow, Southern voice that quivered slightly when she spoke. When we visited, she always wanted to make sure that we were fed. I wasn't much of a cook growing up; in my parents' house it was the adults who cooked and us kids who helped clean up. The older I got, the less interested I became in cooking, even when learning opportunities were presented to me. Like most kids, I was more concerned back then with hanging out with my friends. Recently, however, I have begun to reclaim my relationship to cooking and nurturing myself adequately.

This has been a journey of its own, because when I first began to cook, I'd constantly think about what was "healthy" or "unhealthy."

It would cause me so much stress that I couldn't make much of an effort at all. But as I have put in the work to divorce myself from thinking about food in those rigid binaries, I have become better able to be in relationship with the process of preparing and joyfully experiencing the food I cook. On those days when I do decide to step into the kitchen, I can feel my grandmother's presence and all of my ancestors' energy come through in every dish I make.

I now see cooking as an artistic medium. What nourishes us is not only about what our eyes can see, but also about the unseen: the energy we bring to the cooking, the way we speak over the food, and the care we take throughout the process. It is the blending and meshing of different cultures into one pot, adding in different ingredients with rich and vibrant colors, taking pride in the design of the final presentation as you serve up dishes that were passed down through many generations and are now reflected in you. It is in the way that we use our tongue to decipher where each flavor comes from.

As farmer and food justice activist Leah Penniman once explained, "With the seed, our grandmothers also braided their esoteric and cultural knowledge. For our ancestors, the earth was not a commodity, but a family member. They did not tuck a seed into the ground and expect it to grow without requisite prayer, offerings, song, and propitiation. They did not see themselves as master of creation but as humble members of a delicate web of sacred beings."

To be nourished and sustained by a lineage and ancestry of plants, herbs, and animals is sacred. The energy that we obtain from these entities also becomes a part of our bodies' ecosystem and vitality. I am constantly reminded that being in the kitchen is a spiritual and emotional experience that connects me to ancestral memories of growing up in the South and to living in reciprocity with the land.

WHAT IS HEALTHISM?

Healthism is the idea that a person's health is entirely within their control—and it places a moral importance on maintaining limited definitions of "good" health. We live in a culture where there is a heavy emphasis on health being connected to personal value and worth. The idea that health or the lack thereof is the result of some moral failing contributes to ableism. It falsely requires us to put the quality of our health into a box in which far too many of us do not fit, particularly those of us who have been marginalized by society. Having a moral obligation to be healthy typically represented by having a thin body and the absence of all disease, illness, or disability can have negative consequences, and lead to issues like eating imbalances and negative body image.

Tying health issues in Black communities to the types of food we eat without first examining the impacts oppression, trauma, and stress have had on our bodies—and the bodies we come from—totally misses the point. As we've just discussed, contrary to widely accepted mainstream narratives, fat is not unhealthy and there have been no empirically based studies that have proven that fatness leads to poor health. However, what has occurred is that studies that look at health outcomes like diabetes, high blood pressure, and heart disease primarily focus on proving that fatness is diseased and draw conclusions based on correlations. It is important to note that correlation is not causation.

A 2020 study by the Centers for Disease Control (CDC) found that African Americans aged thirty-five to sixty-four are 50 percent more likely to have high blood pressure than white Americans, and that African Americans aged eighteen to forty-nine are two times more likely to die from heart disease than whites. In 2017, another CDC study showed that in comparison to their white counterparts, young African Americans are living with more diseases, such as high blood pressure, diabetes, and stroke, that are usually more common in individuals at older ages.

These data findings point us to the fact that Black bodies are disproportionately dealing with life-threatening illnesses at higher rates than their white peers, and experiencing these symptoms at younger ages. When we discuss Black people's "health," the main default is to blame these illnesses on our food choices and our weight. But if it is assumed that the "American diet" is to blame for what the medical-industrial system describes as the "obesity epidemic," then there should not be any disparities at all between Black and white Americans; the data should be similar across all races and ethnicities. So if it's not food, we have to contend with systemic and historical factors that contribute to these disparities.

Healthism often becomes amplified through orthorexia nervosa, which is a focus on eating in a healthy way. While eating nutritious food is fantastic, if you have orthorexia you obsess about it to a degree that can damage your overall well-being. Dr. Steven Bratman coined the term and defined orthorexia nervosa as "a fixation on righteous eating," as diagnosed through compulsive behavior and/or a preoccupation with a restrictive diet to promote optimum health. A violation of one's self-imposed dietary rules can cause an exaggerated fear of disease, a sense of personal impurity, and/or negative physical sensations, anxiety, and shame. Over time, this type of dietary restriction may come to include the elimination of food groups and an overindulgence in cleanses. Weight loss commonly occurs, but the desire to lose weight is often not the focus.

Someone dealing with orthorexia may constantly check ingredient labels and nutritional information, cut out eating entire food groups, express increased concern about the "health," "cleanliness," and "purity" of ingredients, frequently engage in "cleanses" intended to rid the body of "toxins," avoid eating with others if they cannot control the menu, raise concerns and have anxiety about food preparation, experience extreme feelings of guilt and shame when consuming "unhealthy" or "unsafe" foods, and/or experience stress in social situations where food is involved. The side effects of orthorexia can be gastrointestinal problems such as constipation and/or bloating, electrolyte imbalances that can lead to irregular heartbeat and seizures, decreased estrogen/testosterone/thyroid hormone, weak and brittle bones (osteoporosis), kidney and liver damage, muscle loss and weakness, fatigue, and lack of energy.

Another part of healthism we cannot overlook is how it demonizes our cultural foods and labels them as "unclean" or "bad." We see this in how the soul food our people have put their blood and sweat into for generations is now being replaced with what nutrition expert, coach, and food activist Dr. Kera Nyemb-Diop describes as "white people food." My mom has had to navigate this kind of healthism. She shared with me the story of the time she went to her white woman doctor for a routine checkup and, after the doctor noticed her weight had changed slightly, asked her what she was eating. My mom casually shared some of the cultural foods she'd eaten recently; the doctor soon demonstrated her biases by turning up her nose in disgust and commenting that my mother needed to see a dietitian who would "teach" her how to eat properly.

Even the current obsession with veganism in our communities has its roots in healthism. Certainly, embracing our history of farming culture, having access to land, and growing our own foods can be an essential part of our healing. The issue arises when there is a shaming narrative that "everyone needs to and can engage in this lifestyle," and that those who don't are "less than" or even dirty for what they consume, a phenomenon that I have witnessed in mainstream vegan communities. It reinforces the idea of food being good or bad, a concept that is then laid on individuals and communities, without considering and deconstructing other challenges these communities might be facing—such as food apartheid, colonization, and access to land.

THE FALSEHOODS SURROUNDING OUR FOOD

We have been taught that during enslavement, Black people had nothing to eat but the leftover scraps of what had been thrown away by the slave owners. That is a myth. In my own unlearning of this falsehood, I came across the work of award-winning culinary historian and food author Michael Twitty, who has written at length on this subject. He reminds us that even as we were captured, Black people still had the presence of mind and ingenuity to stash and bring along with them the grains and spices that were a part of their culture, and incorporated them into the food they ate as slaves. He says we knew what to do with the meat that was described as "the unsavory parts," because we were resourceful and did not waste food. It really wasn't about the fact that we were eating scraps; it was that we were innovative with the minimal amounts of food we received during slavery and used what we had to create our own cuisine—what's now known as "soul food."

Twitty says there is no soul food without the food of the enslaved because that food is a blend of our African heritages. The narrative that enslaved Africans were just making do with the scraps given to us denies our resistance, agency, ownership, and stewardship—both before the plantations and throughout our enslavement. It ignores the fact that our ancestors curated the passing down of culture from Africa to America. The culture and spirit of our food practice is portable, he says. We should celebrate the fact that the memory of this culture also resides in our hands and feet when we march, dance, cook, preach, sing, and reinterpret the reinterpreted. It is imperative that we remember all the bits and pieces so that we can put together the full mosaic of our cultural and social story with food. Because this story has been marginalized, redefining it should be our lifelong work and responsibility.

Without a doubt, white people are the culprits behind the movement to stigmatize soul food. With limited skill and understanding of our culinary heritage, they conspired to appropriate our food culture and recast it for their own purposes as Southern cuisine. In doing so, they also introduced leftover options into the mix—i.e., pig's feet, souse, chitterlings, and scrapple. Historically, of course, our ancestors utilized the entire animal for efficiency, and that continued into our lives on the plantation. But then white people turned this practice back on us by claiming that we were responsible for the "unhealthy" diets that are part of our cultural tradition.

As a Southerner, let me tell you: There is a difference between Southern food and soul food. The former is often associated with large-scale chains like Kentucky Fried Chicken. These fast-food restaurants typically have a white originator, even though the recipes were often both created and prepared by Black hands, then co-opted and popularized in Southern white culture. Soul food, on the other hand, is a way of life; a tie that binds us within our communities; an expression of who we are and what we've endured.

In a society where white culture is the dominant one, foods that are crafted and designed by white people are often the types of foods that are considered closer to power and privilege. These are the foods that get labeled as "healthy," "clean," and "good." But this, of course, does not stop white people from coming into Black neighborhoods to consume our culture and food, then take what is profitable and bring it into white dining spaces, while never crediting the original stewards.

Soul food, on the other hand, has been castigated as unsophisticated and less than. Controversial conversations on social media platforms such as TikTok have done little to change this perception; in fact, some viral videos have gone so far as to label our food "low vibrational." This interpretation suggests that Black food is not only bad, but also literally brings down our energy level. The assertion is not only false, it also fails to consider the energetic relationship to cultivation Black people have established and put into the food we are harvesting.

For example, all food holds its own energetic vibration and molecular structure. Those structures and vibrations are influenced by the soil, fertilization, chemicals, pesticides, genetic modification, environment, and the relationship to nurturing and nourishing the plant, animal, water system, or whatever entity becomes the resource to provide energy and fuel to our bodies. Much like humans are impacted by the care we receive growing up, plants, animals, and water systems are also impacted by the care *they* receive, along with their biology, lineage, and environment, which ranges from the breeding, harvesting, and production process to when it arrives in our local supermarkets and/or farmers markets.

When we return to our ancestral worldview and view food in an ecological way, we contend with the journey, story, and life span of food in America and how different factors have impacted the quality and sustainability of what we are ingesting. Acknowledging this interdependent relationship is a more holistic framework than the reductive approach of dichotomizing and assigning food moral value based on race and access. It goes against labeling a food item as "good or bad," "healthy or unhealthy," "clean or dirty" when technically we are all accessing the same large-scale chemicalized food ecosystem—even though class, zip code, land ownership, and racial background have determined the prevalence of chemicals one ingests. I am more interested in addressing how capitalism has contributed to mass production, which has tainted the quality and genetic makeup of what we are consuming.

Soul food is most often associated with so-called hole-in-the-wall locations that have been embedded in our communities for generations and are frequently owned and operated by Black people. These are the places only local folks know about, mostly through word of mouth—places where pictures of Black public figures such as American presidents, rappers, singers, actors, activists, and athletes, as well as revered elders, are proudly displayed on wood-paneled walls. I'm talking about dining establishments such as Stephanie's in Greensboro, North Carolina, or Ben's Chili Bowl in Washington, D.C.—places that serve as portals into our

ancestral food lines. These restaurants are brick-and-mortar tributes to Black liberation and joy and serve as safe spaces for Black
people to just exist outside of the white gaze and express themselves freely in community with one another. They're also prime
examples of how we as a community can lovingly nourish one another.

A critical part of this conversation, too, is America's overabun-
dance of fast-food restaurants—which often appear within Black
communities, especially in low-income areas. While it is true that
fast food can be one of the few accessible, affordable options for
some, it is also true that it doesn't offer a variety of nourishment.
And limited job opportunity in low-income, Black communities
only further inhibits our ability to purchase more nutritious meals.
In this way, the cycle perpetuates itself. Breaking this pattern—
reconnecting us to our food in a way that sustains us in a truly
comprehensive way—requires a level of institutional investment
that our communities have never been afforded: more fertile land
for community gardens where we can grow and harvest our own
food; more consideration from business owners regarding what
they're doing to ensure that they are employing diverse people
who need jobs, creating opportunities for upward mobility; more
funding to support culinary school enrollment for Black folks;
more Black chefs owning Michelin-starred restaurants that represent a variety of cultural foods. What are those with the most advantages doing to invest in neighborhoods that are underresourced?
And how can we insist on having nuanced conversations about
food and nourishment that address the history of colonization, enslavement, and capitalism?

With their obvious connection to the inequitable distribution of
food and resources, the topics of food deserts and food insecurity
are certain to arise in public health discussions about systemic racism and structural oppression. However, related concepts, like
food sovereignty, food justice, and food apartheid, are rarely mentioned, if at all. This is not coincidental, but by design, according to

fat liberationist, writer, and educator Marquisele Mercedes, also known as Mikey, whose 2020 article "Public Health's Power-Neutral, Fatphobic Obsession with 'Food Deserts'" looks at how even the public health field is loath to call this inconsistent access what it truly is: food apartheid.

Mikey goes on to say that public health—as an academic field, profession, and apparatus of the state—is not interested in the political nature of food sovereignty, food justice, and food apartheid. It is not interested in acknowledging that oppression and anti-Blackness are two of the major forces behind the way some humans, backed by the concentrated power of corporations and institutions, have decided to deprive others of the access that should be everyone's right. The term "food desert" neutralizes the threat by turning it back on us, equating the Black community's inequitable access to diverse food as our community's natural state.

Using a term like "food apartheid," coined by activist Karen Washington, instead would push this point to the forefront of the conversation. But to admit that the inequitable distribution of food is deliberate and intentional would then warrant a reconsideration of public health's entire approach to our health and welfare. It is easier, it seems, for some people to have access to "healthy" food, for others not to, and to just leave it at that. It is less controversial to vaguely gesture at injustice by using terms like "food deserts" rather than to work to dismantle the injustice altogether.

These concepts are important to understand not only broadly, but very specifically, in the way they impact those in our communities with eating imbalances. When people experience food insecurities such as inconsistent access, followed by compensatory eating when food finally becomes available again, it can often spark a cycle of restrictive eating and food portioning. It is a survival response that Black folks have leaned on since the time of slavery— when food on the plantation could be withheld as a form of control and punishment of the enslaved. It is further proof that food has *always* been a political tool for the oppressor. And that the body, especially the Black body, has always been one of its many battle-grounds.

WE ARE NOT WHAT WE EAT

As I reflect on Mikey's scholarship, I think more and more about the toxic messages we've received throughout our existence in this country. Society teaches us that all we have to do is simply look at someone's body size and be able to tell how much they eat, what they eat, and if they are healthy or not. I've experienced this within my own family. Once, during a family gathering, someone approached me—quite unsolicitedly—and asked whether I was working out. When I asked why they wanted to know, this person said that it was obvious that I was not healthy because I had gained weight, and they were just concerned. I remember being so full of anger during this encounter. There were so many levels to what they were saying to me that were rooted in healthism and fatphobia, wrapped in "good intentions."

But scenarios like this one illuminate those toxic, often moralizing messages we receive that if someone is larger-bodied or has gained weight, they must have an unhealthy lifestyle. The concept of food hierarchies, the notion that there are "levels" that we should attribute to food and its value, can lead us down this toxic path as well. There's sometimes little awareness or consideration of the fact that everybody is different, and everyone is entitled to make their own dietary choices, no questions asked. Some bodies require meat to survive, and from an evolutionary perspective our precolonial ancestors were not mass-producing or riddled with overconsumption when hunting and gathering.

We must also make room to allow for economic barriers at play that can impact people's choices. Not everyone, for example, can access a vegan lifestyle, due to lack of financial and geographical access. I have also learned that a "healthy" choice in one body can lead to harm or inflammation in another. As an example, crucifer-

ous vegetables are described as leafy greens that are good for inflammation and have anticancer properties, but if I consume too
much of these veggies it can actually trigger an overactivation of
my thyroid gland. Everybody is truly unique, and the most trusted
source for expertise about what your body needs is the wisdom and
discernment of your own body.

The idea that everyone needs to follow the same diet can lead us
to reject our ancestral foods, which then leads to further food disconnection. When we view our relationship with food as solely
about survival and take the spiritual and emotional components
out of it, we miss so much that can help heal us. Spiritual and emotional issues often manifest through our physical bodies. There
may be emotional needs that our bodies are trying to communicate, and we may need to consume comfort foods in order to address them. Food could be the pathway to help us slow down and
understand what we need at that moment. Our relationship to
food—in its most generous, loving state—is medicinal and regenerative. Dr. Tao Leigh Goffe explains it this way: "Soul food is a
recipe as much as a resource for the future of Blackness itself, for
survival and sustenance, for a multiplicity of Black futures."

But the Americanized mindset around food has been distorted
to the point where we rely on food labels and other people to be
the experts, instead of listening to our body and allowing it to guide
us into what it needs. American culture is quick to label food like
pasta as a "bad" food that leads to poor health outcomes; however,
there are areas in the world that entirely contradict this thinking—
like a village in Sardinia, Italy, where people consume pasta every
day and are living to be more than a hundred years old. In these
areas where folks are living past a hundred, also known as "blue
zones," the key to longevity and health is connected to how the
food is made, as well as there being a balance and variety within
diets.

Other telling contributing factors include embodying a
community-oriented mindset and not living in a hyperproductivity

culture—both of which are conspicuously missing in American culture. The truth is, modifying our diets in a helpful way is often-times less about what we remove from our list of "acceptable" foods, and more about what we can add into our diets—and our lives—to better support our bodies.

We live in a culture that is significantly undernourished, whether through the limits we have around food based on who determines what foods are sourced in each country, the financial cost of access-ing food, the limits we put on ourselves around what we allow our-selves to eat, or our increasing sourcing of vitamins and nutrients from things other than food because we are not getting enough of what we need in our diet. Instead, we are constantly told to con-sume less and eat less to achieve thinness. But in actuality, we should be eating *more*—getting more variety, more of what we love, more of what nourishes our souls.

In the busy hustle and bustle of our days, however, we barely have time to check in with ourselves, much less eat. There have been times, particularly early on in my career, when during the workday my body was screaming "feed me"—via stomach rumbles, headaches, an inability to focus, even shaky hands—and my brain would answer only after much delay. Or I'd often spend thirty min-utes on Google just looking through menus trying to figure out where to get some semblance of an affordable, nutritious meal. As I struggled to make the "right choices," it became harder and harder not to realize that food access, from both a financial and locational perspective, is inextricably tied to privilege.

LISTENING TO WHAT THE BODY KNOWS

While we can't always get around the systemic factors that lead us to neglect our bodies—work culture, food hierarchies, and food accessibility, to name a few—there have been some subtle shifts in social attitudes. In recent years, a movement known as "intuitive eating" has become popular, mostly with white women. Intuitive eating, a concept popularized by Evelyn Tribole and Elyse Resch, is a non-dieting approach to changing your eating habits. Intuitive Eating is designed to follow a linear flow where someone begins with rejecting the diet mentality and concludes with honoring their health through gentle nutrition.

For example, we might decide to reject the diet mentality by throwing out the diet books and magazine articles that offered us false hope of losing weight quickly, easily, and permanently. We can choose to keep our bodies nurtured with adequate nutrition, because excessive hunger will only lead us to overeat. Learning to honor our bodies' signals sets the stage for rebuilding trust in yourself and in food, so that when those thoughts come around that police us and bombard us with messages that you're somehow "good" for taking in fewer calories and "bad" when you indulge in a special treat, we are better prepared to reject them.

We also have to listen to our body's signals that let us know when we are full. Looking for fullness cues is as easy as pausing in the middle of a meal to check in and see if our hunger has been satisfied. When you eat what you really want, in an environment that is inviting, the pleasure you derive will be a powerful force in helping you feel satisfied and content. By providing this experience for yourself, you will come to understand when you've had "enough." We all have a genetic makeup that is uniquely ours. Once we acknowledge that there is no "one size fits all" approach to eating, we can begin to respect our bodies for what they are.

Within the eating disorders field, many practitioners encourage their clients to engage in intuitive eating. According to the National Eating Disorders Association, intuitive eating is about trusting your body to make food choices that feel good for you, without judging yourself and without the influence of diet culture.

But while I have found that the principles of the movement have been helpful for some folks, I have publicly pushed back against the oversimplification of intuitive eating. I have found that, when working with groups that experience marginalization due to their social identities, eating intuitively can be challenging if we do not first work together to establish a relationship where we are actually listening to our bodies. When we have been taught to shut down, dismiss, or disconnect from what our bodies are telling us through our cultural conditioning, intuitive eating will not come easefully. People who struggle with depression, anxiety, PTSD, or even the effects of Covid-19 may not feel hungry or have an appetite. However, it is still important that they nourish their bodies. This type of eating instruction also encourages eating solely for the purpose of obligation. It does not honor that many people eat for different reasons, and it doesn't always have to be obligatory; it can also be because we want to consume food that is pleasurable, even when we are adequately nourished.

From a body-based trauma perspective, to be in connection with our bodies in a way that is intuitive requires us to look at what intuition is, and how it has historically been disembodied in our culture. It is widely accepted that our senses are sight, smell, taste, touch, and sound. However, it is less accepted that intuition is also a part of our senses. There is a reason for this: Intuition, which is the ability to understand something immediately without the need for conscious reasoning, is antithetical to our patriarchal society, which is rooted in the logical, measurable way we've been conditioned to think. When it comes to systems of oppression like patriarchy, white supremacy, and capitalism, we are all swimming in their deep waters. The only way for us to get free is to recognize how we got there.

Intuition is a matriarchal and feminine energy of embodiment. In a culture that demonizes the feminine, it is less likely that we are listening to our intuition and more likely that we are second-guessing ourselves in the pursuit of patriarchal and Western facts and evidence to back up what we know to be true. We have been disconnected from intuition, which likely occurred with the oppression and subjugation of non-men, which created a wound based in cultural trauma. This wound is what keeps girls, women, and femmes out of connection with our bodies and not knowing how best to take care of them.

When popular theories are developed with good intentions that tell us to "intuitively eat" without examining the impact of patriarchy, colonization, white supremacy, and capitalism on our Black bodies—and how that has in turn impacted our ability to listen to our intuition—it feels more like a Band-Aid than a balm. This kind of surface solution lacks the critical and layered analysis necessary when considering the efficacy for other communities.

Before we can even get to a place of trying out intuitive eating, it's first important for us to develop trust with ourselves and recognize the ways our intuition speaks to us when it comes to our relationship with food. At this point in my life, I can tell when my body desires and needs a green smoothie, something savory and sweet, or a light snack, but it took a lot of listening, while also detangling the threads of diet culture and fatphobia, to get there. I had to learn how to listen to my body without second-guessing and thinking, *Is this bad? Will this make me gain weight? How many calories does this have?*

It took time for me to recognize how my body responds to certain foods and to not feed into the simplified narratives of "I am so bloated, or inflamed," when in fact it actually was my body responding to a longer period of food restrictions that contributed to stress and was exacerbating those symptoms. Over time, I began to experience my body as a micro ecosystem influenced by what I was consuming not just through my diet, but through my thoughts, the media, and conversations that I had. This vast approach allowed me to see, for example, that if I lived in an area with increased exposure to mold, chemicals, or pollution, those issues would also impact my gut health and digestion, that it wasn't solely the food.

While the barriers to accessing intuition can be particularly high in Black communities, I would argue that our culture generally discourages us from validating our intuitions. For example, from a young age we are told when and what we should eat. But as babies, our nourishment revolved around pleasure, desire, and when we were hungry. I have so many friends who have shared that their newborn dictated their feeding schedule; that they had to adjust to respond to the needs and hunger of their baby, and that typically it did not involve waiting for hours before they decided to feed their child. When the baby was crying out for nourishment, the parent(s) knew that it was time to feed the little one.

But something interesting happens over time: Those little ones grow up and are told what foods are good or bad for them, and meals become more structured in terms of what time food will be served and what is on the menu. This is important, because as we get older, we move away from our body's intuition and fall into the expectations of family routine and convenience. I have spoken with many parents who are also professionals in the eating disorders field who decided to take a different approach. They started out by offering their child a few options and set boundaries around a time frame of when those options would be available. They didn't dictate how much or how little their child could eat, and they were very cognizant of asking their child, "Does your tummy like that?" or "Do you want more?" or "Do you not like that very much?" All the while, they were reinforcing that all foods provide nourishment and pleasure, and that enjoying a variety of foods is important to one's ability to play, experience fun, and move one's growing body.

These parents shared with me that even reframing the way they talk about food and their bodies has been helpful in guiding children to establish a better relationship with their bodies. They don't comment on their children's appearance, but instead celebrate them for who they are and support them in cultivating a practice of nourishing their bodies. For example, one colleague told me that her eight-year-old son frequently helps her in the kitchen, and that she's had conversations with him about listening to his body and letting her know how the food that he consumes feels in his body. These parents are teaching their children the importance of body awareness. They are fostering the connection to the child's intuition and offering them the language to communicate with others what is going on in their bodies.

Many of the clients I have worked with as adults have not had this experience. Rather, they often share that they grew up hearing their parents tell them they needed to lose weight or be on diets, or that they were greedy and "too fat." Some were told that certain foods like cookies, chips, and cakes were junk food, and that they should avoid them. Others said they grew up like I did, in a "clean-your-plate household," where they had to finish everything on their plate or they would get in trouble. Many spoke about not being able to afford food and having to scrape by on the bare minimum, and shared that the kitchen was not a place of bonding, but a place of obligation. These early experiences shaped the way they learned to listen to their bodies and nourish themselves, and ultimately contributed to some of their imbalanced eating experiences.

UNPACKING THE "HEALTH JOURNEY"

I've noticed that when clients first begin to analyze diet culture and are in the early days of challenging their notions about fatphobia, many land on describing this evolution as a "health journey." While on the outside this may seem like a safe landing place, I would encourage us to untangle this idea a little bit. In the case of my client Alexis, a small, fat biracial queer college sophomore, landing on what she considered a lifestyle change became a slippery slope that led her right back into her imbalanced eating patterns. Alexis was witty, adored by many of her peers, and held leadership positions in many campus organizations. But while she was accepted and admired by her college peers, she shared that in her home life her mother would constantly comment on her size and how concerned she was about Alexis's health. Their relationship was very complex; her mother, who was in a straight-sized body, was always trying to lose weight, and as a result, Alexis never felt good enough around her. Alexis told me she grew up watching her mother restrict foods and then consequently experience physical symptoms such as dizziness, moodiness, and low energy. When Alexis turned nine, her mother began to restrict Alexis's food as well, and to make negative and disapproving comments when Alexis's attempts at restriction led to even more weight gain.

Alexis was coming to therapy sessions because her mother had signed them both up for a 5K run and was constantly checking in with her daughter to make sure that she was preparing for it by watching her food intake and working out more. Alexis shared that she felt depressed and anxious and was avoiding her mother. As we unpacked the emotional distress associated with this dynamic, I introduced to her the idea that her health and weight were not synonymous. While she initially resisted this idea, after we talked about other social determinants of health such as racism, zip code, and socioeconomic status, she began to come around.

Alexis told me that she was sick of her choices around eating, mostly because restricting her diet was not helping her, especially in school. She noticed that it was harder for her to concentrate and focus when she was not adequately nourished. Although her academic performance and grades were more important to her than restricting her diet, she continued to label her food as either "healthy" or "unhealthy," and told me that at the university café she would only eat what she deemed healthy foods. "You know, salads," she responded when I asked what kinds of foods she was eating. "No sweets, no junk, just clean food." I told her that while she might think this was a "healthy" choice, by allowing herself to eat only salads she wasn't providing for a lot of options in her food choices. She acknowledged that sticking only to salad was "pretty boring," but said she couldn't allow herself to eat "bad" foods that would make her fat and unhealthy.

As I worked with her, I tried to get her to understand that her "health journey" was actually one with self-imposed limitations and rules that were just as unhealthy as dieting. We decided to

focus on expanding her food choices and discussed the fears she
had developed around certain foods that caused her to avoid them.
After a few sessions, Alexis admitted that when she thought about
eating foods she had labeled as unhealthy, she began to feel sick
and got a stomachache. We began to explore that anxiety and
where she was holding it in her body: her belly area.

The expression that says we have a "gut feeling" about something is actually biological. The belly area is often associated with
vulnerability; it is also a place where we tend to store the energy
that allows us to digest and metabolize and is associated with the
emotions of confidence, self-esteem, and empowerment. Whenever Alexis did allow herself to eat sweets, she felt as if she was
doing something wrong, and shared that she would often eat
quickly so that she wouldn't feel as guilty or get in trouble with her
mother—and that this would often cause her to have a bellyache.

Once we identified this concern, we began to work with her
inner girl, who feared getting in trouble or being a disappointment
to her mother for eating sweets, or "bad foods." It took about six
months before Alexis was able to expand her diet and introduce
foods into her routine that initially elicited fear. She discovered
that one part of the eating imbalance voice that she had internalized belonged to her mother; she heard it on repeat, constantly
judging and critiquing her body. Alexis was able to set boundaries
with that voice and began to make more space to listen to her own
inner voice, which was much more body-affirming and encouraging in her recovery.

We worked together to unblock the area in her throat where her
own inner voice had been suppressed, and gradually helped her
speak in her truth. As a result, Alexis was eventually able to set
boundaries with her mother and tell her that she did not want her
projecting her own body insecurities onto her.

One of the last things Alexis and I worked on was her fears
around taking up space. These fears were significantly enmeshed
in her complicated relationship with her mother, but they also de-

veloped because she was one of the only Black women in a dance program she was enrolled in at the university where I was seeing her. She shared that most of the other women in her classes were white or thin, and that this made her feel isolated as a Black woman in a larger body. She told me she consistently walked around sucking in her stomach and would tell herself that she should only take opportunities to move her body when they did not put her in the spotlight.

I listened to and helped Alexis sort through the racial trauma she felt in her body by being one of the only Black women in her class. We worked on the toxic messages she had internalized around not being good enough, and those she received from her family about having to work twice as hard to be just as good as her white peers. Alexis also felt she had to shrink her body in white spaces and noticed that when she was among her white peers she tried to hide and isolate herself so as not to be seen. This was a manifestation of ancestral trauma—the kinds of survival skills often required of Black folks in front of white people during the Jim Crow era. We had to be productive, entertaining, and accommodating to white folks, a commodity but not an actual human being.

To counter this trauma, we began to practice "power poses" in my office, to allow her body to feel what it was like to take up space and feel confident. Alexis would try physical poses like standing upright with her hands on her hips, her head uplifted, her heart and belly exposed, and her feet spread wide apart. It took a while before she felt comfortable in that pose, but we would set aside time at each session to practice, and then use the power of that stance to uncover other places within her body where she felt stuck or uncomfortable. Sometimes she felt a blockage in her shoulders or her hips; in those instances, she shared that she felt burdened in her shoulder area, or that when she stretched her hips she felt sadness and wanted to cry. I'd always check in with her to assess her capacity so that we didn't push her body too far, which I knew would have caused her to shut down.

Before Alexis graduated, we scheduled a closing session to wrap up our work together and send out good intentions for the journey ahead of her. Right before the session ended, she pulled out her phone and began looking for something, smiling widely as she said, "I have got to show you something—you're going to be so shocked." As I waited, I rested one of my elbows on the arm of my chair and smiled as I thought about how much she had grown over the last two years. I thought about how I was going to miss her—most endings with clients are bittersweet for the therapist, too. It wasn't long before she turned her phone toward me and showed me her graduation photos. She paused on one photo where she was staring squarely into the camera with a confident smile on her face: her chin high, wearing her graduation cap like a crown. Her hands rested firmly on her hips and her stance in her high heels was wide—she was fully embodying the power pose we'd practiced in therapy.

As I held my hand over my heart, I was so proud of Alexis and felt such excitement that she was embracing her healing and truly taking up space. I expressed my joy, offered her some kind words, and gave her a hug before sending her off into the world. As I returned to my desk to record the final notes from our session together, I thought, *It is moments like this one that remind me why I do the work that I do.*

A NEW WAY OF THINKING ABOUT FOOD AND HEALTH

I often ponder over how contradictory it is that our culture has used body size to signify health using the equation that eating less, plus exercising more, will equal a slim or fit body. At the height of the period in the eighteenth century during which the Black body was associated with fatness, our ancestors were already eating less due to starvation, malnutrition, and undernourishment, and were one of the most physically active groups in America, yet they existed in an *array* of body shapes and sizes. The math, as they say, isn't mathing. It doesn't add up, and completely topples the idea of what we deem "healthy" in our society, and the generic messages we often receive when it comes to the pursuit of health.

We can redefine what health is while also not moralizing it. We do not owe anyone healthiness, which may even be impossible to achieve by societal standards. I have come to believe that health is defined by how connected I *feel* to my body on a holistic level. My mental health, for example, is based on having good boundaries with people in my life, continually accessing my emotional capacity, and keeping up with therapy appointments. My spiritual health is determined by my connection to God and my ancestors, and being mindful about the energy that I am consuming (like news, personal conversations, and social media). My physical health is defined by making sure that I am adequately nourished and rested, and that I engage in some type of body-affirming movement.

Throughout this chapter I have emphasized why it is so important to connect with our food on a soul level, from my treasured experiences growing up and cooking alongside my grandmother to the lessons we've learned around what a positive connection to food can look like. I have unpacked the contradictory imbalanced relationship that we've had with food and offered suggestions and reflections to facilitate harmony in the way we nourish ourselves. I'd like to end this chapter by encouraging you to lean into patience and self-compassion along this journey.

As you continue to listen to your body, I invite you to first identify, research, and investigate what foods, recipes, and practices already exist and have been passed down in your family. Perhaps there is a particular gumbo recipe or a way that you make collard greens, or a way that your family has paired food together. I have friends of Caribbean descent who frequently cook together and talk about the passing down of foods like mofongo, which was carried to the Caribbean through the African diaspora. Other Black folks I know who grew up in areas like New York and Washington, D.C., talk about frequently eating jollof rice with beans, and people from Southern states like Mississippi playfully argue about the "right" way to make corn bread. All of these items were brought to us through our ancestors, and we bring it forth into the future by unlocking it through our cellular memory.

I often hear people say things like, "Well, what about folks who are adopted and know nothing of their ancestry or family traditions?" To them I would say that everything you need to know is already within you. Many folks of the diaspora do not know who our people are, or where we come from, but we share the same ancestral memory. I was well into my early twenties before trying plantains for the first time, but when I tasted them there was something warm and intimate about the experience. It wasn't just that they were delicious; there was also something familiar about them—something that felt ancient and sacred. After that first bite, my heart began to swell and tears came to my eyes. I offer this example as a way of reiterating that we are holding the energy of thousands of stories and desires, lifetimes of wisdom and love, within us, just waiting to be awakened, and no one can take that away from us. We are more than just who we show up as in this physical form. As beloved ancestor Maya Angelou once said, "I come as 1, but stand as 10,000."

If diving into your family traditions around food poses a challenge, I recommend checking out local Black-owned, African, and Caribbean restaurants near where you live and taking the time to be intentional with your meal. Notice how many flavors you can taste and if anything is familiar. If there is an item on the menu that sticks with you, just know that food is the connector back to the motherland. For folks who have dietary restrictions or adaptations, I would recommend finding ways to infuse those adaptations into the food. There are many soul food restaurants nowadays that are also vegan, vegetarian, and pescatarian.

There is also a larger-scale movement rooted in food justice toward food that is sustainably sourced. I identify as a lifelong learner, so I am continually in pursuit of new information. For me it was helpful to get an African cookbook to read about and connect with the lineage and legacy of Black food. For some, connecting with a Black anti–diet culture dietitian or nutritionist may also be helpful in this journey. We are returning to and reclaiming an era when food was not just food, but was also rooted in the wisdom of Black and Indigenous communities, centering the full ecology of our existence.

Food connects us to our roots. But it's not so much about connecting to a place; it's more about connecting to a journey. The links between our African and ancestral foods and the foods we eat today register in our ancestral memory. Studies show that our taste preferences are influenced by what our parents ate while we were in the womb. Writer and activist Dara Cooper describes Black food as resistance: "Our resistance looks like the reclamation of our rightful place as leaders within our own food systems. The ways in which we've created beautiful meals to feed our loved ones despite it all, the markers we've created to counter the Jim Crow foods that saturate our communities, the cooperatives we've created to pool our limited resources, the burning of corporate (sterile) seeds donated to us in our most vulnerable moments are all forms of protest and resistance that lead us to what we know as food justice. It gets us that much closer to the taste of actual freedom."

GUIDED PRACTICE #6

While participating in eating imbalance support groups, my clients have shared that one helpful method they've employed to heal their relationship with food has been the practice of mindful eating. Mindful eating invites us to be fully present as our bodies are being nourished; it allows us to slow down and be in relationship with what we are eating. I often use a script I adapted from integrative somatic psychotherapist Christine Milovani as a compass to guide clients into mindful eating; I invite you as well to change it as you see fit, in whatever way feels affirming for you.

For this practice you will need a food item—it can be anything, whatever is accessible to you at the moment. I like to engage in this practice with something sweet, because it allows me to increase my feelings of joy and pleasure. You can sit or stand for this activity, whatever feels most comfortable for you. To the best of your ability, choose a location that is convenient for you and will allow you to be comfortable.

Begin by connecting to your breath and body, feel your feet on the ground or feel your backside connected to a surface, and notice your experience in this moment.

With your awareness in this moment, notice any thoughts, sensations, or emotions you are experiencing. *Pause.*

Tune into the awareness or sensation that you have in your body of feeling hungry, thirsty, or maybe even full. If you were going to eat or drink something right now, what is your body hungry for? What is it thirsty for? Just pay attention and notice with awareness the wisdom you gain from these sensations and impulses. *Pause.*

Now, bring your attention to the food item in your hand or on your utensil and imagine that you are seeing it for the first time. Observe with curiosity as you pay attention. What do you notice about the color, shape, texture, and size? Is there anything else that you sense or feel? *Pause.*

I invite you to reflect on the journey of how this item got to you, what it took to get into your hand: sunshine, water, time, processing, shipping, and more. You may choose to offer thanks and gratitude to everyone involved in the cultivation and preparation of this item of food. Reflect on the hands and the labor that harvested it: often migrant, undocumented folks and Black, Brown, and Indigenous people. All of these forces conspired together to nourish you at this moment.

Spend a moment offering thanks and perhaps a kind word, affirmation, or blessing to those hands. Reflect on the land that took time to process and cultivate this nourishment. Is·there something you can offer to the spirit of the land? You may choose to bring in your own gratitude or spiritual blessing. *Pause.*

Now place the item between your fingers and feel its texture, temperature, and ridges. You may notice smoothness or stickiness. Again, observe if you have any thoughts, sensations, or emotions at this time. What you are feeling and experiencing is valid. Continue to breathe and be fully present in this moment. *Pause.*

With full awareness of your hand's movements, place the object into your mouth without chewing or swallowing it. Just allow it to be there; try rolling it around to different parts of your mouth and tongue. Notice the taste and texture. You may pick up on the different seasonings used or the variety of flavors. Notice the physical sensations within your body, especially your mouth and your gut. Continue to breathe as you explore the sensation of having this item in your mouth. *Pause.*

Next take just one bite, staying mindful of its flavor and texture. Then very slowly begin to chew this piece of food and take note of what parts of your mouth are involved in this activity. Notice the sound and movement of the chewing as you continue to notice the sensations and flavor. *Pause.*

When you are ready, swallow the food item and notice the path that it follows from your mouth and throat into your stomach. Notice the sensation and taste that may linger in your mouth. Connect again to your body and your breath and notice your experience in this moment. *Pause.*

Next, I invite you to pick up another food item, and choose to eat it however you wish. Notice your choice and your experience. Notice how it compares with the previous practice.

Pause and reflect on what your experience was in engaging in this practice. Journaling may be helpful. Perhaps there are memories associated with the taste and flavor. Observe if those memories are favorable or unfavorable—the associations that we have with food are also important to our relationship with it. We want to lean into food that has been associated with favorable experiences for our bodies. This practice is also a way to reintroduce or try new food items in an environment and with a tool that can create more favorable transformation. Perhaps there is no memory, but the item you are consuming still feels familiar to you. This could be an ancestral memory that has been passed down through your taste buds. As time goes by, you may be able to find a link back to your ancestral roots through this ancestral data.

QUESTIONS FOR REFLECTION

1. Food tells a story; it has a history and an ancestral lineage. What is the story behind some of your favorite foods?
2. What foods did you grow up eating in your family? What foods did your parents and their parents grow up eating?
3. When you make a favorite dish, what sensations are activated?
4. What are some ways that you have internalized healthism through the values, thoughts, or beliefs you have around food?
5. What's one thing you can do to rewrite your definition of "healthy" that would be self-affirming?

· SEVEN ·

Black Bodies and Beauty Standards

"We must reject not only the stereotypes that others hold of us,
but also the stereotypes that we hold of ourselves."
                    —SHIRLEY CHISHOLM, congresswoman, activist,
                                    and 1972 presidential candidate

I RECOGNIZE MYSELF AS SOMEONE who is in the middle when it
comes to privileges connected to beauty and body ideals. My
skin tone is medium brown—I'm not light-skinned or darker-
skinned. I am currently on the higher end of straight-sized, meaning that I am not slim, but I also would not be considered fat, nor
have I experienced the degree of systemic oppression that many
people in larger bodies do. I have features that are perceived to be
"attractive" or "pretty," and hair that is a combination of kinky,
curly, and frizzy, but that I can manipulate to be more desirable to
society in a way that may not be afforded to others with tighter curl
patterns or kinkier textures.

Being in this specific range also means that I have been constantly told by society that if I work just a *little* bit more on the
areas "within my control," and tweak myself in *just* the right way, I
can move into a stratum with even more privilege. It's devastating
to think about. And it is also the way society continues to create
power structures within communities. These kinds of body ideals
have perpetuated my own imbalanced eating. My attempts to control the way that I ate and my body size were aimed at receiving

affirmation and compliments. When it came to dating, I knew I would receive better treatment if I could modify my body to what society deemed desirable and attractive at that time. My experience with beauty ideals is just one reality among many—there are millions of Black women and femmes who experience even more marginalization within these complex, narrow standards. It is imperative that we center their stories, experiences, healing, and guidance in eradicating these systems at the places where they do the most harm.

This conversation is as relevant today as it was back in the 1940s when Black psychologists Kenneth and Mamie Clark created and conducted a series of experiments known colloquially as "the doll tests" in order to study the psychological effects of integration on African American children. Using four dolls that were all identical except for their skin color, the doctors questioned children between ages three and seven about their racial perceptions. In most of the studies, the children were asked the same eight questions. The first four were designed to reveal the children's racial preferences, while questions five through seven were used to test the children's knowledge of racial differences. The last question addressed how the children self-identified. The subjects were also asked to identify both the race of each doll and which skin color they preferred.

The results were indisputable. Most of the children, regardless of their racial background, preferred the white doll, and assigned positive characteristics such as "nice" and "pretty" to it. Negative characteristics, however, were primarily attributed to the Black dolls. The Clarks concluded that "prejudice, discrimination, and segregation" had created a feeling of inferiority among African American children and damaged their self-esteem.

This experiment may have been performed more than seventy years ago, but at this moment, global anti-Blackness is as pervasive as ever. Colonization created a power structure where those with skin tones that have been labeled as white sit at the top of the ladder. They are granted access to a socially designed power and privilege that is based on the white patriarchal definition of success and belonging. That same ladder puts Black people and Black bodies at the bottom rung, with the intention of eradicating Blackness in every space where it exists. Even those of other racial/ethnic groups who may find themselves in the middle of the ladder—and who may even experience racial marginalization and exploitation—are encouraged to reject anything that explicitly represents Blackness.

In these cultures, whether we're talking about folks who are Latine, Native American or Alaska Native, Asian, Native Hawaiian or Other Pacific Islander, or Middle Eastern, people who are lighter-skinned and have straighter hair and features that we have accepted to be "European" in nature are more likely to get married, establish financial security, and access advantages in society than those within the same racial or ethnic group who are darker-skinned. Consider, as an example, the well-established practice across the diaspora—including Africa, India, and the Caribbean—that encourages darker-skinned girls, women, and femmes from a very young age to use beauty products that bleach their skin.

Our society still accepts this distorted status structure in which the closer you are to presenting yourself as white, the more social advantages you attract. This is not to say that non-Black people don't have a hard time, or that life is easier for them. But it *is* to say that a society that centers white-dominant beauty ideals as the litmus test for what is desirable and attractive invariably creates boundaries that exclude those with darker skin.

In my maternal grandmother's generation, being light-skinned was considered either a pathway to the financial security of marriage—as lighter-skinned women were thought to be better marriage material—or a pipeline to certain clerical or office jobs that paid more than other low-wage jobs. Some of my clients have also shared that their first experience of bullying or feeling as if they weren't enough came from those elders in their family, who often held on to and perpetuated old beliefs about skin shade, facial features, and hair texture. I believe that for these elders, shaming someone for their hair texture, facial features, body size and type, or skin color was really an extension of the trauma they themselves endured during the height of oppressive policies such as segregation, busing, and integration. In many Black families there are still remnants of anti-Black racism and conformity to Eurocentric ideals that impact family dynamics—especially when adults are still telling kids not to go outside in the summer to avoid getting dark, or shaming those with fuller lips, wider noses, or other features that they have been taught are "too Black."

These attitudes have also become ingrained in work environments. A 2019 *Harvard Business Review* article that looked at how beauty biases transfer into the workplace revealed that these biases are still alive and well. The article, which cited an experimental study conducted in 2012, reported that those who are "traditionally" considered less attractive—meaning they lack a thin nose, slender facial features, straight hair, light skin, or a small physique—are more likely to get fired, and also less likely to be hired in the first place.

Researchers sent out eleven thousand curricula vitae (CVs) for various job openings, including identical CVs accompanied by candidate photographs of different levels of attractiveness. What they found: "Attractive" women and men were much more likely to get a callback for an interview than those who were considered unattractive, or candidates with no accompanying photo at all. There is also a well-established association between attractiveness and long-term income, with "above-average" beauty translating into 10 percent to 15 percent higher salaries than "below-average" beauty.

I say all this to point out that the internalization of white-dominant cultural values around worthiness, desire, and attractiveness is not merely a psychological hurdle that can impact our overall sense of self; these widely held systemic values impact our very survival. Another way to look at this topic is through phenotypical ideals. "Phenotype" refers to an individual's observable traits, such as height, eye color, and blood type; "pheno" simply means "observe." People's phenotype is determined by both their genomic makeup (genotype) and environmental factors. Studies have shown that only a small percentage of our DNA accounts for phenotypic observable differences, such as our skin tone, eye color, hair texture, and facial features. It is our social and cultural beliefs and subsequent social constructions around race that have contributed to the common phenotypic definitions of race and ethnicity.

Although the media, entertainment, and advertising industries are making some attempts to put forth more diverse representations, the internalization of anti-Blackness in mainstream society and in Black communities still holds sway. It especially shows up in the historical wounds we bear, the colorism, texturism, and featurism we experience, and the ways we've embraced the ever-evolving "slim-thick" ideal. I have heard from my clients of color who experience more discrimination than others that when they try to discuss these topics with family members who enjoy more privilege because of their skin color, hair texture, facial features, or size, they are met with a lot of defensiveness. These family members believe that having their relative advantages pointed out suggests that they've never had to struggle.

But the truth is, talking about these issues neither downplays nor excludes the fact that *all* Black folks have struggled with them to some degree. There is a system at work that was designed from its very onset to annihilate those who are considered "less than." We perpetuate this annihilation within our own communities when we gaslight or dismiss the concerns of dark-skinned girls, women, and femmes, or reject those who do not align with the Eurocentric standards of beauty.

I have to confess that approaching this chapter required me to do a lot of my own inner work. I had to look at how I have internalized a lot of the societal attitudes we're examining, both outside of and within the Black community. And I had to reconcile what is being discussed in our communities with what I've been taught through my academic education. In short: I had to sit with my own stuff.

You, too, may have some inner work to do around your beliefs in and acceptance of certain beauty ideals. This is not uncommon. We are constantly being told—brainwashed, if we're being completely honest—that we *should* alter our appearance, sometimes by any means necessary, whether that be by purchasing bleaching creams, having cosmetic surgery, or changing the texture of our natural hair.

Let's resolve together that as we move through this chapter, we will protect ourselves by making space for the discomfort that is sure to arise in our hearts and minds as we do this work, but also by rejecting any tendency we might have to rush to judgment, either of ourselves or of others who have perpetuated these opinions and beliefs.

LET'S TALK ABOUT INTERSECTIONALITY

We've already established that our society has shaped its worldview of beauty through a decidedly Eurocentric lens based on desirability. I've already mentioned how author and fat deconstructionist Da'Shaun L. Harrison shed light on this kind of desirability politics in their book *Belly of the Beast: The Politics of Anti-Fatness as Anti-Blackness.* Yet, outside of size and shape, there are other levels of privilege that often intersect: the constructs of colorism, texturism, and featurism. It is important to note that these three constructs are not always separate, and often work in tandem.

COLORISM is prejudice or discrimination against individuals with darker skin tones; it was created by white supremacy culture on the plantation and spread globally through colonization and imperialism. It is both an interracial issue impacting people of different ethnic or racial groups, and an intra-racial issue impacting people of the same ethnic or racial group.

TEXTURISM is a preference for hair with a straighter texture, and the discrimination against people with kinkier, coarse hair within the same race or ethnic group. When it comes to "curls," looser ones are idealized and fetishized for their proximity to Eurocentric standards.

FEATURISM is societal acceptance of or preference for certain features over others. It is the preferential treatment of people with features that have historically been considered more attractive and that of course hew to Eurocentric standards of beauty (thin lips, small noses, light-colored eyes, long, straight hair). Nahar Khan, executive director and curator of theblackstory.com, points out the intersectional nature of this kind of discrimination. "Like colorism, featurism is often gendered. Women are disproportionately affected by this type of discrimination due to unfair beauty standards."

Featurism exists, in part, because so many young girls with more prominent noses and lips (before larger, plump lips were trendy in white culture) suffer from self-hatred and insecurity about their features. Many folks in the modeling and acting industries have also shared that they have been encouraged to get nose jobs and other facial enhancements to streamline their Black-associated features in order to seem more desirable and attractive. These are all tools of anti-Blackness and, whether we choose to recognize and acknowledge it or not, the perception that we have fallen short of these racist, narrowly defined beauty ideals has had a negative impact on the self-esteem of all Black women.

Many of my clients come in describing these intersectional issues. The women and femmes I have worked with who have non-Eurocentric beauty features such as darker skin, a broad nose, and/or kinkier hair feel like they have to at least make their bodies smaller and toned to be considered desirable or worthy. Managing food choices is the one measure they feel that they can control to fit into these Eurocentric standards, which in turn gives way to an eating imbalance.

COLORISM'S UNSAVORY STING

The construct of colorism was first built, and then later evolved, on the plantation. Many enslaved folks who were darker-skinned were often outside doing brutal manual work in the fields, while the lighter-skinned women and femmes were inside of the home doing house chores, nursing the slave owners' children, and/or cooking meals. This dichotomy came about because many white slave owners sexually abused enslaved women and, as a result, their offspring were multiracial children who still carried the status of a slave. These offspring were often given preferential treatment, and typically worked inside of the home, closer to the slave owners. This doesn't mean that these offspring never experienced any trauma; in fact, there is evidence to show that many of them endured sexual violence, torture, and harm at the hands of the slave masters' wives, who resented them.

The legacy of pitting Black people against one another—light versus dark—continues to this day. For decades, hip-hop and R&B artists have pushed forward messages about what is attractive and desirable in Black women, with songs dedicated to and referencing lighter-skinned Black women and femmes. We see it in songs like "Redbone" by Childish Gambino, and in the extreme skin-lightening and plastic-surgery featurism of artists like rapper Lil' Kim. Recent female artists such as American rapper Latto, who shortened her name from Mulatto after claiming she did not know the history of the name before taking it on, have been called to the carpet.

Artist DaniLeigh, who identifies as Dominican, has also come under fire for her song "Yellow Bone," which she described as a song for light-skinned women, who she felt also needed an anthem. "Why can't I make a song for my light skinned baddies??" she replied to one social media comment that criticized her choice. "Why y'all think I'm hating on other colors when there are millions of songs speaking on all types. Why y'all so sensitive & take it personal . . . gahhhh damn."

But in a *Vice* article entitled, "Is Hip-Hop Ready to Address Its Colorism Problem?" writer Kristin Corry offers this answer: "There's a lot to take personally. The legacy of being a 'yellow bone' isn't rooted in a preference, but instead is the result of decades of color bias placing lighter skin, which is closer to whiteness, as superior to darker complexions." When confronted on Twitter about her ethnicity, DaniLeigh wrote, "I'm Dominican, I'm Spanish. I'm black, I'm white. leave me alone." Corry's response: by "trying to separate her Dominican identity from Blackness, she is erasing Afro-Latinx who identify as both, and fails to understand the difference between race, ethnicity, and nationality. Being Dominican doesn't absolve you from perpetuating anti-Black rhetoric, regardless of your skin color."

Still, both DaniLeigh's song and her response to the backlash were backed up by many Black men on social media platforms such as Facebook. They commented that darker-skinned Black women were too sensitive or jealous of lighter-skinned women and were hurling critiques at DaniLeigh just to be divisive. These same commenters also proclaimed en masse via social media that they "preferred" light-skinned Black women to Brown and dark-skinned women; in fact, many of their comments labeled Brown and dark-skinned women as masculine and hard and undeserving of protection, and often compared them to objects and animals. Lighter-skinned women, in contrast, were described as more feminine and soft, and described as "beautiful," "pretty," and "desirable."

In addition, women and femmes who appear to be more ambiguous and "less Black" in proximity to whiteness, those who are multiracial, and those who are non-Black People of Color, are also often lifted up as the gold standard. Patriarchy, misogynoir, and white supremacy have heavily influenced desirability politics, and it doesn't just stop at cisgender heteronormative relationships and partnerships. I have heard from a lot of Black women and femmes in queer and gender-expansive partnerships that the overlapping constructs of colorism, texturism, and featurism have impacted their dating and relational experiences as well.

After I completed graduate school and landed my first job in the mental health field, I found myself working in an environment that was heavily dominated by white feminists who thought that because they identified as liberal or progressive, said all of the "right" things, and featured performative diversity, equity, and inclusion initiatives in their marketing kits, they should automatically be trusted—despite the ways they exhibited behaviors, beliefs, and actions that were heavily rooted in anti-Blackness, misogynoir, and internalized patriarchy. One of the white women was pregnant by a Black man, and I remember overhearing another white woman congratulate her by saying, "Your biracial baby is going to be so pretty and have good hair." The age-old belief that whiteness can dilute Blackness and serve to make an unborn child "pretty" or have a more desirable hair texture is not only absurd, but it is rooted in anti-Black beliefs that whiteness is better—and that having a biracial baby, and therefore being "less Black," is inherently more deserving of praise.

These constructs have shown up in my own family, specifically on my maternal side. My grandmother, who grew up during the 1950s, shared that it was not unusual for those with lighter skin to have more privilege and better access. The ability to "pass" as a white woman made all the difference when it came to financial mobility, job security, housing, child care, and generally being treated with respect, dignity, and protectiveness and made to feel that she belonged—all things that many Black women and femmes were not afforded during that time (and now).

My grandmother also talked to me about the "Paper Bag Test," a concept passed down through Black oral history in which an individual's skin tone is compared against a brown paper bag—

thereby determining the privileges they could be afforded. It was thought that those with a skin tone lighter than a paper bag could move about the world with more freedoms. They had access to more job opportunities and career advancement. They might be allowed admission or membership privileges to certain organizations and social institutions, such as sororities, fraternities, and churches. Many of those Black folks who met the requirements of the paper bag test were even granted the ability to transcend their race entirely by "passing"—as in passing for white in larger society if they chose to. These experiences were an intra-community way of continuing the prejudice and discrimination that was first implanted in us during slavery.

I grew up around lighter-skinned cousins and friends and remember that, by the time I got to middle school, I was acutely aware of the way colorism and texturism worked differently for them than it did for me. They were never told to stay out of the sun; they were not afraid of their hair texture transforming with the touch of water, so they never worried about getting their hair wet at the pool during summertime or being caught in the rain. And other children never gawked at or bullied them because of their facial features.

Historically within Black communities, there has also been a cultural stigma attached to being the only dark-skinned child in a family of light-skinned parents and siblings. In these scenarios, the father might have rejected or disowned the dark-skinned child, believing that the child's skin tone was indisputable evidence that his wife had stepped out on him with another man. Some family units, driven by this deep-seated fear rooted in anti-Blackness, treated children who were lighter-skinned with more favor, while the darker-skinned children were subjected to a disproportionate amount of punishment and violence.

Thus, survival during my grandmother's time was inseparably tied to the shade of one's skin. In fact, it wasn't uncommon for family members to discourage their relatives from dating or marrying people with dark skin; they didn't want their offspring, who could potentially also be born with darker skin, to have to endure those same social disadvantages.

Colorism still shows up today in dating "preferences," such as when people say things like, "I will only date a light-skinned, non-black, or white person," while simultaneously using this illogical reasoning to denounce dark and brown-skinned people. I have heard from many dark-skinned women that colorism is more often enforced within Black communities than when they have dated folks outside of their race. Many share that they are expected to engage in more emotional effort to prove to their partners the validity of their experiences with colorism, while also experiencing more emotional abuse from partners who are still working through their own internalized anti-Blackness and colorism issues.

Historically, the entertainment industry has repeatedly reinforced the imagery of this ideal, consistently pairing Black leading men with female love interests who are ultrafeminine, lighter-skinned, and thin or very slim with pronounced curves, and who have straighter or looser curl patterns. We saw this in sitcoms like *Girlfriends, Family Matters, The Fresh Prince of Bel-Air, Living Single,* and *Martin.* Often when there were characters in these shows who did not fit into those boxes, they were cast as the antagonists, or were displayed as sexually ravenous, loud, or aggressive—essentially playing into stereotypes of being the Sapphire or the Angry Black Woman. Just consider the Gina and Pam characters in *Martin.* Gina is the good-girl, lighter-skinned love interest of Martin, while her darker-skinned best friend Pam is treated terribly by him, often called a dog, no less, and depicted as masculine, ugly, and undesirable.

Prior to these shows, lighter-skinned people who could pass for white were some of the first Black people to get jobs in the entertainment industry. That pattern has continued, and many actors have come forward to share experiences of colorism in the industry, generally connected to being cast in stigmatizing roles, or hearing comments that it takes more effort to capture their skin shade because their team has to shoot their scenes in a different light.

The experience of colorism shows up globally in every racial and ethnic group, with a preference toward those who have skin tones that are lighter and closer to whiteness. We have all been injected with implicit biases that may spring up unintentionally, but that nevertheless affect our judgments, decisions, and behaviors.

THE TEXTURISM CONUNDRUM

Conversations around texturism are so complex and multilayered that it's hard to know where to start. So, I'll simply begin with a bit of background. The history of Black hair in the U.S. has always been politicized, even though statements from non-Black people, such as "It's just hair," are often used to downplay our experiences. Prior to colonization and enslavement, Black hair, particularly for African women, was a sign of tribal affiliation, class status, self-expression, spirituality, and mourning. Hair told a story and communicated who you were without words. During the period of enslavement and colonization, however, one of the first things the slaveholders did to enslaved Africans was to strip them of their identity and culture by cutting off their hair.

I wrote this chapter while I was in the middle of taking out my faux locs. I'd had them in for about two months and my roots were noticeably growing out; I knew that it was time for something new. There was also a desire to change some of the energy I experienced during the two months I had them as I recovered from an illness and dealt with some deep trauma work. I wanted to cleanse myself of that energy and clear out my aura; it was time to release the locs and let all of that go.

As I struggled to remove each individual loc without cutting the natural hair that was tucked into each extension, I thought about what it means to "have your hair done" in the more traditional sense. Growing up as a young Black girl, having your hair done usually meant that it would be straightened with a very hot comb that sizzled and smoked from all the products that had been added to it. Using a perm, or relaxer, to chemically process your hair until it was straight was another often-used method.

I received my first perm/relaxer when I was six years old and attending a private Christian academy where most of my peers had permed hair. It had somehow been drilled into us that straight hair was prettier, more presentable, and easier for our caregivers to manage, whereas kinkier, tightly curled and coarse hair was viewed as being unmanageable and was treated harshly, often being brushed or combed with brutality and contempt. Almost every Black woman I encountered back then complimented me on the length of my hair when it was relaxed or permed, telling my mother, "Please don't let her ever cut off all of this beautiful hair, she's such a pretty girl." I heard these statements so often that I began to equate my ability to be pretty with how long and straight my hair was. I'd already learned through my patriarchal and binary conditioning around gender that to be a girl meant that I was to have long hair and that only boys had short hair. I also observed that girls with longer hair were more favored by the boys, who were also indoctrinated into this patriarchal view around gender politics. Girls with shorter hair were assumed to be boyish and less feminine, or assumptions were made about their sexuality. Once, when I was in elementary school, my mother got her hair cut to shoulder length and someone questioned if my sister and I were her children because our hair was a lot longer than hers.

And so, from an early age, I received messages that my natural hair was ugly, an inconvenience—"too much to handle"—and that altering my texture through chemical perms was a necessary correction. I remember many trips to the salon, where my stylist would assure us I would have straight flowy hair as she'd apply the perm/relaxer. When the chemicals would begin to burn my scalp, which literally felt like fire ants had built a hill on my head, I would speak up and ask my stylist if she could just rinse it out. She'd tell me to stop being so sensitive and dramatic and to wait it out just a bit longer so that the effects could have more time to take hold. I was expected to sit still and bear the pain, or else I'd be labeled "tender-headed." Either that, or she'd blame the pain on the fact that I must have been scratching my scalp a few days before the treatment, and if I'd only stop doing that it wouldn't burn as much.

Historically our community has associated straight hair with being "put together and proper," particularly for special events like weddings, church, picture days, and holidays. Recent studies, however, have shown a correlation between the chemicals used in straightening products, like perms and relaxers, and an increased risk of breast, ovarian, and uterine cancer; for Black women, that risk is more than doubled. Still, I remember sitting in salons well into my early twenties, holding back tears from my scalp burning, while convincing myself that it would all be worth it in the end, that my straightened hair would be "pretty" and easier to deal with once it wasn't so "nappy" at the roots. To be feminine or to be a girl meant that my hair had to be long, straight, and flowing; essentially, I had to have what folks often describe as "good hair." When I was in middle school, the white girls would often describe their hair as clean and soft but say that Black girls' hair was "coarse" and "dirty" like a Brillo pad. Imagine comparing someone's hair to a household cleaning item used to remove tough stains.

When I was younger, I wanted my hair to be associated with positive characteristics, and I knew that in order to achieve that goal and also receive the social acceptance of the peers in my advanced curriculum classes, I had to make sure that my hair was clean, straight, and soft. By the time high school came around, I'd stopped moisturizing my hair altogether so that it wouldn't be "too greasy" or "too stiff." I continued to keep up with my perms every six weeks, while also straightening my hair in between with heating tools like flat irons.

It's no wonder, then, that my hair began to suffer from all that trauma I was inflicting on it. The dandruff that I also started developing worsened and, over time, my hair started breaking off from the heat damage. Treating our hair in ways that are not in alignment with what our particular hair type needs can cause long-term damage to our hair follicles, and for some, their hair may never recover due to the trauma. The Black hairstylists and dermatologists I've spoken with have shared that the prevalence of scalp issues in Black women is greater than we think, and is often connected to a lack of nourishment and education around how to truly nurture our hair, stemming back to childhood.

These early experiences taught me that I had to disconnect from my body's natural state in order to achieve a certain beauty ideal. Whenever I had my hair braided so tightly that I felt nauseous but endured it because I needed to preserve the style for the next day, I was denying my hair's natural state. Even when the pain was so intense that not even painkillers could help me sleep at night, I held on, because I was told I needed to tough it out so the styling would last. I've put my hair through the damaging straightening process even when I knew my natural hair needed a rest, just to conform to society's beauty standards. And don't get me started on the number of times I've had a hairstylist tell me that my hair texture was "just too much" to work with, as if I were asking them to do me a favor by "wrangling with" my natural hair.

As a culture, we have to take a deeper dive into how we think about and treat Black hair. When I was working in white-dominated spaces and frequently changed my hairstyle or hair color, both my white and non-Black coworkers would act as if they didn't know who I was because I'd changed my hairstyle. At one of my jobs, I started with braids, but one day took them out to give my hair a break. I was wearing my natural hair, and when I came into work, a coworker loudly exclaimed, "I barely recognized you! I thought we were going to have to call security to get this random person out of the workplace." Nothing had changed in my overall appearance. However, for this white woman—who likely did not have many

Black people in her life—my hair change could have caused her to call security on me.

This type of microaggression speaks to the lack of diversity and representation of Black culture in certain spaces. Why can most white and non-Black cultures switch up their look over and over again without commentary, yet when Black folks do it, it's jolting and unfamiliar—even to people you've worked with for years?

Another workplace microaggression, one that is a leftover from enslavement, is the way white and non-Black women feel comfortable and entitled enough to touch our hair, often without our consent. This pattern is rooted in the long-held idea that everything about the Black body, and the spaces Black bodies occupy, is open to the interjection of whiteness. This energy of ownership over Black people has been passed down to people in white bodies for generations, and, if not challenged, will be explained away by white women as simply innocent good intentions. Indeed, if we dare to set boundaries around our physical space, these women will take offense and say they're confused when they are told they cannot touch our hair.

"What if a man just came up to you and grabbed your breast?" I've asked white women when trying to make my point about boundaries. "And then when you spoke up against his actions, he responded in shock and disbelief toward you." Though many admitted that they would feel angry and violated—some even proclaiming that they would file a police report—when white women come into our space with their fetishes, fascination, and curiosity and put their hands in our hair, they expect us to just sit back and accept it.

I've had enough experience working with, holding space for, and studying "well-intentioned" white women to know that those of us impacted by their ignorance often know them better than they would care to admit. I write about this because this generation of Karens know how to play the victim while also using the power of whiteness, white innocence, and fragility to their advantage. These are the things I began to think about when I first went natural and found that whenever I would style my hair in a large fluffed-out Afro, I'd attract undue attention from white women, who would invade my space and treat me like a pet instead of a human being.

Under their white gaze, I'd get questions like, "How did you get your hair like that?"—as if a white woman had the ability to change her hair into an Afro. Or this favorite of theirs: "Is that your real hair?" Once, when I wore my hair up in a pineapple style, a white coworker passed me in the hallway, loudly and excitedly put her hands in my hair, and said, "Wow, your hair is so . . . festive."

As a result of all this, before leaving the house I began to alter my appearance in order to avoid the intrusiveness of white women, especially when I was working in white-dominated spaces where my financial security depended on my ability to remain cool and collected. Navigating these spaces often put me in a nervous state of "freeze and appease" just to get by.

Many of my clients have shared similar stories with me, saying that their families, particularly their grandmothers, mothers, and aunties, were the first ones in their lives to perpetuate a lack of self-acceptance about their hair. Clients have described sitting in a chair or between their mothers' legs on the floor and having a comb or brush ripped through their hair while negative comments were made about their hair being too difficult to manage. They shared that their complaints and cries were often met with violence as their mothers, caregivers, or stylists smacked them with whatever styling tool they were using at the time, telling them that they needed to stop being so "tender-headed." Those with tighter, kinkier hair textures would be even worse off, to the point that their hair became extremely damaged, and in some cases led to irreversible hair loss.

It is no wonder, then, that many of us grew up not knowing how to properly nurture and nourish our hair without its being seen as a burden or inconvenience. I say this now as someone who regularly sees a dermatologist to help rectify the damage my scalp suffered after years of perms; I've had to work hard to reverse my scalp's flare-ups and inflammation as it continues to balance itself out.

Which brings me back to my loc situation, standing in front of my bathroom mirror trying my best to take out my faux locs, knowing it will take me an hour and thirty minutes to remove them, then another two or three hours to wash, condition, and fully detangle my entire head of hair and style it into two-strand twists. As I did my best to be gentle with my hair, I was already planning my next protective style and estimating how long I would have to give my natural hair a break before I could go back to braids, wigs, or some other style. Part of my dilemma was that I wanted to avoid dealing with the texture perceptions I myself have attached to my natural hair. The rest period between styles always feels like an inconvenience because, as one popular music artist has said, it's important to keep your nails done, hair done, and everything done to give off the impression of being desirable and put together at all times. At least that's what I found myself thinking in this particular moment.

I thought about how I would look after the locs were removed—with only my natural hair pattern, which is tightly curled when it is not manipulated into a twist-out. I receive so many compliments on my hair when it is straightened or in a protective style, but that treatment is different when I wear my hair naturally, especially when it comes to dating. The anti-Black ideals that have been ingrained in us influence how we treat one another and who is considered desirable or attractive—and none of us in the Black community are exempt. I thought about my own participation in this system through my willingness to damage my hair to be more acceptable, while also reminding myself that it's not just about desirability but also about accessibility and survival in this anti-Black world. Much as with fatphobia, in a lot of sectors of society the ability of our hair to fit into a particular box often determines how we are treated or labeled at any given moment.

One of my favorite influencers described it best in this Instagram post:

> "We need to be honest with how the world treats Black people with different styles of hair. When I had straight hair, I was perceived with the least amount of pushback and most praise. Here is the ranking: at the top is straight long hair, then I was treated better/moderate with protective styles (i.e.: box braids, twists), then at the lowest is when you wear your natural hair and it's kinky and short. And beneath that is when I had Freeform locs and they were shorter, and people didn't know where to place it. There's a hierarchy with how we get treated with our hairstyles as Black people."—Mayowa aka @mayowasworld on Instagram.

This assault on Black hair began when enslavers would cut off the hair of Africans to strip them of their cultural identity and status prior to auctioning them off. The practice of oppressing Black hair continued into 1786, when Governor Esteban Rodriguez Miro of Louisiana created the Tignon law, which mandated that Black women must cover their hair with a knotted headdress and refrain from adorning it with jewels when out in public. The hope was to calm white men's desires while also acting as a class signifier.

A hairstyle change can make all the difference in receiving a job opportunity or enjoying favorable treatment by people in positions of power. But it wasn't until 2020 that we saw positive steps like the CROWN Act, which stands for "Creating a Respectful and Open World for Natural Hair." The act, which as of June 2023 had been signed into law in twenty-three states, prohibits race-based hair discrimination, which is the denial of employment and educational opportunities because of hair texture or protective hairstyles, including braids, locs, twists, or Bantu knots. That means there are another twenty-seven states where it is perfectly okay to discriminate against natural hair. In those states, it is legal for employers to deny you a job, to write you up, or to fire you because they don't like the natural hair growing out of your head and think it is "unprofessional"—which translates to "does not conform to standards created by white culture."

This bias also applies to the world of education: In 2018, a young Black girl was kicked out of school for wearing her natural hair, which was described as "disruptive." This is not an isolated incident; over the last five years, all over the world, stories have emerged in the media about young girls being bullied, harassed, and expelled from school because of racism around their hair.

I can't say for certain, but it's quite possible that all of this public animosity toward natural hair could be a knee-jerk reaction to that watershed moment in the early 2000s when Black people once again began to embrace natural hair as a personal and political statement, much as we did in the early '70s. Black people of every gender variation were transitioning out of their permed/relaxed hairstyles and embracing natural styles, whether they were getting Sisterlocks, going for a shaved or bald look, or picking their natural hair into a massive Afro. There were also a lot of "big-chop videos" that started popping up online, as some people, including myself, decided to cut off all of our hair and start from scratch. Around the same time, sites like YouTube began to soar in popularity, helping those with natural hair to find and build community, as well as learn how to take care of their natural hair.

Among this new wave's many pluses was that it gave so many people permission to unpack the narratives we'd learned in the past about our hair being too difficult to manage. We'd suddenly found our tribe, and connected with groups of people who could relate to our stories of growing up going to the hair salon to get a perm, or who also went through some intensely frustrating detangling sessions.

But there have been some downsides, too—particularly that a lot of the same anti-Black messages we'd seen in the mainstream media made their way into the natural hair movement. For example, when magazines would feature stories on how to embrace one's natural hair, they'd often center on natural hair that was looser in texture or wavy—the kind of textures typically worn by light-skinned, often biracial women and femmes with slimmer features. The faces of the natural hair movement began to look more like people such as Tracee Ellis Ross, Zendaya, or Lisa Bonet. We see this in media representations of natural hair looks, for example TV's obsession with showcasing multiracial kids. These things, of course, also intersect with colorism and featurism, and the message is clear: Don't look too Black.

I am still working through my internalized beliefs around conforming my hair to so-called socially acceptable standards, even if that means damaging it. And while I am self-employed and do not have to concern myself with the threat of a biased employer, the fear of not "being desirable" still shows up in my body as a trauma response. It shows up in the way that I often style my natural hair, because I recognized early on in my journey that even in the natural hair community, hair that is more defined—meaning curls that are less kinky and frizzy, or that have been manipulated to create a more symmetrical look—is considered more presentable or attractive.

I remember going through some intensive detangling sessions, then using heavy curl creams and gels to twist my hair into a more defined look before job interviews so that my hair would appear less threatening or not too much for white people to take in. I did this throughout my undergraduate and graduate school years, in order to present the image of being a "put-together, neat, orderly Black candidate," and to be perceived as a "safe" Black person. My internalized belief even extends to the amount of money I've been willing to spend pursuing such Black beauty and body ideals—the $400 faux locs and the expensive Black hair care products that cost more than products marketed to people with straight or looser hair textures.

Somewhere along the way, we have literally gotten it twisted. The idea that people with tighter or kinkier hair textures and patterns should damage their hair texture in order to loosen it up and be seen as having "good" or "pretty" hair is really not that different from the anti-Black Eurocentric ideals that have been forced upon us for centuries. Hair is a deeply layered conversation in Black communities. Even if we think we are accepting and proud of our hair, it is important that we continue to examine the ways in which we have internalized and been conditioned to feel about it.

THE FEATURISM PHENOMENON

I have had clients share that they developed eating imbalances as a way of escaping the trauma and oppression they've experienced because either their family or everything in the culture was telling them they were unworthy and did not deserve to be seen or take up space. They'd traded in nourishing and nurturing themselves in order to be able to seamlessly fit into society's rigid and limited beauty ideals. Much like the whitewashing of skin tone and hair texture ideals, when it comes to Black beauty standards, featurism is also rooted in anti-Blackness.

The complicated dynamics surrounding featurism are fascinating. Lifting up certain features as desirable and worthy while diminishing other features that we view as "too Black" has created deep wounds of mistrust in our communities, ones we have yet to reckon with. Much of this pain has been embedded in us for centuries through white culture, and still shows up in the way the outside world sees us, and in how we see one another. Those marginalized among us may see altering their bodies as the only thing over which they do have control.

While our mainstream culture has normalized fillers and Botox for young white women for years, many Black women, femmes, and other women of color have recently responded to the trend with both buy-in and bitterness. They've shared on social media how upsetting it is that it's now okay to have big, full lips, when in their own experience growing up, they were teased, bullied, harassed, and terrorized for having "Black facial features." However, getting fillers and Botox is common and trendy now, and is even considered a part of routine self-care and maintenance. This is impacting folks across the racial spectrum. With the rise of social media, the pressures to achieve this look—slim, youthful features and plump, full lips—has moved outside of celebrity and influencer culture and been internalized by many, including teens and young girls, who often do not have awareness of the long-term implications of these face-altering services.

I once had a client who grew up in an Afro-Caribbean family that put her on a diet around the age of eight, encouraged skin bleaching, and taught her to hate both her hair texture and the shape of her nose. She would often show up to our sessions dressed in oversized hoodies to hide the fact that she was cutting her wrists. She would wear only black or gray clothing, had been in and out of hospitals for attempting suicide, and had just been released from her second round of treatment for a persistent and acute eating imbalance. She had a pattern of self-neglect and denied that she had needs, yet would be resentful when others did not show up for her in the same way she showed up for them.

By the time she reached middle school, she was regularly engaging in purging, followed by what she described as eating large amounts of food. Over the years, as her weight fluctuated up and down, she said she'd receive the most praise from her family when she was smaller and deeply into purging. Even when she did finally get into treatment for imbalanced eating, she was the only Black femme in her program and often felt isolated. At the root of her eating imbalances was the racialized trauma she'd experienced from an early age. And those factors that contributed to her eating imbalance had not been addressed by any of her treatment providers before she started working with me.

I also worked with a teenage client who shared that she could not wait to turn eighteen so that she could get lip fillers. She shared that as a Black person who identified as such, she felt that her lips were not desirable enough to fit the standard of fullness seen in the social media filters on Instagram. She had already been dieting to "lose the roundness from her face" and to create more defined, slim features. She believed that once she got the fillers, and if she could continue to lose weight, she would have more access to dating partners.

When we talked about representation, she shared that social media is filled with Black women and femmes who might start off looking like her, but who as they advance in their industry transform—getting nose jobs, slimming their bodies, and engaging in all kinds of other cosmetic procedures. The specific type of Black representation this young woman looked up to showed her that bodies and faces that were altered were the only looks considered beautiful, desirable, and successful. Acceptance was what she wanted most. She was sure that she had never had a romantic relationship because she didn't embody the "socially acceptable type of Black girl."

WHERE DO SLIM-THICK BODIES FIT INTO ALL OF THIS?

We've already discussed how Black women and femmes have had to deal with the pressures of healthism and fatphobia founded in anti-Black racism. But we also need to talk about the pressures we're under to conform to having a body type that has "curves in all the right places": a tiny waist and stomach, and ample curves everywhere else. This body shape composition is common in only about 3 percent of the general population, and is heavily influenced by genetics, hormones, and age. But this "slim-thick" body ideal has been made *the* gold standard to meet throughout Black culture. We often see fitness influencers selling the message that if people would only work out enough and eat a certain way, they would achieve this slim-thick ideal. As consumers of the fitness industry, we view these influencers' bodies and think that if we just follow their regimen, we will look like them.

But the truth is, we really don't know much of anything about these people—not their genetics, hormones, stress responses, or history of body alterations through surgery, and whether or not they have eating imbalances or are managing disordered eating patterns. As many Black folks have shared on social media, our bodies are not business cards: Even if we all ate the same way and worked out the same way, our bodies would still each be different. Most fitness trainers will tell you that you cannot target a specific "problem area" of the body and change that alone, and that the fitness journey requires whole-body exercise. The slim-thick ideal also goes against most folks' genetics and, even with the most rigid diet and exercise practice, is unobtainable for most. The pressure to conform and compare our bodies to those of fitness influencers can lead to extreme food deprivation and control issues, which can also contribute to more eating imbalances and other adverse health effects.

If Black women and femmes can't achieve the slim-thick ideal through exercise and diet, more and more of us in Black communities are turning to body altering surgeries like Brazilian Butt Lifts, breast augmentations, liposuction, or body contouring. Many of us even opt for rib repositioning, breaking our ribs to reshape the waistline. And the deeper implications of this trend aren't impacting just adult Black women and femmes, but also our young girls and teens. Studies show that children's opinions of their bodies form at a very young age and suggest that children as young as three years old can have body image issues. But there are many other things that influence how children see themselves as well, and parents play a critical role in helping them to develop a positive body image and high self-esteem.

While exploring Black body aesthetics and ideals, I have noticed that the history of the "thick in all of the right places" trope has shifted over time. Hip-hop and rap music in the late '90s and early 2000s—heavily influenced by the male gaze and the oversexualization of Black women's bodies—regularly referenced the Coke bottle shape, making women feel they needed to have a "slim waist, pretty face, and thick behind."

As the wider celebrity culture began to co-opt Black body ideals for itself, they came to be adopted by society at large. These are the same ideals that hypersexualized, fetishized, and degraded Black women's bodies. Kim Kardashian, of course, immediately comes to mind. She is often credited for creating and popularizing the "slim-thick" ideal that started in Black communities. When she got butt implants and modified her body to mimic that desired pear shape, she was not only celebrated and seen as beautiful and attractive, but she also caught the attention of a Black man, Kanye West, which added another layer connecting the internalization of anti-Black racism to the appreciation and celebration of the Black aesthetic among whites.

This has been seen throughout the media and entertainment industry and continues through social media. Some may argue that Kim Kardashian's decision to alter her body has nothing to do with race; however, more recently, in 2022, there were many media outlets, articles, and social media content with headlines such as "Kim Kardashian Is Becoming a White Woman Again." But when did Kim Kardashian represent anything *other* than a white woman, and what made that possible?

While Kim Kardashian and other non-Black folks receive the benefits of trying on "the Black aesthetic," other Black women have had the opposite experience, with critiques that often reinforce the view that Black women are not protected and are often invalidated or gaslighted in society when we show vulnerability. Look at the example of singer and actor Chloe Bailey, who in 2020 began to post herself on social media, confidently taking up space in her body through her sensuality and freedom of expression in the way she dressed. She was immediately slammed for coming across as what people perceived as being "too promiscuous." Many commenters also leveled critiques against her body, saying she was *too* thick to be doing what she was doing. Chloe expressed on social media how hurtful the commentary was and how emotionally vulnerable she felt—and was labeled as being dramatic and overly sensitive.

Meanwhile, Kim Kardashian became an enormously famous celebrity—revered in some circles as a cultural icon (directly *because* she appropriated Black culture)—after the leaked release of a 2002 sex tape made with her then-boyfriend Ray J. This is not to shame sex work or women and femmes being in our sexuality and sensuality in whatever way that is consensual and affirming to us. But it *is* to say that Kim Kardashian was considered socially redeemable. She became a household name, got a TV show, and earned countless endorsements. Whereas Black women like Chloe, Lizzo, and Megan Thee Stallion have been boxed into being "too sexual," "too dramatic," and largely unworthy of compassion and grace. Although there were many fans who loudly supported these women and called out the hypocrisy of the criticism, it continued. This is one of the ways anti-Blackness shows up in the politics of desirability—or the ways in which our narratives about beauty, intelligence, and kindness have mostly been centralized on white people.

There are other examples I can cite of white people appropriating previously vilified Black-originated aesthetics and making it acceptable in wider society (see: box braids, absurdly credited to the Kardashians; nail designs, once labeled as "ghetto" or "unprofessional" for Black women to wear but that later became mainstream through TikTok culture; or the usage of African American Vernacular English (AAVE) that has spread throughout Gen Z, which often abandons the history, struggle, and resilience behind the "trends"). I have even been challenged by non-Black People of Color trying to make the comparison that demanding proper respect and reverence for Black culture is a double standard because Black women wear blond weaves.

My response to them and anyone else out there who has similar sentiments is that Black people have one of the most phenotypically diverse gene pools in the world. There are many places throughout the globe where features that are considered "white" by modern-day standards have always existed in Black culture. There are indigenous aboriginal Black people in Australia who have blond hair and blue eyes, as well as tribes in Africa who naturally have a similar gene variation. The same is true for red hair (a fact that made the world erupt in 2022 with the casting of Halle Bailey as the fictional mermaid in the movie *The Little Mermaid*.) Red hair does not belong to white people; it is a recessive gene that is also very common in Black communities. Global anti-Blackness has associated white skin, blue eyes, and blond hair as "a white thing," when in fact all those recessive features are a response to a genetic mutation that became adaptive over time. The invention of race as a social construction has had historical and systemic implications that still impact us today.

The rise of social media has slightly altered the slim-thick ideal, and not necessarily in a good way. While a new movement that is seemingly more culturally inclusive of size has emerged—brought on as more positive associations with this body type have spread throughout the white, thin, able-bodied "body-positive" movement— the ideal is still problematic. The "body-positive" movement has moved the needle in terms of expanding our view of what is desirable by showing thicker bodies, but this aesthetic is still not inclusive of larger bodies, the kind that have been the most marginalized. There is still more work that needs to be done. The expectation to be toned, tightened, and sculpted, while also maintaining the thick-in-all-the-right-places with a smaller-waist body type, is still a cultural value that rewards a shape that is unattainable to most without cosmetic intervention.

As a teen I didn't have an awareness of all the ways bodies—Black bodies especially—have been politicized. I simply thought there was something wrong with *my* body because it did not fit into popular ideals. It wasn't until I got into this work and began helping folks heal their eating imbalances that I realized our bodies are constantly working in ways that support us, even when they model an aesthetic that is not deemed desirable by modern beauty and body standards.

WHEN APPEARANCES CAN BE DECEIVING

I would be remiss if I did not mention that the pressures to conform to beauty ideals can also contribute to body dysmorphia. Body dysmorphic disorder is a mental health condition in which you can't stop thinking about one or more perceived defects or flaws in your appearance—though they can't be seen by others. Nonetheless, you may feel so embarrassed, ashamed, and anxious that you may avoid many social situations. I feel certain that I experienced body dysmorphia myself as a teenager. No matter how thin I was, I continued to feel that I was not thin enough. These feelings were only compounded by the other shame I felt around not having curves "in all the right places," which led me to constantly isolate body parts that I would try to fit into those standards.

When you have body dysmorphic disorder, you intensely focus on your appearance and body image, repeatedly checking the mirror, grooming, or seeking reassurance, sometimes for many hours each day. Your self-perceived flaws and your repetitive behaviors cause you significant distress and impact your ability to function in your daily life. You may seek out numerous cosmetic procedures to try to "fix" your perceived flaw. Afterward, you may feel temporary satisfaction or a reduction in your distress, but often the anxiety returns, and you may resume searching for other ways to address this supposed flaw.

Body dysmorphia is rooted in Eurocentric beauty standards, fat-phobia, and our body's ability to maintain its youth. Our culture is obsessed with anti-aging, which under patriarchy has been associated with desirability and worthiness. In the media, we don't even see Black women and femmes represented as starting new careers, finding their purpose, or having suitors after a certain age. Operating under this lens of ageism, it is assumed that life for women and femmes stops as we get older. Our roles are then relegated to being a mother, wife, partner, or someone in a position of servitude. It is rare that we are viewed as having our own lives, separate from what we can do for other people, and we are often judged and criticized when we attempt to define ourselves outside of those expectations.

On top of this, we live in a culture obsessed with the "before" and "after." There is constant comparison of our current bodies to the way they were at some *other* stage of life—typically when we were younger, or before the weight gain, or before a pregnancy—and as a result, we feel a nonstop pressure to somehow get back to those departed versions of ourselves. Even people recovering from illness or disease feel the push to be in a desirable body size once again, as an indication of their "overcoming" story.

Body dysmorphia, then, often gets activated when those toxic messages we're constantly inundated with convince the brain that the only way to survive is to fixate on the body and continue to alter it. No amount of cosmetic surgery or procedures are ever enough. I often wonder about the connection between body dysmorphic-related plastic surgery and the ancestral trauma of body mutilation that occurred to Black women, femmes, and girls throughout the transatlantic experience, the trauma in response to body mutilation that was not allowed to be expressed through the body at that time. Perhaps the body dysmorphia many of us have is that unresolved trauma in Black communities replaying itself through the repeated pattern of cutting off, altering, and injecting into oneself.

Eating imbalances are very common in people who live with body dysmorphic disorder, and serve as an attempt to alter the body into a shape, size, and weight that is deemed socially acceptable. Our biology shows that in response to a period of restriction or food deprivation, our evolutionary response will kick in and we will often overcompensate to give our bodies what they need. Some of us may see this as binge eating, food addiction, or overeating, when it is really our bodies getting what they need. When those signals are not communicating with one another, it can lead to *more* imbalance in eating, as people may begin to feel "out of control" with food and notice that "keeping off the weight" becomes harder and harder to manage.

Most treatment teams for the body altering or weight loss surgeries people feel they need as a result are not trained in eating imbalances, and if they aren't, they don't often approach treatment, prognosis, and recovery from an anti-diet, inclusive, or liberation framework. If they did, they would be more intentional about recommending these surgeries.

Culturally we pursue these body ideals under the guise of wanting to get "in shape," but this also means that we are internalizing and uplifting the message that we need to literally get into a shape that does not embody the fullness of who we are. While I always think it is important to examine our intentions and make sure that we are not making decisions based on our oppression, all of these conversations are very layered.

I believe in body autonomy, and if someone decides, for example, to have a surgery that they feel will enhance their life and allow them to exist without daily body terrorism, I am in support of living an enhanced life with less harm. I also think that it is important that people in straight-sized or thin bodies do not get to dictate or police people with lived experience of fat oppression, nor should they tell them what to do with their bodies. Similarly, I have advocated for gender-affirming care and surgeries for many clients. People deserve to feel congruent with and free within their

bodies, and as a cisgendered-bodied person I will use my privilege
to support that process.

THE BEAUTY INSIDE ALL OF US

My own healing from the constructs of colorism, texturism, and
featurism has allowed me to examine the places within my body
where I am holding these interlocking constructs, the wounds that
originated in cultural oppression and were injected into our family
histories, and that were then reinforced by the way that we talk
about our bodies and pass those beliefs down from mother to
daughter. I have also worked to not only *uproot* my inherited narratives about body and beauty ideals, but to *release* the energy of
trauma that I inherited, which is connected to the fear and survival
I inhabited when I held on to those ideals.

Growing up, I was not exposed to a lot of diverse representations of Black women and femmes, and I had internalized a lot
of anti-Blackness connected to my identity. As an adult, I am perpetually doing the work to unpack these issues within myself. I
didn't grow up knowing about Black feminists like Audre Lorde,
bell hooks, Toni Morrison, Octavia Butler, Zora Neale Hurston,
or others—but now I have reclaimed their stories, which have
helped me understand and see myself. I have pictures of ancestor
Harriet Tubman on my ancestral altar, and an image of the Black
Madonna—ancient depictions of the Virgin Mary with dark skin—
because I want to surround myself with the existence of Black
beauty and boldness in all the wonderful, myriad ways it has manifested throughout time.

Recently, I ordered a book written by Catherine E. McKinley
called *The African Lookbook: A Visual History of 100 Years of
African Women*, which is full of African women existing in their
bodies. It was amazing to see women in a variety of body shapes,
sizes, skin tones, hair textures, and features—wearing a variety of
adornments—taking up space. Some of the photos were of women

and femmes unbashful about their bare chests or bottoms being exposed. They were not sexualized or objectified, because being in their bodies was common and had spiritual connections. The book also shows representations of Black women and femmes sitting down and gazing directly into the camera within postures of rest, joy, and confidence. Some postures even represent the physical experience of taking up space as they sit with their legs open and their arms resting on the back of a chair in a way that Western society would deem unladylike.

These images continue to remind me that Black beauty and the Black body cannot and should not be contained inside a box—and that our ancestors have *always* been expansive and embodied. We now have the opportunity to reclaim what was lost and to remember what has been misremembered about our bodies.

Healing ourselves from colorism, featurism, and texturism requires us to both examine the places within our own bodies and families where we have been holding on to these damaging constructs and to begin the hard but necessary work of unpacking them. By making an honest assessment of the way these constructs show up for us, and then working to amplify the narratives of those who experience the most social oppression around these beauty ideals, we can finally address the wound. This is how we stop directing our anger and rage—whether conscious or subconsciously—toward each other, and instead join together to take down the power structures that have instigated our separation from one another and from our own bodies. In this way, we liberate both ourselves and our communities.

GUIDED PRACTICE #7

In this practice, let us now affirm that your features, your shade and skin tone, your hair texture, and your body shape and size are a beautiful reflection of all of the ancestors who came before you.

While you may never know who all of them were, you can choose to acknowledge them by acknowledging yourself, and by showing appreciation for all the beauty, love, possibilities, and pain it took to create you. One place to begin is at the top, by honoring our crown. The crown—our hair—is a statement associated with regality and the essence of being a queen. It includes those of us who have crowns that are buzzed, bald, or cut short; that appear as fades; that are wavy, tightly coiled, or curled. It is used to revere and reclaim an area of our bodies that has long been politicized and policed.

Nowadays a lot of Black people have reclaimed the practice of cutting off our hair and recasting it as a form of rebirth and empowerment. Cutting our hair is a part of many cultural initiations, representing liberation and nonconformity to the limited standards offered to Black women. It has also served as a way for us to release certain energies and emotions that were tied to our hair but no longer serve us. Many have described shaving their head as a way of living with more ease and developing an intimate acquaintance with their body, by familiarizing themselves with the hair that naturally grows out of their scalp. As Black women and femmes, we change our hair for a variety of reasons, from liberation to dealing with illness, and it really isn't anyone else's business or prerogative to comment on how or why we do it.

Don't worry: In this practice I won't be asking you to do the big chop (unless you're moved to do so!). But I do want us to create a space to celebrate our hair—our crown—for the magic and energy it holds. One of the things that I have done recently is to affirm my crown during "wash day," an often all-day process of washing and styling one's hair. I have begun to treat this day as a spiritual event that affirms the relationship I have with my hair and helps heal the trauma and pain that I've experienced with it.

In this exercise, I invite you to do the same. As you cleanse your hair, imagine that you are energetically clearing out the residue our hair holds on to. You might want to play some calming music as you tend to your hair. Remember, we are electromagnetic beings. We operate on a vibration, a wavelength, and our bodies respond to sound. In indigenous African spirituality, sound is used to open a particular space and allows certain energies to partake in the rituals being performed, because sound is a form of existence. Sound, quite literally, shifts our state of being.

As you move from washing to styling, think about your crown chakra, which is located at the top of the head. "Chakra" means "wheel" and refers to energy points in your body. These points are thought of as spinning disks that should stay "open" and aligned, as they correspond to bundles of nerves, major organs, and areas of our energetic body that affect our emotional and physical well-being. The crown chakra, which is represented by the color violet and linked to every other chakra (or every organ in our system), represents awareness and intelligence. It is considered the chakra of enlightenment and represents our connection to our life's purpose and spirituality.

While nurturing your scalp, give thanks to the indigenous South Asian stewards and keepers of the wisdom and origin of the chakra system. Speak positive affirmations to yourself or think kind thoughts about the process of taking care of your head and hair. While this may seem like a small action, healing and uplifting our crown can be restorative in our relationship with our hair, especially after years of not having had such a loving and tender relationship with it.

QUESTIONS FOR REFLECTION

1. Has society made you feel as if your body shape or size needed to be altered? If so, which system has impacted you the most (i.e., the slim-thick ideal, colorism, texturism, featurism)?
2. How have these systems shown up in your family relationships, your workplace, and/or your personal life?

3. When you consider these systems, which ones do you feel are most harmful, and why?

4. How have these systems shown up in the relationships that you form with others?

5. If you could teach your younger self anything about these systems, what lessons would you share?

· EIGHT ·

Toxic Fitness and Exercise Culture

"The word 'fitness' is often used to designate which bodies are fit (acceptable) and which bodies are unfit (unacceptable). This classification of bodies is intrinsically linked to colonization and is harmful."

—ILYA PARKER (HE/THEY), owner of Decolonizing Fitness

F ADS COME AND GO, but fitness and exercise culture always seems to generate (and regenerate) more than its fair share of them. From Jack LaLanne and Jazzercise to Jane Fonda's Workout, Beachbody, and Peloton, the one common philosophy they all share is that in order to be healthy, we must take a structured, almost militaristic approach to moving our bodies. Messages such as "no pain, no gain," "feel the burn," and other catchphrases have become just as interwoven into our collective consciousness as dieting itself.

What's rarely admitted is that this messaging is intentionally designed to foster guilt and shame. Fitness and exercise have become synonymous with intentional weight loss which, for those of us already struggling with imbalanced eating, can evoke extreme emotional discomfort. Some may immediately feel anxious or completely turned off by the idea, because of the way the fitness and exercise industry operates. Others may find it invigorating, especially those who have been taught that we have to keep our bodies in shape and, therefore, need to push them to the limit in order to mold them into what we want them to be. The mainstream fitness and exercise community compels us to sit in judgment of ourselves and others, which can lead to the development of habits—often unhealthy ones—meant to correct what is "wrong" with us.

I spent many years in a toxic relationship with movement. When it came to my physical body, I was always in and out of the gym, trying to meet some ideal, whether the goal was to have a slim-thick body or to achieve a "revenge body" after a bad romantic breakup. After one particularly rough end to a relationship in college, followed by months of destructive habits like binge-drinking to numb the pain, a good friend invited me to join her in a kickboxing class.

I committed to going to the class with her every Wednesday for about a year, and I noticed that through routine practice, the anger, resentment, and hurt I felt were released from my body. I believed, for a time, that my body was healing and that I was getting mentally and physically stronger. But this healing focus soon turned into a preoccupation with slim-body aesthetics as I pushed myself harder and harder. I eventually damaged my knee and aggravated a hamstring injury that still affects me to this day.

A few years later, I decided to move from North Carolina to Maryland. It was my first time living alone, and I knew it was time for a change of scenery. I had been reading and thinking about making some changes in my life and slowing down. Moving away gave me an opportunity to put that into practice. A lot of my relationships—both platonic and romantic—shifted in the process, including my relationship with my body, which was telling me it needed something different. My nervous system was in a state of hyperarousal, in fight-or-flight mode.

Rather than hard-core kickboxing, I knew I needed something gentler. So I decided to listen to my body, to slow down and go into healing mode, something I could not do when I was constantly pushing my body to move quickly and ignore any discomfort or pain. I decided to center my healing instead, and as I put this into practice, over time it became embodied and automatic.

I decided to try restorative yoga and, as my heart began to heal, I was able to move into more vinyasa flows and other forms like aerial yoga (more on my yoga practice later). In every season the body may need something different in order to process, heal, and grieve. I had to do the work to detach myself from body aesthetics, and instead give my body what it was really seeking in that moment.

Over time, I've learned a few things. First: We are always in movement as human beings; Second: Movement can be cathartic and help release emotions; Third: Balance is imperative and slowing down and resting is important; and Four: *Listening* to the body, letting it guide you, is the best way to discover what it needs. I transitioned from working out obsessively, as I discussed in depth in earlier chapters, to discovering other ways to embrace movement as a means of liberation.

I know the subject of fitness and exercise can be a controversial one, especially in today's society. And I am not here to suggest that it does not have value. *Toxic* fitness and exercise culture, however— the kind that drives far too many of us to aim for certain body ideals to our detriment—is another societal ill that intersects with everything we have discussed so far. People who live with imbalanced eating often describe working out as a form of punishing their body for not fitting into a subjective ideal; they feel that they must work off their food or earn the right to nourish themselves. In my work with Black women and femmes, this mentality is rooted in a deprivation mindset they have inherited that keeps them in a deep ancestral pattern of feeling like they are unworthy or undeserving of taking care of their bodies if it is not connected to harm or punishment.

The industry's incessant marketing around toning up and trimming the waistline through intense workouts perpetuates the idea that our bodies must be tight and hard, and that normal softness or body rolls are not acceptable. But, as our community is beginning to urge Black women and femmes to embrace more softness, tenderness, and ease within our bodies, I believe we are ready to consider alternative points of view that honor and celebrate *ease* in our movement, too.

HOW TOXIC FITNESS AND EXERCISE CULTURE GOT ITS START

Here I return once again to our collective ancestral history. We cannot talk about toxic fitness culture without first acknowledging white supremacy and the oppressive colonialist roots upon which America was founded. Which brings us, for the purposes of this chapter, to the subject of eugenics.

Developed largely by nineteenth-century statistician, sociologist, and anthropologist Sir Francis Galton as a method of "improving the human race," eugenics is the study of how to arrange reproduction within a human population to increase the occurrence of inheritable characteristics that white-dominant culture regards as desirable. Simply put, it is scientific racism. Eugenics was created as an explicitly supremacist project that basically said white Europeans who were Christian, able-bodied, gender-conforming, and heterosexual were naturally fitter, stronger, and better predisposed to living than People of Color, Black people, Indigenous people, queer, trans, and disabled people, who were considered inherently inferior and therefore *un*worthy of living. In the twentieth century, eugenics became increasingly discredited as unscientific and racially biased, especially after its doctrines were adopted by the Nazis in order to justify their treatment of Jews, disabled people, and other minority groups.

America also has a long and complex history of murdering, sterilizing, and torturing Black and Indigenous people and People of Color to create the "perfect" human race. Fake science has defined human inferiority based on skull shapes and sizes; it has sterilized disabled and neurodivergent people and placed them in institutions; it helped introduce Jim Crow laws that sterilized poor single mothers of color; and it introduced the concept of gay conversion therapy. In contemporary terms, eugenics naturalizes social discrimination as a fact of biology. It enforces false ideologies, such as that people of color are poor because they are naturally less intelligent and therefore predisposed to criminality. Or that people in larger bodies are naturally gluttonous, that they are lacking in discipline and restraint. Even today, Black personal training clients are often viewed as lazy and noncommitted, and blamed for the chronic illnesses they carry, especially if they exist in larger bodies.

The belief that Black people are naturally stronger, faster, and bigger is a different side of the same eugenics coin that has for centuries been used to dehumanize African people and to justify their enslavement. This "biological science" is rooted in the same lies white supremacy spins over and over again, positing that the Black body can endure more force, more pressure, and more pain without any breaks, rest, or recovery because of the superhuman abilities that have been ascribed to the Black body as a way of disconnecting us from our humanity. And it still allows for Black athletes to be dehumanized, punished, and criminalized to this day. As Venus Davis, founder of The Strong Academy, has pointed out, "Our ability to perform physically is never questioned due to our history of being viewed as having been bred as 'athletes.' Unfortunately, that stereotype is accompanied by a less flattering stigma of being born without brains."

Toxic fitness culture feeds into these stereotypes by telling us we have to push our bodies to the limit and ignore any pain or discomfort that accompanies the process. Achieving the "right" body aesthetic becomes paramount. So we push our bodies to the extreme until we can't take any more, and define that extremism as success, as if exceeding the limits of what our bodies can reasonably handle is something to celebrate. The downside: early injury to the body, and not learning to trust what your body is telling you because you refuse to accept its limits.

To add even more layers to this conversation, we must also investigate and explore the relationship between Black people and our ability to engage in movement at all. Dating back to global colonization and human trafficking from Africa and enslavement throughout the transatlantic, everything about the way we moved as Black people was policed. Many of our ancestors had a gun trained on them by an overseer from sunup to sundown, which meant about eleven hours a day of manual and excruciating work. Getting tired or wanting to stop and take a break could get someone killed. I think about who was most impacted by this work structure: those who were disabled and/or had chronic health conditions, pregnant people, or those who were menstruating. Imagine the amount of intentional effort it took to ignore hunger and the need to release one's bowels, and the consequent effects of infections and other challenges that came along with intentionally ignoring a body's natural cues in order to survive.

If a slave was killed, for example, it was typically done quickly, and those on the plantation were then forced to dig holes in the ground, bury the dead bodies, and get right back to work, without any allowance to grieve their loved ones. Enslavers and colonizers literally worked our bodies to the bone: When anthropologists examined the graves of enslaved Africans, they found that our ancestors' bodies had been worked so hard that many of their extremities were detached from their sockets, and many skeletons showed extreme muscle damage from overextension and overwork. Can you imagine engaging in so much physical labor that your muscles and bones detach from themselves?

Today's gyms tend to replicate this dynamic of pushing our bodies to the limit, with exercises designed to encourage us to achieve a certain "body goal" that has been determined by a white-dominant culture that cares nothing about Black bodies. The contradictory messaging Black people have internalized says we are "lazy," while never acknowledging that our ancestors literally built America (and never received reparations for that labor). As my friend and colleague Erika Totten once shared, "Black people can't be lazy.

We have been born into a capitalist society that requires us to work as a means to survive. We overwork, overachieve, and put our bodies on the line for our jobs. Black people are tired."

In modern society we say that building strength can only be done by exerting force. We question how you can take care of your body by embracing ease. And even easy workouts aren't considered "real" work, because we tell ourselves that our bodies have not been through enough for it to count.

It is time for our bodies to rest.

Let this serve as an invitation to pause, to check in—and to divest from overproductivity. I would like to think that our ancestors' wildest dreams included rest, abundant nourishment, and the ability to listen to their bodies.

WHAT TOXIC FITNESS CULTURE LOOKS LIKE TODAY

Toxic fitness culture can best be described as a way for a dominant society to deny support, access, and services to people whom they deem unworthy. The health care, diet, and fitness industries are all interlocked in this pursuit. Each institution capitalizes on our vulnerabilities by creating unattainable versions of what "healthy" and "fit" bodies should look like. Wellness products and services are sold as solutions to the "problem" of not being able to maintain one's health. But, contrary to what the diet and fitness industries want us to believe, health and wellness are not commodities. They aren't items on a checklist or a place for you to one day finally arrive at.

Most fitness programs that are marketed this way, or as the only way are using a tactic rooted in the belief that there are always things we can and should do in order to improve ourselves. Fitness professionals have a unique opportunity to either thoroughly uphold the dignity of every single person they serve or to become a source of great shame and pain. Unfortunately, I've seen far too much of the latter.

Without any insight into the individual lives of the people they purport to help, many fitness programs send us into a never-ending feedback loop of dissatisfaction, rigid rules, impossible standards, threats of failure ("falling off the wagon"), disappointment, and punishment. And they're usually completely devoid of the compassion and flexibility we actually need in order to keep up with the unpredictability of human life.

Toxic fitness culture consists of two binary groups situated on opposite ends of the fitness spectrum. On one side are those folks whom the mainstream fitness community intentionally exploits; this group often has limited access to the resources and representation that would make them feel included and supported, and typically includes larger-bodied Black women and femmes. On the other side of the spectrum are those who are traditionally accepted as "fit": non-disabled, thin-toned, attractive, young, cisgender, heterosexual people who are often upheld as the gatekeepers of who should—and should not—be embraced by fitness culture.

White cisgender, heterosexual, non-disabled, athletic men are most often positioned as the body ideal. This is not surprising when you consider that the fitness industry is dominated by white cis men, which is likely why 90 percent of studies surrounding fitness and what we know about the body are conducted on cis men. Those results are then disseminated via major news outlets as applicable to everyone. It's not a coincidence that almost all exercise tutorial videos are led by cis white males who have a very specific body type. You can't expect an industry dominated by white male coaches, personal trainers, athletic therapists, physical therapists, and other exercise science–based professionals to be devoid of white-centric patriarchal bias.

The gatekeepers are only seen as experts because they have bodies that often align with Eurocentric beauty standards. Because of their whiteness, credentials, and years of experience, many of these "professionals" who espouse toxic fitness and exercise practices escape responsibility for what actually happens to those who follow them. Their limited view of what fitness is, and should be, is buttressed by personal training certifications that often don't include any education about or support for how to work with diverse body types or eating imbalances. In fact, in many personal training curriculums, students are only exposed to those with diverse body sizes as a way to highlight the difference between "healthy" versus "unhealthy."

The result is an entire culture that distinguishes between those who look fit and those who supposedly need help getting fit. Even movement studios, which have been seen as more benevolent and "liberatory" spaces for diverse body types, can be problematic. Far too often they're just spaces for cis white women that center hyperfemininity with deceptively harmful language like "People are people," or "We are spirits, not bodies," or "Yoga is inherently inclusive," all while simultaneously profiting from and whitewashing the South Asian and East African indigenous cultural practices they've appropriated.

And of course, social media spreads these messages even further. How often have you been scrolling and noticed that your feed or time line has suddenly been infiltrated by fitness ads, before-and-after body transformation pictures conveniently connected to a gym membership, or fitness and weight loss products (pills, powders, waist trainers, etc.) coaxing you to buy into the "latest thing"? They inundate us with messages like "Natural bodies are made in the gym," but those natural bodies always represent limited body ideals.

The celebrities and social media influencers who are the faces of the "Fitspiration," or "Fitspo," movement (a movement that is obsessed with fitness and enforces healthism) often post about what they eat in a day or offer their viewers a simplified way to eat and work out just like them, all with the promise that their followers will achieve the same body, desirability, and power.

But as consumers of these products, we are encouraged to buy in to these promises without ever considering how our individual genetics impact the way our bodies exist and are shaped. Then inevitably, when our bodies don't conform to the formula we've been sold, the industry turns its back on us and makes it a personal issue, telling us that if only we'd tried harder or had enough willpower and determination, we would have been able to alter our bodies to fit into these limited ideals.

And it doesn't stop there. We act as if we should "work off the meal" we just ate, as if our bodies are input/output machines that must be countered by walking, running, or working out as soon as we finish eating. Fitness "gurus" are asking us all to believe that by "burning off" what we've just ingested, the food will immediately and magically leave our bodies, as if our multidimensional and complex digestive systems can be reduced to a simple calculation of calories in, calories out.

Even the way we describe our food these days can be highly problematic. The fitness and exercise industry has begun to use the language of "lifestyle change" and "eating clean" to make it seem as if its intentions are based on wellness, when in fact this approach is designed to perpetuate diet culture under the guise of being health-focused. The mantra drummed into us that "You are what you eat" has racial implications, too, as we examined earlier in this book. The truth behind this message exposes an ugly reality—that the clean, healthy foods we are to aspire to consume are concentrated in zip codes belonging to affluent, white, able-bodied people. The foods labeled as "unhealthy" or "dirty," in contrast, are more often found in low-income and non-white communities of folks with fewer choices because of the economic cards white supremacy has dealt them.

"The fitness industry and all industries are impacted by systemic racism, because all industries are managed and run by people," says Cheryl McCarver, executive director of the Cooper Street YMCA, in Arlington, Texas. "People come to the spaces they fill with thoughts, beliefs, and behaviors that represent what they have learned, been taught, and experienced from the day they were born. With more diversity at the leadership level in our industry, [these] thoughts and actions will be challenged."

We can only hope that is true. At present there are myriad microaggressions we might experience as anti-Blackness within toxic fitness and exercise settings. Some examples:

- Paying for amenities that don't serve you, such as shampoos in gym locker rooms that don't work for your hair type.
- Having to ensure you always have your membership card on you while in your gym because more than once you have been asked by staff to prove you are a member.
- Having to ensure your clothes are brightly colored and unmistakably running clothes when going for a run or walk outside, to help guard against a possible stop by a police officer asking where you live and what you are doing there.
- Living in Black communities that are considered fitness deserts, with low walkability and little to no green space for physical activity.
- Walking into fitness spaces that boast about their diverse hiring practices, yet only place white people in visible leadership positions.

TOXIC GYM CULTURE AND EATING IMBALANCES

When I talk to folks who are heavily into fitness culture, I often hear them say, "Diamonds are formed under pressure." The idea is that if we just work hard enough, we can alter our bodies into what society has deemed acceptable, desirable, or attractive. For many, however, that pressure can be too much. The pressure to contort our bodies into a shape that is socially accepted is especially hard for Black women, because we are expected to heavily ignore our bodies and conform to conventional ideals—in almost a life-and-death way. When we work out and don't see those ideals reflected back to us, we may turn to coping methods like extremely restricting our food intake or engaging in other compensatory eating behaviors.

Toxic gym culture, in particular, can contribute to eating imbalances, because it thrives on the idea that you must be thinner or in a fit body to be desirable or healthy. It also teaches folks to ignore their internal body cues in favor of a subjective ideal. The "Don't stop until you drop" mentality, which is connected to pushing our bodies to the point of exhaustion or harm, and the idea that "If you don't work out you are lazy" moralize movement and stigmatize those who are not able-bodied or who experience disability and illness. Toxic gym culture puts all of the blame on the individual, especially Black people, who have been told since colonization that we are lazy. To prove the dominant culture wrong, we overwork ourselves—often at our own expense.

Personal fitness trainers often are not dietitians, professional mental health therapists, or body-based practitioners, yet they tend to hold a lot of opinions, and are often complicit in messages that tell us our bodies are unlovable and unworthy. Many of them encourage us to alter ourselves to fit into a narrow box of beauty standards and tend to perpetuate weight stigma, eating imbalances, and fatphobia, both intentionally and inadvertently.

Working out can be triggering for folks with eating imbalances, not only because they are counting calories, but because numbers are often associated with achievement and worth. They often track how many hours they have been in the gym and how many calories they've burned, and punishing their bodies as a result. I have heard some folks say that they force themselves to work out for a certain amount of time each gym visit before they allow themselves to do other activities they would also find enjoyable, such as spending time with family, engaging in self-care, or pursuing hobbies.

I often compare notes with a colleague of mine who works in the mental health space and works with clients who struggle with fatphobia, weight stigma, and fitness culture. Kanoelani, a woman from Oklahoma of Hawaiian and African American descent who self-identifies as super fat, has made it part of her mission to help other people in larger bodies learn how to advocate for themselves. She agrees that the fitness and exercise industry is rife with bias, which she herself has experienced.

Kanoelani also happens to be a powerlifter, and once described to me what it was like for someone in a larger body to walk into a gym setting. "Gym spaces can be very violent—especially at the beginning of a year. All of that 'New year, new you' stuff, thirty-day weight loss transformation challenges, even before-and-after pictures all over the place," she says. "It's toxic and really harmful, because it focuses on the aesthetics of the body, not the person inside."

Kanoelani says she's had to learn how to do her own legwork and research to find spaces where someone who looks like her can feel affirmed. "Living in Southern areas can be so oppressive," she told me. "I feel lucky that I've found a space here where I can work out. But when I visit other gyms, there are still those very backward beliefs." Unpacking gym culture allows us to acknowledge that as a society we have elevated the gym to a space of moral superiority. What once was meant to be a haven where we could focus on taking care of our bodies with intention has become a place that is largely mechanical and that excludes certain bodies.

We often use words like "discipline" to justify gym culture; there have been times when I've pressured myself to go to the gym in order to feel disciplined, when what I really needed was rest, or a different type of movement practice. Words like "discipline" and "willpower" are the same words that fuel eating imbalances. It's the idea that if someone has enough discipline and willpower they can achieve a sense of control, thinness, and safety. It's a cycle that enforces a hierarchy of "good" and "bad"—good, healthy people go to the gym, and those who choose not to are bad, unhealthy, lazy, and unattractive. Even declaring that you are going to the gym confers a societal seal of approval, because the act of going to the gym is often associated with our desire and commitment to improve ourselves.

Toxic gym cultures make you feel guilty when you don't follow a strict workout regimen. Many of the representatives of toxic gym cultures themselves have unrealistic goals for their bodies that are rooted in extreme exercise and restrictive diets, and experience a feeling of deep shame if they don't see tangible results. We obsess over the idea of a rigid routine, instead of honoring that our bodies move in ebbs and flows and that as humans we are meant to change, not stay in one state forever. And because of the way that exercise has been blanketly rewarded—considered a responsible thing to do—*compulsive* exercising becomes particularly tricky to spot. More often, people who fall prey to this compulsion are simply lauded for their discipline.

The popular perception in our culture that "More is better" can make it difficult to remember that too much exercise can make you *less* healthy over time. Overexercise, which is any form of activity or movement that is performed when nutritional needs have not been met, can cause the part of the body that manages stress—the adrenal glands—to secrete high levels of cortisol on a regular basis. High cortisol can cause bone loss and muscle breakdown, and lead to insulin resistance, a prediabetic condition that causes high blood sugar.

For others, excessive exercise causes low cortisol. In this instance, basically, the adrenal glands become exhausted from overuse and can no longer function properly. Low cortisol can lead to reactive hypoglycemia (dizziness, lightheadedness, and irritability between meals), muscle weakness, difficulty recovering from workouts, and a weakened immune system that makes one more susceptible to viruses and other infections.

Ask yourself these questions whenever you're wondering if you may be venturing into inappropriate overexercise territory:

- Am I attempting to exercise when my body is injured?
- Am I attempting to exercise when my body is sick?
- Am I attempting to exercise when my body is undernourished?
- Am I attempting to exercise when my body needs the energy for something else?
- Am I attempting to exercise out of fear, guilt, or any other shaming practice?
- Am I attempting to exercise when my body is crying out for a break?
- Am I skipping social events or familial connections to exercise for recreation?

Again, this is not to say that gyms are bad or that people should not go. What I am asking is for us as Black women and femmes to have this awareness and to be empowered in listening to our bodies, even in spaces that were designed to keep us from doing that.

I also want to point out some red flags that might indicate that the gym you are going to may be more focused on a narrow idea of body movement than on an expansive view that considers and affirms different body sizes and shapes. For example, if you are working with a personal trainer and come in with certain goals to work on that are not connected to altering your body, does the person you are working with honor that, or do they recommend food restriction and weigh-ins—things that tend to trigger eating imbalance patterns? Some other things to consider when you are trying out a gym for the first time:

- In group class settings or while you're working with trainers, do they encourage you to listen to your body?
- Do they say it's okay not to participate or offer more supportive options and choices?
- Does the equipment fit folks in larger bodies?

- Are there weight scales all over the gym or marketing tools promoting weight loss or moralizing specific food items?
- Do the instructors and staff represent a diverse array of body shapes, sizes, and abilities?

A WORD ABOUT ABLEISM

As I defined earlier, ableism is a set of beliefs or practices that devalues and discriminates against people with physical, intellectual, or psychiatric disabilities, and that often rests on the assumption that disabled people need to be "fixed" in one form or the other. Ableism is everywhere in our culture, due to its many limiting beliefs about what disability does or does not mean, how able-bodied people learn to treat people with disabilities, and how disabled people are often not included at the table for key decisions.

Within an ableist system, value is assigned to people's bodies and minds based on societally constructed ideas of normalcy, productivity, desirability, intelligence, excellence, and fitness. These ideas—as abolitionist community lawyer, educator, and organizer Talila Lewis often points out in her work—are deeply rooted in eugenics, anti-Blackness, misogyny, colonialism, imperialism, and capitalism. In our society, people whose bodies cannot move, look, and perform productively in accordance with ableist standards of capitalism are neglected and often used—nonconsensually—as props.

"Ableism is connected to all our struggles, because it undergirds notions of whose bodies are considered valuable, desirable, and disposable," says Mia Mingus, another organizer whose work focuses on disability justice. Morality around types of body movement, then, is principally rooted in ableism.

As a culture, we have taken body movement and reduced it to the boxes of exercise and fitness. Instead, I challenge us to expand those terms so that the experience of being in our bodies can be more accessible to folks with a variety of bodies and access. Every person carries a unique experience of how their body shows up in this world. The choice to exercise (or not) should have no impact on a person's intrinsic value. Everyone has the right to cultivate (or not) movement practices that suit their needs.

It is important to remember that our bodies are *always* in movement: Our heart is pumping, our breath is expanding and contracting our lungs, and our eyes are constantly moving and taking in new information. Considering movement as both an internal process and a deliberate outward expression holds space for those who may not have access to those gross motor movements. For example, those who experience paralysis or some other chronic or acute condition that may limit mobility may experience exercise and fitness as a space that is exclusionary because of what is required to participate. However, when we begin to tap into these micro movements, more possibilities become available within the body.

I first learned about the concept of our bodies constantly being in movement through my work in somatic therapy. A teacher described to me that for folks with severe injuries, there was evidence to show that recovery was substantial when it was guided and supported by the body organically, through accessing micro movements and celebrating and supporting the body in the way that it wants to heal, according to its own timing. It is a process of moving with the body and listening for the impulse, the sensation, that tells us where in the body to go next. There is nothing wrong with enjoying movement and the many non-aesthetic-related benefits it can bring. However, toxic fitness culture emphasizes using movement to become your "best self." The job of a fitness coach isn't to help people "get better," or to "fix" them with fitness, as all humans are whole and complete, with or without engaging in these kinds of activities. It's ableist to assume otherwise.

We all deserve to experience health and healing that derive from our own autonomy—whatever that feels like for us. We deserve to be part of wellness institutions that reflect the wholeness of who we are and who we can become. Working from a place of awareness and healing, we can liberate our ideas around health and exercise from what we have been conditioned to believe, and from what many of us have experienced through systematic oppression and state-sanctioned violence. The following disability justice framework created by Patty Berne, executive director of Sins Invalid, offers this powerful affirmation to keep in mind:

- All bodies are unique and essential.
- All bodies have strengths and needs that must be met.
- We are powerful, not despite the complexities of our bodies, but because of them.
- All bodies are confined by ability, race, gender, sexuality, class, nation state, religion, and more, and we cannot separate them.

THE POWER OF INTENTIONAL MOVEMENT

When working with Black women and femmes, I've found that we must expand our perceptions around what it looks like to be in movement. There are *many* benefits to moving our bodies, especially in ways that are enjoyable, pleasurable, foster a sense of freedom, and honor our embodiment. Our ancestors knew that body movement was a way of processing grief and trauma in their bodies. We see this in activities like the "ring shout"—a worship practice used by enslaved Africans to be in reverence to the divine that involved moving in a circle while shuffling and stomping their feet and clapping their hands. (This practice is still prevalent in many Black churches.) It wasn't described as somatic practice back then—as moving the body to release emotions and stuck energy. But shouting and running around in church, praise dancing, shaking the body, and other iterations of movement to release or express emotion have shown up in Black communities across the diaspora, in every region of the world, forever.

Moving our bodies has always been tied to our liberation and healing. We see threads of these ancestral practices even today in dance routines that go viral on TikTok. We only need to reframe what movement is and divest it from the toxicity of using it to alter our weight, shape, and size for the purpose of assimilating to Westernized standards of beauty and health. Imagine how it would feel to work with a personal trainer who used language that shows sensitivity, such as asking, "Do you have the capacity for one more repetition?" Then imagine yourself having the intuitive listening to ask yourself: *What does one more rep mean for me? Am I shaking? Do my muscles feel like they are expanding or cramping? Am I experiencing tension somewhere in my body that makes me think if I push too hard I might snap?*

A good friend once told me that when she thought about her wish list for the perfect fitness trainer, it included more invitations than pushes and involved more consent from her. She wanted frequent check-ins throughout activities to make sure she was okay. She imagined developing a safe word that she could use—and that would be honored by the trainer—whenever the movement was getting too intense. In her ideal scenario, clients would get to set the boundaries around how they're spoken to, the language used for motivation, and what counts—or doesn't—as a marker of "success" or "progress." ("I don't want weigh-ins" or "I don't want to count calories," for example.)

I choose to no longer use the terms "exercise" or "workout." Instead, I say "intentional" or "affirming movement practice" to describe the many ways that our bodies communicate to us. As trauma-informed fitness professional Lore McSpadden-Walker notes: "Someone training for a competition moves with intention, as does a person living with chronic pain who cleans their room while being 'aware' of [their] movement patterns. Intentional and affirming movement for someone who experiences paralysis could be tapping their finger; for some folks recovering from injury, it could be slowly gaining rotation in their shoulder; and for others it can be more gross motor movement of lifting weights, yoga, or a brisk walk to enjoy nature."

Over the past three years, I have decided that I want to create a relationship with my body rooted in gentle movement and tender care, which is what led me to restorative yoga. It took a while for me to find this practice, because I had to unpack messages I'd heard that "Yoga is a sin"—another falsehood that comes from Westernized Christianity to demonize body movement, and particularly those that have been associated with other religious and spiritual practices. Yoga is indigenous to South Asia and East Africa and has been practiced as far back as ancient Egypt or "ancient Kemet" in indigenous African cultures.

For me, restorative yoga has been life-affirming and connects me to my roots. It offers me the opportunity to exist and take up space in a world where I am not afforded tenderness, and encourages me to move without a focus on completely burning out. I created a practice of beginning the morning or ending the night with some form of restorative yoga practice and have grown in my practice of intentionally syncing breath to movement. I now have a better understanding of my body: what it needs and where it holds tension and knots. I see yoga as a spiritual practice. It's enabled me to notice a difference in my stress levels and has increased mobility in my joints. Since I've been practicing restorative yoga, I have not had significant weight fluctuations.

But my body hasn't become thinner or more toned, either. In mainstream fitness culture, this would be considered a failure. And yet, I feel completely changed. Restorative yoga helped me develop an intimate relationship with my body. It allowed me to slow down and listen. I learned how to recognize the micro conversations my body was having with me through the sensations I felt throughout the day, and to explore spaciousness with my body every time I showed up to the mat. Experiencing more flexibility and mobility, and feeling more grounded and centered within my breath—and inside my body—was empowering.

We have been conditioned out of experiencing our bodies in mindful or affirming movement. Why does exercise have to be strictly attached to a goal of becoming fit or heavily regimented? Can we redefine exercise as our bodies engage in movement practices, while also honoring that what our bodies need, day by day, will change? As our bodies' needs shift, so does our capacity, and we don't have to feel guilty about it. Holding space for "discipline" can look like so many different things in each season of our lives. Perhaps discipline is thirty minutes of walking outside every three days, or creating a practice of stretching every few hours. Discipline can be a vow we make to ourselves in relation to our bodies that says we are going to give our bodies what they need to thrive as much as possible, according to our own capacities.

The current exercise and fitness industry is connected to numbers (weight, steps, hours at the gym, calories) as a measurement of wellness. It is common to hear, for example, that we should strive for about ten thousand steps per day. We are inundated with Fitbits, Apple Watches, and phone apps that document whether or not we meet "our goal" for the day. There are even office-sponsored practices around exercise and fitness connected to these arbitrary numbers. However, when explored further, the concept of ten thousand steps a day is largely nothing more than a marketing tactic. There have been no studies that have been able to prove that ten thousand steps a day will increase vitality.

But studies have shown that simple body movement alone— regardless of the method—can contribute to better health outcomes. If the "health benefit" of movement is to boost our heart health to reduce our risk for cardiovascular issues, or to improve our mental health, or to support our cells and bones, there are multiple ways to get those needs met. If we are at the gym stressed out about what we are doing because we don't want to be there, we're increasing our cortisol levels, which is counterproductive to what we are trying to accomplish.

Intentional movement, on the other hand, feels affirming, not punitive; it is safe, self-paced, and free of diet culture messaging. An affirming movement practice allows for every person to feel at home and safe in their bodies. And it has many benefits that have nothing to do with aesthetics. Movement can decrease pain; improve mobility; promote emotional well-being by reducing stress, anxiety, and depression; and boost your immune system. It can help release trauma from the body, help us process grief, and offer physiological and psychological benefits that we can tap into if we are not concerned with altering our body by putting it through more pain. The decision to honor your body with movement is always optional and should not adhere to ableist notions of worth. Remember: A movement journey is yours and yours alone, and should ultimately be guided by *you*.

All bodies deserve equal access to compassionate and affordable fitness services. All bodies have strengths, and needs that must be met. I encourage you to find what moves you. It could be taking the stairs if you have access and are in the mood. It could also be cleaning your house, or mowing your yard, or having sex. Also think about your inner child self. What type of movement brought you joy when you were younger? I personally loved to ride my bike, because I felt unstoppable being able to ride fast while my ponytails were blowing in the wind. You can dance, twerk, try indoor wall climbing. The point is, movement doesn't have to be serious—it can also be fun.

GUIDED PRACTICE #8

For this activity, I am going to guide you through a body scan. This practice will allow you to check in with your body while also recognizing its natural movements. You will be able to reconnect to your physical self and notice any sensations you're feeling, without judgment. This activity can also be a helpful tool in strengthening your mindfulness and meditation practice.

I invite you to settle into your body by turning your attention inward, perhaps moving into stillness by finding a seat in a chair or lying down and allowing the earth beneath you to support your body. If sitting or lying down does not feel affirming to you at this moment, you can offer yourself a gentle movement, such as slowly rocking back and forth or swaying side to side.

As you find the space where your body feels the most comfortable, notice your breath. What is the quality of your breath at this moment? Is it expansive, shallow, tight, labored? Just notice what is present for you, without judgment. This is information and wisdom that your body is offering you. Now, ask your body if there is something that it needs—a pillow, a yoga block, or any kind of support that may be helpful.

Take several long, slow, deep breaths, breathing in fully and exhaling slowly. Breathe in through your nose and out through your mouth. Feel your stomach expand on the inhale and relax and let go as you exhale. Sometimes it can be helpful to offer touch to the area, space, or region of your body as you are focusing on it. Begin to let go of noises around you. Begin to shift your attention from outside to inside yourself. If you are distracted by sounds in the room, simply notice this, and then bring your focus back to your breathing.

Now slowly call your attention down to your feet. Begin observing any sensations there. You might want to wiggle your toes a little, feeling your toes against your socks or shoes. Just notice, without judgment. You might imagine that your feet are rooted into the ground, like the roots of a tree. They are sturdy and supported from the earth as you allow breath to flow through your body. Perhaps you don't feel anything at all. That is fine, too. Just allow yourself to feel the sensation of not feeling anything.

When you are ready, let your awareness travel up to your ankles, calves, knees, and thighs. Observe the sensations you are experiencing throughout your legs. Send your awareness there, breathing in and out. If your mind begins to wander during this exercise, gently notice this without judgment and bring your mind back to observing the sensations in your legs. If you notice any discomfort, pain, or stiffness, don't judge it; just simply notice it. Observe how all sensations rise and fall, shift and change moment to moment. Notice how no sensation is permanent. Observe and allow the sensations to be in the moment, just as they are. Continue to breathe in and out, keeping your focus on your legs.

On the next breath, allow the legs to dissolve in your mind. Then move to the sensations in your lower back, pelvis, and hips. Softening and releasing as you breathe in and out, slowly move your attention up to your mid and upper back. Become curious about the sensations here. You may become aware of sensations in the muscles, in the temperature, or in points of contact with furniture, the ground, or your bed. With each outward breath, you may let go of the tension you are carrying. Then very gently shift your focus to your stomach and all the internal organs there. Perhaps you notice the feeling of clothing, the process of digestion, or the belly rising or falling with each breath. If you notice opinions arising about these areas, gently let these go and return to noticing sensations.

As you continue to breathe, bring your awareness to the chest and heart space, and just notice. See if you can feel your heart beating. If you are touching the area, you may notice the rhythm of your heartbeat against your hand; that is your body in movement. Stay here for a moment and just be with your heart space. You may notice that as your heart is beating your chest is moving inward and outward with each inhale and exhale; this is also your body in movement. Let go of any judgments that may arise. On the next outward breath, shift the focus to your hands and fingertips. See if you can channel your breathing into and out of this area as if your hands are doing the breathing. If your mind wanders, gently bring it back to the sensations in your hands.

And then, on the next outward breath, shift the focus and bring your awareness up into your arms. Observe the sensations or lack of sensations that may be occurring there. You might notice some difference between the left arm and the right arm—no need to judge this. As you exhale, you may experience the arm softening and releasing tension. Continue to breathe and shift focus to the neck, shoulder, and throat region. These are areas where we often hold tension. Be with the sensations here. It could be tightness, rigidity, or holding. You may notice the shoulders moving along with your breath. Let go of any thoughts or stories you are telling yourself about this area.

As you breathe, you may feel tension rolling off your shoulders; sometimes it can be helpful to place your hands on your shoulders and notice how your body receives the touch. On the next outward breath, shift your focus and direct your attention to the face, head, and scalp. Observe all of the sensations occurring there. Notice the movement of the air as you breathe into or out of the nostrils or mouth. As you exhale, you might notice the softening of any tension you may be holding.

And now, let your attention expand out to include the entire body as a whole. Bring your awareness to the bottom of your feet—feel them rooted and grounded in the earth—to the top of your head: your crown. Feel the gentle rhythm of the breath as it moves through the body. As you come to the end of this practice, take a full, deep breath, taking in all the energy of this practice. Exhale fully. And when you are ready, gently lift your gaze and return your attention to the present moment. As you become fully alert and awake, consider setting the intention of this practice as building self-awareness.

Even when we are cleaning our house or walking to the car, we are in movement. We can all benefit from a relationship with our bodies that is rooted in ease and flow versus force. Some days our body needs a good stretch; some days it will need stillness and rest. When we begin to divest from worrying about the look of our body or even what our body can do, we can focus on being present with the constant state of movement that our body is already in. What is it like being with the unique flow, rhythm, and movements of the body that you have in this lifetime?

QUESTIONS FOR REFLECTION

1. Think back to the curious and playful movements you experienced as a child. What feelings do you remember? What sensations now become heightened? Think about when you were a kid and felt free to move in your body. Start from that place and imagine what it would feel like to experience that now.

2. Why do you want to engage in movement at this point in your life? (Be mindful of societal pressures and internal motivating factors.) How would you describe your relationship to movement now?

3. Are you someone who is dedicated to movement by way of sports or competition of some sort? How has this impacted your relationship to affirming movement?

4. Do you feel guilty when you don't engage in movement?

5. When thinking of movement, do you have any feelings around lack of safety?

6. What type of body movements bring you joy, ease, and empowerment?

· NINE ·

Making the Case for Body Liberation

"Body positivity . . . is benevolent anti-fatness in that it is masqueraded as some sort of semblance of acceptance for fat people when it is, instead, an opportunity for thinness to reroute—but not give up—its hold on fat people's collective liberation."

—DA'SHAUN L. HARRISON, author, *Belly of the Beast*

I CAN'T REMEMBER EXACTLY WHEN I first heard the term "body positivity," but I do remember being fascinated by it. The idea that we could choose to see and define ourselves in the positive, no matter what size we are, resonated with me as a mental health therapist with clients who were dealing with various stages of eating imbalances. I soon learned, however, that the concept of body positivity only scratches the surface of body affirmation. There are many movements and conversations about this topic that go way deeper than I ever imagined, from the self-care movement, to body positivity and body liberation, to body neutrality. There are also intersectional considerations: Where do movements like fat liberation and Health at Every Size (HAES) fit in? And how do systemic oppression and social justice work play into the conversation? I'm going to outline what some of the movements and concepts we'll be discussing in this chapter look like—and even give you the opportunity to perhaps identify which one(s) you feel most aligned with. Being aware of this doesn't necessarily mean that you've accepted it as your final destination. Consider it a step along the journey. Here are some definitions that may help:

THE MOVEMENT: Body Neutrality

THE MEANING: You neither love nor hate your body. Rather, it's about acceptance and respect, focusing more on what your body can do than on how it looks. For example, when you wake up in the morning you may offer your body gratitude for digesting, resting, and mentally processing all of the things that occurred the day before, because now you have more space and capacity to take on a new day.

THE MOVEMENT: Self-Love

THE MEANING: Those who are centered in this movement believe in being okay with who you are, even if you don't love certain parts of yourself yet. Lizzo is this movement's greatest proponent. It's about accepting the parts of you that you have never wanted to accept. Self-love is important, but it does not address the impact of systemic racism on our bodies.

THE MOVEMENT: Body Positivity

THE MEANING: Those who are "body-positive" quite literally have a positive view of their physical body no matter its shape, size, or other appearance-related attributes. You love your body for what it is, even if it isn't "perfect" according to society's standards. Being body-positive does not require you to take a political stance such as fat liberation, nor does it challenge internalized beliefs around fatphobia.

THE MOVEMENT: Health at Every Size (HAES)

THE MEANING: If you follow this philosophy, you support the idea of a holistic definition of health that doesn't require you to be free of physical or mental illness, limitations, or disease. You believe pursuing health is neither a moral imperative nor an individual obligation. You follow what the Association for Size Diversity and Health affirms, which is that one's health status should never be used to judge, oppress, or determine the value of an individual. HAES supports weight inclusivity and rejects the idealization and pathologizing of specific weights. It advocates for health policies that improve and equalize access to information and services that focus on people's economic, social, spiritual, and emotional needs. HAES promotes flexibility in eating based on hunger, satiety, nutritional needs, and pleasure, rather than some externally regulated eating plan. It acknowledges our biases from an understanding that socioeconomic status, race, gender, sexual orientation, age, and other identities impact weight stigma. And HAES supports physical activities that allow people of all sizes, abilities, and interests to engage in enjoyable movement to whatever degree they choose.

THE MOVEMENT: Fat Liberation

THE MEANING: This movement goes by many names, including fat acceptance, fat pride, fat empowerment, and fat activism. Those who find themselves aligning with this movement seek to eliminate the social stigma of fatness by pointing out the social obstacles it creates. However, it tends not to address intersectionality and the roots of anti-Blackness as a driver of fatphobia and fat oppression.

THE MOVEMENT: Body Liberation

THE MEANING: Those who operate at this level understand the role oppression in the external world has played in society's acceptance of certain bodies as more worthy, healthy, and desirable than others. This movement is activism-focused, as it aims to free us from social and political systems of oppression, even if we have already worked through our own internal struggles with them.

I know it's a lot to unpack. If you're feeling some uncertainty, now would be a good time to engage your senses and take a deeper look within. Feel free to pause and take some time to digest all that we just reviewed. If you need to take a break, please don't hesitate to put down this book and do something else.

When you're ready to move forward with this practice, I encourage you to first notice your breath. Don't judge it—just notice your inhales and exhales. Are they deep, shallow, labored, fast, or slow? Notice what you are experiencing and remember that this is your body offering you information. After a few rounds of breathing, I invite you to call your attention to the sensations you may be experiencing in your body and to remember that all emotions have a sensation. Once you have identified what you're feeling, perhaps take a moment to jot down any notes on what may have come up as you were exploring the current state of your body. Again, where you fall on the spectrum of possibilities may depend on a moment, or your mindset. You can even be in several of these spaces at once.

WHY BODY POSITIVITY HAS BEEN SO CONTROVERSIAL

Now that we've level-set, let's discuss one of the most controversial movements of the moment: body positivity. Body positivity is a term that's been popularized in recent years, particularly with the growth of social media. But it actually has its roots in the fat rights movement of the 1960s. Back then, the National Association to Aid Fat Americans (NAAFA) campaigned for equal rights for people of higher weights and criticized the diet industry. Over time, this campaign has evolved into the body positivity movement. For some, body positivity has been a turning point—finally, a movement centered on embracing bodies that are not thin. It has been a place where people in diverse bodies have finally been able to hear the words "Wear a bathing suit," or been able to walk into stores like Target, Old Navy, and Nike and see mannequins that represent body sizes that look more like them. But for a lot of other folks, especially those who experience more marginalization, body positivity is not enough to eradicate the systems that entrap them.

Unfortunately, the movement has fallen prey to cultural appropriation. While Black women like Sydney Bell and Danni Adams have become some of the body positivity movement's most vocal advocates, a quick social media search reveals just how much the term has since been co-opted by the white-dominated mainstream. On platforms like Instagram, we often see images of mostly white and thin, or smaller, fat, able-bodied women and femmes posing in front of a mirror in sports bras and leggings in an effort to do their best to showcase a small body roll, some cellulite, or a few stretch marks with the caption "body positivity." What's unsettling is that these are the bodies that hijack the social media algorithm, or even become social media influencers in body-positive spaces. They often easily secure financial endorsements and other brand partnerships, because their bodies don't challenge the status quo. These bodies, which are seen as just flawed enough, but not *too* flawed, *too* disruptive, or *too* controversial, are still small enough to be embraced by mainstream society as "normal." Or, as Black model Simone Mariposa puts it, "Body positivity right now is centered around women who are still conventionally desirable."

On the other hand, Black women and femmes living in a patriarchal society are often taught to feel insecure about the same body qualities these influencers are praised for. Our belly rolls, bloating, stretch marks, blemishes, cellulite, and dimpled skin aren't accepted in the same way. The irony? Body positivity was a movement created for and by Black women and femmes. But, as with much of cultural appropriation, our contributions were pushed to the margins. We were not granted opportunities to lead, were often excluded from organizing, and were even ignored when we tried to join forces with white women. The popularity of social media only exacerbated the issue—white women and folks with body privilege have been able to opt into the movement without doing any real work to deconstruct the systemic oppression that inevitably impacts it.

Body positivity, therefore, reinforces white ideals, making it easy for white women to co-opt the movement from fat Black women and femmes without being accountable for their part in body disconnection. It's an especially unrealistic approach to treating eating imbalances in Black women and femmes, because it proposes that if we develop a positive attitude toward our body flaws, we won't engage in imbalanced eating behaviors. Body positivity is grounded in loving your body and being positive, but it does not honor the experiences of people who wake up with the pain of knowing that their lived experiences are not always validated. It sets a precedent that we must be positive about ourselves all the time. But what about those days when we don't wake up and feel good in our bodies?

A more affirming statement without judgment might be, "Have you had a moment today where you have felt free in your body? What was that moment?" Once those moments are identified, we can create more of them to lean into. Every day does not have to be perfect or positive; what often makes us feel the freest is what is most in alignment with our truth. We need to normalize the experience that our body may have many different capacities, feelings, and looks on any given day, and we don't have to feel the same way about it every day, nor should we.

The current body positivity movement will never dig into the systemic oppression that impacts people's ability to simply exist in their bodies, because it was neither intended, designed, nor structured to do so. It proposes that if we can all just be positive and love ourselves—while also striving for the beauty and body ideals that we have been inculcated with through white culture—all of our other issues will disappear. It offers a simple solution without attempting a deep examination into the conditions that have made it harder for certain groups of people to love, accept, or experience positive feelings about their bodies in the first place. Therefore, it puts the responsibility back on the person being impacted by the system and suggests that it's their fault for not loving themselves enough.

It can be difficult to divest oneself from the body positivity movement, mainly because of the massive mainstream buy-in and the way that companies profit off this narrative by engaging with white social media influencers and developing entire campaigns around the concept. For Black women and femmes, however, this movement doesn't truly embrace us. The idea that the body positivity movement is progressive and accepting of all bodies is an illusion, a facade undergirded by fatphobia that tries to mask just how limiting and exclusionary the movement really is. Body positivity, in truth, does not eradicate body oppression.

I am not the first person to name this; there is an entire history of Black, fat, disabled, queer, gender-expansive folks who have put their lives and work on the line to create the possibility for *all* Black folks to be liberated within our bodies. Some of those who have done the work to free *all* Black people did not live to see the fruits of their labor, or to personally reap the benefits, which is why I continue to amplify the voices of those who have been in the movement and have shared their lived experience of fat liberation—vanguards like Tigress Osborn, Ashleigh Shackelford, Stephanie Yeboah, Leah Vernon, Roxane Gay, Sesali Bowen, Joy Cox, and many others. Their work has led me into the work of body liberation—a movement that can serve as the optimal space for Black communities to heal, if we can make it there.

THE FAT CAMPAIGN THAT TURNED THE TIDE

I would be remiss if I did not honor and amplify the history of how I cultivated my ethos around body liberation, and why I align more with folks being liberated in their bodies as opposed to just being body-positive. It is my personal commitment to continue to raise awareness, and to support folks in healing from systems that leave the most marginalized at risk within their bodies. It's important to pull back the curtain and get into the true origins of how this movement really began.

Long before body positivity was a thing, there was fat acceptance, a movement birthed out of the 1960s counterculture. In 1967, five hundred people came together in New York City's Central Park to protest bias against fat people. Together, this group ate publicly, carried signs of protest, burned diet books and photos of uber-slim model Twiggy, and were visibly, publicly, loudly—and yes, unapologetically—fat. That same year, a man named Llewellyn "Lew" Louderback wrote an article for *The Saturday Evening Post* titled, "More People Should be FAT," in response to the discrimination his wife faced. This was one of the first public defenses of fatness to be shared in mainstream media. Louderback would later go on to author a book called *Fat Power: Whatever You Weigh Is Right*.

His article led to the formation of the National Association to Aid Fat Americans, which sought to address discrimination against fat people. NAAFA was groundbreaking, in that it addressed weight bias and discrimination against fat people as a civil rights issue. The organization focused on letter-writing campaigns and providing a social network for its members. NAAFA also launched an annual conference that allowed fat people to meet, celebrate, experience joy, and be in community.

The organization, which changed its name to the National Association to Advance Fat Acceptance in the 1980s, still acts as an important resource around the discrimination fat people face in society, with a focus on bias in health care, employment, and education. It provides key tools to help fat people self-advocate, as well as pushes to make weight a protected class, offering fat people some degree of legal protection from discrimination.

Meanwhile, on the West Coast, a collective of women in Los Angeles came together and formed the Fat Underground. The Fat

Underground began as a more radical and activism-minded chapter of NAAFA, but eventually split from the parent organization. Its type of activism was more confrontational than NAAFA's, as it was informed by second-wave feminists and the gay activism of the 1970s. Many of its members were radical feminists and lesbians who believed that fat people were fully entitled to human respect and recognition.

In 1973, the group released its "Fat Liberation Manifesto," which stated, among other things, "We are angry at the mistreatment by commercial and sexist interests. These have exploited our bodies as objects of ridicule, thereby creating an immensely profitable market selling the false promise of avoidance of, or relief from, that ridicule. We see our struggle as allied with the struggle of other oppressed groups, against classism, racism, sexism, ageism, capitalism, imperialism, and the like."

If you've ever heard the statement "Diets are a cure that doesn't work, for a disease that doesn't exist," know that the phrase was coined by this group. The Fat Underground was closely aligned with the Radical Therapy Collective, which believed that many psychological issues were the product of societal oppression. Some members of the Fat Underground were also members of this collective.

In the academic world, Fat Studies slowly became a legitimate field of study, with many universities throughout the United States offering at least one Fat Studies course by 2009. In 2008, Esther Rothblum, a professor of Women's Studies at San Diego State University, and Sondra Solovay, an attorney and adjunct professor of law who founded the Fat Legal Advocacy, Rights, and Education Project, coedited *The Fat Studies Reader*, compiling articles, personal essays, studies, and work of fat activists from previous decades in order to preserve the cornerstones of the fat acceptance movement.

Much of the focus in fat activism has been on the oppression of fat women, as well as white women who identified as second-wave feminists. Many early fat activists believed that diet culture was a tool of patriarchal oppression, used to exert control over women's bodies and lives. Modern fat activism is now primarily led by and focused on women, but aims to be more inclusive of men and non-binary people.

It's also important to acknowledge the contributions other social justice movements have made to this cause. In 2021 Tigress Osborn, the chair of NAAFA and the second Black woman to lead the organization, wrote, "There are also the champions of other social justice movements—especially Civil Rights, Black Pride, and the Movement for Black Lives—who were or are fat Black women and femmes. It's our duty to learn more about them and to recognize them as important to fat history whether or not they were important to the formally organized fat rights groups of their times. But we also need to be sure we are not co-opting their legacies just so we can say the fat community is diverse. What I mean is this: we must know, acknowledge, and respect the work of fat Black people as liberation leaders in a multitude of ways, but one of those ways cannot be to pretend Black people were integrated into the fat liberation movement in ways that they simply were not. This is also true for our activist heroes of other marginalized identities."

Research has shown, time and again, how important true representation is to marginalized groups—and not the token "checking-the-diversity-quota-box" as we so often see in America. Going forward, it is vital that when we use the term "body positivity" we acknowledge and remember the history behind it. We also need to continue to advocate for Black voices, queer voices, disabled voices, and fat voices in the movement, and to embrace the intersectionality of race, class, gender, sexuality, and weight stigma that is crucial to understanding it.

BODY POSITIVITY VERSUS BODY LIBERATION

Now that we understand how the body positivity movement pushed those it was first created by and for—namely Black, fat, disabled, queer, women, and femmes—to the margins, let's talk about how the body liberation movement has worked to recenter us. This movement, which embraces an expansive, compassionate, truly inclusive praxis, was formed in the 1960s as well, by a group of fat, queer Black women. At its core, it was a fat liberation movement created by and for marginalized bodies that needed a safe space to just be. It was revolutionary for a group of fat, queer, Black women to demand respect from society.

Body liberation expands body positivity, because it isn't merely a movement or a practice: It is both and the same. Body liberation is collective; it is a way of seeing how the collective impacts the individual freedom we have in our body. It connects the external—work, family, friends, media, magazines—to the way that we digest and internalize those things. Whereas the body positivity movement insists that we don't have to address symptoms of oppression, and that we should all just love ourselves, body liberation encourages doing the critical work of naming and examining why we don't love or feel positive about ourselves in the first place. It acknowledges the institutional systems that make it possible for Black, fat, disabled people to be pushed to the margins and most impacted by systems of oppression.

I was first introduced to critiques about body positivity through writers like Ashleigh Shackelford (they/them), whose work has called out how deep this oppression goes, especially in Hollywood: "Darker-skinned fat Black women and femmes are demonized and juxtaposed as the direct opposite of the beauty standards that promote white, thin, femme bodies as a universal goal. Gabourey Sidibe is a primary example of why body positivity and fat acceptance does not privilege women or femmes of color. If so, Gabby would have the platform that Melissa McCarthy or Rebel Wilson has. We never regard Gabby as a forerunner in the body positivity movement, although her representation and presence is imperative for everyone. Seeing a darker-skinned Black woman who is not shaped like an hourglass, who does not have small petite features and who is unapologetic is powerful and necessary."

Shackelford's point resonated with me, because my work is about centering the voices and experiences of folks who have suffered the brunt of marginalization. I want us to continue to push the envelope around who is seen and amplified in these spaces.

The body positivity movement also espouses the belief that we should always be positive or neutral about our body. In many group settings where I have held space for Black folks with eating imbalances, we've discussed that being neutral about one's body is a privilege, because the Black body has always been set up as a political entity and object. To simply view our bodies as neutral not only dilutes and erases the history of our bodies, but it also asks us to ignore what we know: that we must redefine and recenter ourselves outside of the white colonial gaze.

We as a community need real, intersectional representation. I'm not saying thin bodies and white bodies should be excluded from the movement; they just shouldn't be at its center. I struggle when I hear white women speaking out against body politics and centering femininity or womanhood without addressing the fact that even those in larger bodies who are white continue to benefit from internalized patriarchal attitudes and anti-Black racism. To truly be an ally in the work of body liberation requires activists to center the work at the place where it began: with the disdain for Black bodies. Experiencing insecurities in a body that is privileged around size, weight, or shape is not the same as understanding the systemic experiences that folks in larger Black bodies encounter because Black bodies are often labeled as deviant.

OUR PART TO PLAY IN SHIFTING THE PARADIGM

I cannot say this enough: Those of us with body privilege, thinness privilege, or straight-sized privilege must come to terms with the fact that we do not need to be centered in this movement. Our insecurities are valid and, yes, we are all impacted by systems of patriarchy and white supremacy and capitalism that keep us from trusting our bodies and our intuition. But that feeling cannot and should not be compared to those bodies who experience overt and covert harm daily under systems that uphold fatphobia, ableism, and racism. For those bodies cannot easily move in and out of certain places and spaces in the same way as someone who has what is considered an acceptable body size, shape, and weight.

I don't think it is the place of straight-sized people or people with more body privilege to instruct fat folks on how to navigate body oppression, or to offer the kind of advice that says they just need to embrace their bodies and get out of their head. But I do think it is our responsibility to be critical of the ways that we are reinforcing systems, behaviors, and attitudes that limit fat and larger-bodied folks from existing freely, and it is within our purview to challenge and push back when we notice fatphobia, anti-fat discrimination, and weight stigma. Those who enjoy more privilege should challenge themselves to understand and address the systems that don't allow all bodies to experience freedom and liberation. Uprooting these systems is collective work—and we need the whole village to be on the same page.

In my work with folks of many gender identities, I am also cognizant of the fact that it can be invalidating for those who do not identify as cisgender to be told to simply be positive about their bodies, or that they need to love themselves no matter how they are viewed or how they experience themselves in society. Many gender nonconforming and gender diverse/expansive folks have shared with me that they often don't have access to the resources or support to receive gender-affirming care that would offer them more security in housing, jobs, and access to community. They have the right to not be positive when you consider the conditions that have made it more difficult for them to be in their bodies as they seek liberation from constructs of oppression.

I also think about those folks who are disabled or dealing with chronic illness yet constantly receive messages that they can only be happy or positive if they are aspiring to the so-called norm. Being in their bodies may often feel painful, and their bodies are often blamed as the problem, without any examination of how society is structured to not make space for disabled bodies to exist. I once had a client who was in a wheelchair who shared that she felt like a burden or inconvenience everywhere she went, and that it was exhausting to know that there were just certain places that were intentionally designed to keep her out. She developed a restrictive eating imbalance so that she could physically take up less space, because everything around her told her that she needed to make herself smaller and more invisible.

How so? By society not providing wheelchair-accessible ramps or creating office spaces large enough to fit her chair. By people being annoyed that they had to adjust their space so that she could fit, or being irritated with her—or refusing to service her entirely—because the support she needed was "too complicated" to address. Simply being positive and having more self-love does not change that reality.

There are many people who have an issue with not being able to project their lived experience onto someone else; they find it unimaginable that people don't move through the world as they do. What I suggest to folks who may be having these feelings is to imagine that you are having a conversation about how Black beauty and body ideals stem from white-dominated culture, and a white woman comes up to you and says, "I just can't see why Black women and femmes can't just accept and love yourselves—you all are beautiful to me."

The comment may be rooted in good intentions, but its impact and how it is received is what really matters. While she may sincerely view Black as beautiful, it is also irresponsible to not acknowledge the way the system that was set up to benefit her simultaneously works against us. The comment is heavily influenced by her experience as a white woman who lives in a society that rewards her for matching up to the Eurocentric ideals of beauty. Obviously, these ideals still may negatively impact her, but not to the degree that they impact Black women and femmes.

I have even heard smaller-sized able-bodied health practitioners and peers toss off the simplified solution that people in larger bodies should just love themselves or not be too focused on their bodies, or not allow their bodies to be a barrier, as if we have any idea what they go through on a daily basis. While some, again, may have good intentions and want to offer solutions, the issue with providing solutions from a place of privilege is that we often bypass lived experience and assume that we know what is best for people—which ultimately *dis*empowers folks. It also blames the people themselves for the behaviors they adopt to survive, without investigating the barriers and conditions that are in place that activate them into survival mode. I want all of us who hold privilege in these areas to consider these examples when we are offering advice to folks without taking the time to really honor their lived experience and to see how we may benefit from those very systems that continue to push them further into the margins.

Earlier in this chapter I described the Health at Every Size (HAES) movement as one framework many in this field have followed for a more inclusive alternative to the body-positive movement. In my early career, I utilized this weight-inclusive practice with my clients, and also found it helpful with incorporating social justice into the work I was doing. Still, for me it did not go far enough. HAES has received a lot of criticism because the curriculum was based on the experiences of white people and, therefore, still felt exclusionary to Black providers. The supervisors and training instructors were also all white, and the process of becoming certified as a HAES provider was costly and cumbersome for many.

My critique of HAES is that it mirrors body positivity by being a stop along the way to liberation. It proposes that if we accept our bodies at whatever our size is, it will lead to better self-esteem, but it still does not address the fat discrimination and fatphobia that continue to exist within our society. It promotes the idea that if you have achieved health no matter your size, you have "arrived," while overlooking that prejudice, discrimination, and stigma will still persist. It does not address how illness and health issues disproportionately impact Black bodies due to systemic and generational oppression. It also does not say that at the root of fat oppression is anti-Black racism.

Until we address the root of anti-Black racism, we have simply put a bandage on a deeper wound. Sociologist Deborah Lupton put it this way: "Whatever one's own attitude about one's body, the external societal meanings will remain unchanged, and prejudice, discrimination and stigmatization will continue to exist. Fat people themselves, however hard they try, may struggle to accept their body size in such a punitive social environment. Their inability to 'love themselves' may well become yet another source of shame and guilt."

Despite its flaws, I have come to appreciate the contributions that HAES has offered to the field, by moving away from a strict weight-loss and weight-centric treatment modality for eating imbalances. It is scientifically based and has been well accepted by the medical community. Some of my clients have shared that they do not resonate with the HAES model because they feel that it is still very health-centric, and that health has been moralized. There are others, however, who have shared that they would not have recovered or healed from their eating imbalances were it not for models like this one that did not stigmatize their bodies.

Let's finally dismantle the idea that we have to be positive about our bodies in order to feel whole, when what we truly want is to be liberated within our bodies. We can do this by detaching ourselves from the systemic narratives that tell us we are not enough, and lovingly leaning into those revolutionary systems that will help us heal.

GUIDED PRACTICE #9 AND QUESTIONS FOR REFLECTION

Body liberation requires more than a simple mindset change or perspective shift. The liberation we often seek requires action and change on many levels: intrapersonal (within ourselves), interpersonal (with one another), institutional (focusing on policies or behaviors within an organization), systemic (focusing on oppressive values or practices founded and perpetuated throughout systems) and structural (focusing on cultural values in a society so ingrained in daily life that they are seen as "the way things are"). Before we can create that life, we must first envision it. For some people that might mean visualization, while others may choose another pathway, such as intuition, sound, smell, touch, or taste.

For this guided practice, I will take you through a visualization exercise. Once we envision what we want to see in our lives or in the world, it can make achieving that intention or goal much more obtainable. First, let's think about:

1. What does liberation mean for you?
2. What does it look and feel like?
3. How will you know that you are liberated?
4. What things would be different?
5. How would you feel in your body in this liberated vision of yourself?

Then ask yourself, What is one thing that you can take from this liberated world and begin to implement today? Sometimes it may require help from other people, and that is okay; it's fine to lean into community.

To take the exercise even further, you might consider creating a vision board that represents the liberated world you've envisioned. Traditional vision boards are usually created with a piece of cardboard—folks may find photos or pictures cut out of magazines to represent the things, ideas, goals, and dreams they would like to manifest in their future. I also know people who create digital vision boards. Please don't be limited by the framework that I have provided; if a vision board isn't your thing, you may be inspired to create music, poetry, or some other way of bringing more body liberation into the world. Be as creative and expansive as you would like.

I hope that as these calls to action begin to manifest themselves, you will see how the power of dreaming and envisioning can be a tool for liberation, and that it may someday begin to cultivate collective change.

· TEN ·

Embodiment Is a Revolutionary Act

"What coming back to self really means is coming back to the root, to the source, to the truth of who and what we are, the 'we' that we were before society told us and taught us who they desired us to be."

—JOÉL LEON, performer, author, and storyteller

THE FIRST TIME I became aware of using helpful and positive coping tools to support my mental health was when I was in graduate school studying clinical mental health therapy. I came across an app called "Shine," which offers mental health support for folks who struggle with stress and anxiety. It is also a community for people suffering from mental and emotional illnesses like depression, panic attacks, and severe anxiety. I loved the app, because every morning I would receive uplifting affirmations and motivating stories that would support me in getting through each day. Reading these stories became a part of my daily self-care practice.

One story touched me profoundly: *Honor Your Imperfections with the Japanese Art of Kintsugi* by Candice Kumai. She describes the artistic practice of Kintsugi as "repairing broken vessels by sealing the cracks with lacquer and carefully dusting them with gold powder . . . The Japanese believe the golden cracks make the pieces even more precious and valuable." Instead of throwing away the broken pieces of the vessel or viewing it as damaged or something that should be disguised, Kintsugi treats breakage and repair as part of the history of an object. Kumai explains that Kintsugi teaches us to be kind to ourselves and helps us love and forgive ourselves as we become whole again. The vessel helps us mark our progress, and as we change our mindset about all that has happened in the past, we come out of those struggles with a much more beautiful and refined version of ourselves. Your Kintsugi cracks become gold. Kintsugi helps us learn from our mistakes, reminds us that no one is perfect and that our imperfections are what makes us golden.

I come back to that story time and time again when I need to be reminded that I am enough just as I am right now. It's beautiful to think of this practice as a metaphor for your life's journey, to see the broken, difficult, or painful parts of you as radiating light, gold, and beauty. Kintsugi teaches you that your broken places make you stronger, even better than before. When you think you are broken, you can pick up the pieces, put them back together, and learn to embrace the cracks.

As we continue to move toward healing and liberation, we can now name and identify how we got here, examine the limitations that we have adopted, and redefine our freedom. We have befriended and understood the protective measures we developed to help us survive and have honored what they have done for us. But the real work ahead is to find a more present and adaptive coping mechanism that offers us a sense of belonging, safety, body autonomy, and dignity. As we regroup, reconcile, and reshape this new reality, it will create more space for possibilities and transformation to occur.

OUR PATHWAY HOME

We began this journey by exploring how we got so disconnected from our bodies in the first place and traced the roots back to the impacts of colonization, enslavement, and capitalism on our bodies as Black people. We explored how this disconnection was then implanted in us from the womb, through our genetics, and through the familial and cultural conditions of our childhoods—and how the disconnection shows up in adulthood. We discussed larger systems such as patriarchy, religious dogma, fatphobia, healthism, and diet culture that particularly impact Black women and femmes. We investigated beauty and body ideals that were given to us by the white-dominated culture, then transitioned into a conversation about how we can begin to explore a different kind of relationship to movement. Our journey led us to take a critical look into how we view liberation and concluded with a larger vision of our embodied selves—one that takes into account our earthly and ancestral lineages.

I hope you feel, as I do, that we have been on an enriching and beautiful path together. As I neared the end of writing this book, I felt a deep excavation and rebirth. The feeling was raw, but also tender and freeing. I felt overtaken by the love that was poured into each chapter like warm honey, knowing that I was replanting new seeds in fertile ground and, as in Kintsugi, using the gold to help seal myself—and hopefully you, too—back together again. This journey has asked us to heal deep-seated ancestral and cultural trauma within our relationship with food and our bodies— trauma that we ingested and accepted as either belonging to us or simply just the way it is.

Though our time together is coming to a close, the work is far from done. It is never simple. I hope that this book becomes a part of your continuing emotional, mental, energetic, and physical work, and that you will come back to it now and then as you learn and grow.

OUR BODIES, REDEFINED

"Being in our bodies is a daily art of coming home. Some days we come home, and we'd rather be anywhere else but there. Some days we return home and gratitude fills us with warmth. The goal, then, is that we build gratitude more and more each day that we return back to ourselves. It doesn't mean we will always love being there but hold a deep sincere gratitude for it."

—Poet, actor, and author ARIELLE ESTORIA

The Black body is a manifestation of many rose gardens that had the strength—the audacity, even—to force their way through the concrete. Our bodies are a tapestry of love, healing, blessings, survival, pain, and resilience. Our survival in the face of circumstance and deprivation is a testimony, proof that we are here on purpose and that our Creator took her time with us when we were designed. We are the family recipe that has been passed down from generation to generation: The vast hues of our bold melanin forms the base; our culture provides the spices that impart flavor; the stories of how we came to be who we are provide the step-by-step instruction; and the variety in our textures and features is what makes our personal recipe different from all others. We can fortify ourselves with our own delectable iteration of Black existence.

Embodiment is primarily a physical sensation; we can feel it in the depth of the emotions that arise. It is a combination of emotions, movement, and impulses in the present moment. It is both transformational and meaningful. Embodiment integrates our internal and external being, our relationship to space and gravity. It is an ever-changing dynamic between the self, the other, and the environment. Our conscious awareness of what we are experiencing within our body enhances the journey. The journey of our embodiment can be lifelong, and often requires repeated practices of being present in your body.

We can make it our personal practice to continue to notice what our body is communicating to us and focus on regulating our nervous system. When our nervous system is flexible and can return to regulation, we may notice reduced inflammation, balance of immune response, emotional regulation, stress resilience, more optimism about our well-being, increased capacity for friendship and connection, increased social support, and more self-compassion and empathy.

For some, the idea of giving up one's pain can be threatening to the nervous system, which is why I encourage you all to move slowly and identify and seek out resources for support, because sometimes we can get so familiar with our pain that it feels addictive. We may struggle to let go of what we have known and used to survive. Even when it is hard to be in your body, it can be helpful to engage with your environment through gardening or spending time in nature. And while it doesn't take the pain away, it offers space for anchoring and grounding.

Embodiment principles involve going slow, noticing and bringing awareness to what is happening within your body, and using mindfulness to tune inward. This bottom-up approach to receiving this information teaches you that you can rely on your body and that you have choices around how much, when, or why we need to regulate. That is why it is important that we stay curious by listening to our body and asking it where it wants us to go now, all the while following those instincts and using your intuition to hold space for the truths that come to you.

OUR PERSONAL JOURNEY

As Black women and femmes, there are several areas we must overcome so that we can experience ourselves as whole and recognize that the wholeness we cultivate and embrace within ourselves is mirrored in each other. A friend of mine, Lyvonne Briggs, shared something that has stayed with me: She received a compliment about her personality and appearance from another Black femme, and in response she offered gratitude, saying, "I am a reflection of you, sis." Imagine if we regularly reacted to one another this way, instead of tearing each other down, reacting violently, or bonding over our perceived flaws and insecurities.

I want us to bond over being divinely enough to just "be." Think about where else our energy could go if we already knew that we were whole. I envision that we could expand our emotional capacity to do the deeper healing work that would allow us to not only address the trauma that we have inherited, but to embody the blessings, gifts, and medicine that are our birthright. I dream about a society transformed by just being in the energy of free Black women and femmes. I see us living without constraints, confidently speaking our truth, trusting ourselves and one another, moving in our bodies with ease, abundantly nourishing and nurturing one another, advocating for joy and peace, and defending ourselves and one another when we need it. I see us embracing softness, sensitivity, rest, and the need for tenderness while also wielding our power and honoring our inner warriors. These are all characteristics of who we already are and where we have been—and how we have the capacity to emerge again.

We have inherited a lot from a culture steeped in anti-Blackness. We are responsible for what we do with what we have absorbed and how we choose to move forward. Throughout this book, we have unpacked oppressive systems and constructs that have kept us from being free in our bodies. It is now up to us to contend with these constructs, and to collectively heal ourselves and offer a new narrative for those who will come after us.

The personal journey toward healing our relationship with food and nourishment is recognizing that it's not just about the food or solely about our body image. Our Blackness carries its own interconnected web of stories and, depending on our socialization around Blackness, determines how we have embodied it. But remember: Beyond this body we are connected to a lineage and a larger story. The most radical thing we can do at this time is reject the lies we have inherited about ourselves and surrender to the practice of being Black and embodied.

In an environment steeped in colonialism, we still have a choice to come up for air and locate a new home within ourselves. The personal journey we have embarked on throughout this book has been intentional about both recognizing and unpacking the ways we have internalized social patterns and beliefs that do not serve us. I don't say this to suggest that these things will be easy to overcome and, as I have stated throughout this book, the work will be multilayered for people who experience intersectionality within other identities that have been marginalized. As we move forward, it is important that we do not replicate those same systems that we have worked to divest from. During the good work we've done together here, we have brought awareness to those issues, uprooted the seed, and prepared our hearts to receive embodied practices that are in alignment with our truth and values.

Those of us who live with eating imbalances and body image concerns must make every effort to validate for ourselves that we are not flawed, broken, or damaged. You are dealing with a normal adaptive response to surviving in a system that was invented to deem your existence as something that should not have survived past the plantation. I repeat: It is *not* your fault. While I have used the word "disordered" throughout this book to describe a clinical term, there is nothing disordered about you. I invite you to breathe into my words, and even if they do not feel believable right now, continue to repeat them to yourself, write them on a sticky note, and intentionally place them somewhere where you will see them regularly.

This journey toward becoming embodied may be challenging, as we are told to take up less space, that we don't belong here, are shown that we are not safe, and may not feel as if we have much control. These things will continue to rise up as long as we exist in a racialized society under colonialism. However, I would encourage you to interrogate mainstream messages, and to refine and listen to the voice within. Then, come back to this book, and know without a doubt that by working to detangle yourself from the clutches of these oppressive systems, you will be taking back your power by saying that despite the environment and social conditions in our headwinds, you will continue to heal.

This journey is not meant to be perfect; there will be times where we are tired, when we decide to do what is easier, where we go back to surviving. (Personally, I decided to take a sabbatical from being a therapist to write this book, because the requirements for showing up and holding space for others while tending to the needs of developing this project did not always support each other—and so I had to make a choice.) No one's journey is linear, and we are human beings, not humans constantly *doing*. What is important is that each time we live out of alignment with our values, we recognize it as an opportunity to reexamine what activated or triggered us, and to then make a different decision next time. Choosing to heal yourself, despite the circumstances, so that you can be happy, experience peace, and access liberation is the true definition of a badass: This is the path less traveled.

OUR CULTURAL JOURNEY

The work that we do to free ourselves also begins to free others. When we show up as more embodied and whole, it helps to regulate and create safety for other bodies to envision and practice turning inward. I am relieved to know that while I am addressing bigger cultural issues, my personal path of choosing healing is enough; my own work creates a ripple effect that begins to touch the collective, body by body. As each of our bodies returns inward and experiences safety, we also begin to decolonize a culture impacted by white supremacy, colonialism, and capitalism. We begin to return home.

Most of the thinking patterns, beliefs, and behaviors that have become adaptive originated in messages that we have received about our bodies, particularly the Black body. As time has passed, those messages and beliefs have become normalized, and the context of those messages has disappeared. It is time to recenter the context and history associated with why we have not been embodied, and to work as individuals and communities to begin to make

cultural changes around the way that Black bodies, disabled bodies, gendered bodies, and all bodies are treated.

As Black women and femmes, we must investigate what we have
unquestionably accepted about ourselves and believed to be true.
We have to put in the work to change those narratives. Non-Black
folks must also show up and support Black women and femmes
existing and healing in this anti-Black society without tone policing, silencing us, or expecting us to coddle and be caretakers. What
would it be like if you supported and took care of Black women and
femmes without trying to gain extra credit? What would it look like
for you to align your heart to center our liberation?

Dr. Sara King, an internationally recognized thought leader in
the interdisciplinary field that examines the roles of social justice,
art, somatics, and mindfulness in neuroscience, has shared: "The
path to the end of suffering is located in the relationship to our
body. Our bodies are the key to our individual liberation. Because
of our fundamental interdependence to one another it is also linked
to collective liberation. Our bodies are a site to be an agent to healing in society itself."

OUR ANCESTRAL JOURNEY

Holding space for the ancestral impact on our bodies can be approached in many ways. Admittedly, there is a lot of cultural stigma
and taboo around communing with ancestors—and a lot of that
fear is a product of Westernized indoctrination into religion, which
labels religious nonconformity as demonic. Even still, I tell folks
that honoring the impact of those who came before you can show
up as seeing yourself as a representative of the lineage and choosing to take care of your body for yourself and for those who live
through you. It can also look like diving into family histories or
doing genealogy work. Or it can take shape as an examination of
patterns of trauma and healing that have been passed down for
generations through conversations with elders. And yes, for some

it will be a deeper journey into spirituality and understanding the energy that exists around us. Spirituality is not about religious beliefs; rather, it is about people who perceive themselves as spiritual beings, whose spirit needs energizing. It is recognizing the mind, body, and spirit as interconnected parts of the whole, and recognizing that healing *me* is also healing *you*, and vice versa.

When I began to work with trauma through a somatic therapy lens, I realized that through my body, I intimately know many bodies. I learned that the body does not hold experiences on a linear time line, and that it often takes our "thinking brain"—our prefrontal cortex—to organize time. When I think about generational trauma from this perspective, I realize that the trauma and healing are not stored in our body as a time line, but as many different experiences happening all at once when activated by a specific trigger, environment, or event. That's why when people say, "Well, that happened so long ago" to invalidate people's experiences of racial trauma, it doesn't necessarily add up: The body truly does keep the score. We carry our ancestors with us, even in the facial expressions we use to communicate emotions, or the way their lack of nourishment showed up in their bodies, and now ours. The impulses, sensations, and emotions may come from our present experiences, but they are also one piece of a larger tapestry that I get to understand through my human iteration in this lifetime.

When I dream of returning home, I think about the home of my ancestors and what they might feel through my existing on their land again, breathing the air, and consuming the food culture. We now have the ability to get on a plane and travel to the lands of our ancestors. Perhaps a part of healing our relationship to our bodies is going back to those places, and reconnecting to the stories that became fragmented. We always leave an energetic footprint; therefore, the energy of the land stewards holds imprints of those that came before us. The information is not lost, it is just waiting to be rediscovered. The land, the ocean, and the universe all have a memory—these energetic imprints are never forgotten.

Cycles of generational restriction can only be broken by cycles of intentional generational abundance. A part of healing our bodies is loving one another as we fully are. To heal we need to center our liberation and work through racial trauma, ancestral wounds, and intergenerational trauma.

In order to begin this work, it may be helpful to connect with those who came before you to seek out guidance and healing. Or, if that does not feel affirming, you may also try developing a family tree and seeking guidance from family or family friends to fill in areas that are unfamiliar. For folks who are adopted or may be estranged or not know their family, I ask that we decolonize the definitions of "family," "lineage," and "inheritance" and include those who are our *chosen* family and those we are aligned and connected with in many different forms. Our inheritance is not just biological, but connected to our social learning and environment as well.

Ancestral connection has had the greatest impact on my own recovery from imbalanced eating. I learned to be in my body while also seeing it as a portal to relationships with those who came before me. A big part of what was driving my imbalance in eating patterns were situations that had been normalized in my family and community, cultural and ancestral inheritance, and the internalization of scarcity and lack. All of these factors came together to implant a belief that at my core I was not safe, not good enough, not accepted, and had limited options. The imbalanced eating patterns were an attempt to alter my body and have a relationship with eating and food that I perceived was within my control, even though it eventually began to consume me.

For me, seeking spiritual divination was what started to loosen some of these shackles. I recognized that I was not alone—instead, I had a whole spiritual team that was rooting for me. This truth catapulted me into a journey of seeing myself beyond just my body, and deepening long-forgotten connections through spirit. I also received confirmation that pursuing self-love, truth, and inner authority were my life's purpose in this lifetime, which gave me direction and made what I was experiencing make more sense. I stopped asking *why* this was happening to me and started reframing my thoughts into what this experience was teaching me and guiding me toward in my journey to living in my purpose. I started viewing the storms as life initiations and my healing journey as a rite of passage.

One of the most impactful experiences that I had happened early on in my ancestral healing journey. I enrolled in a six-month intensive ancestral healing class to heal each of the four lineages along my family line, tackling one at a time. About four months into working with my maternal mother's lineage, I was sitting at my sacred altar space in a deep meditative trance, communing with my ancestors. I had just finished my initial proposal for this book and was seeking guidance and favor as I prepared to move into the next stage of pitching it to publishing houses, when suddenly I started humming a song. Time seemed to disappear while I was in this state, and I received an image of four seemingly feminine figures holding hands, their hearts all connected in the middle, with their voices singing in a soft rejoicing and uplifting tone.

A light energy was flowing from their center, where they were all connected. While being fully present in my body and connected elsewhere spiritually, I also began to sing in a language I was unfamiliar with, and it initially caught me off guard. However, I was familiar with "speaking in tongues" from my Christian upbringing and wasn't fearful of tapping into the ancestral memory and linguistics through song. A particular phrase was repeated throughout, and after closing off the space and offering gratitude, I decided to look it up. For the purpose of preserving the sacredness and potency of the moment, I will not share it here. But it very loosely translates into "It is yours." It was the confirmation I needed to continue this journey, knowing that I was protected and divinely guided.

For those who may be interested in pursuing the ancestral journey, the first step is learning to be in and with your body. Allow yourself to experience your emotions as they come up and notice the way your body responds. It might give you chills or cause you to tense up; you may experience ringing in your ears. Relax and get curious about those responses in a nonjudgmental way. While these bodily responses have physical explanations, there are spiritual explanations as well. In my own experience and while working with clients, I have found that in a fast-paced society that is always on the go, it can be a challenge to move into noticing and experiencing your body in this way, because there is so much external noise that rewards us for not listening to our bodies in service of "productivity."

I would encourage you to start with a small mindfulness practice, three to five minutes a day, of checking in with yourself. No cell phone, no other distractions; if possible, just you and your breath. You may ask your body what it needs at this moment and take what it offers you as truth. Mindfulness can be helpful for supporting this practice, and nowadays there are so many apps that you can download on your phone or videos to watch on YouTube. There are also studios that offer in-person mindfulness and breathing practices. This journey will lead you into the practice of listening to and honoring your body.

This is how you begin to establish self-trust and show up for yourself in the way that you may have wished that others would have shown up for you in the past. It is also important to grieve and heal the survival wounds that we have inherited from family and those that came before us. The most freeing thing I have experienced in my own healing journey is reminding myself that those who came before me did the best they could with the tools, emotional capacity, and wisdom they had at the time, and that it is okay for me to experience a myriad of emotions and feelings about the impact of what they didn't know or didn't do, or actions they took that were harmful. This is a both/and situation where we can offer compassion while also holding space for our experiences.

When you know that you are a part of something bigger, you move with the awareness that folks are rooting for you, always; and that when you win, they're part of that win as well. That is empowering. To be whole, we will have to commune with our ancestors and ask them what they need to heal these wounds, and ask for knowledge around coping that is rooted in their healing modalities. A part of healing is honoring all the components of who we are—including our spiritual selves. I will reiterate that when we heal our relationship with the body and food, we repair the relationship with nourishment that our ancestors passed on through their bodies to us. In turn, we heal the connection for future generations as well.

OUR ENERGETIC JOURNEY

Energy is the unseen vibration we carry with us that can collect residue throughout existence and emanate out into the world. Every entity has an energy, which was why it was important for me to call the energy of my eating imbalances into ceremony to get to know it better and understand how it had shifted and changed over time. I came to understand that beyond what could be quantified, the reason this entity had been around for so long was because it needed something, and the dysregulation and lack of balance was a pathway into my healing. We are conduits to alchemize the vibration of the eating imbalance within our bodies, in tandem with the collective, our ancestors, and our larger ecology.

To keep our bodies in flow, we can be aware of our energy and, when it is stuck, we can learn how to release it. Practices like yoga, acupuncture, qigong, tai chi, massages, and Reiki can be helpful for this. We can also reframe our Blackness—seeing it not only as a race, but as an energy that exists to take up space. When we examine, for instance, the statement "As above, so below," we come to see that the space where the cosmos and the unknown meet are spaces of blackness, as are the deepest crevices of earth, where the most gems and treasures and rarities are found. I recognize that by embodying the layered ecology of Blackness, I am an expansive and mysterious being. Blackness cannot be encapsulated; it just is.

Energy is also felt through our bodies when we encounter other bodies. I believe that the liberation we cultivate within ourselves is infectious. How can we move through the world with so much liberation that others are inspired to change as well?

This kind of energetic relationship also extends to the one we have with the land. A wise teacher once shared with me, "Nature is our teacher, healer, and sustains our human form." As we near the end of our time together, I'd like to leave you with this one thought: that our bodies are an ecosystem. If you remember, back in chapter One I shared that our eating and its imbalanced energy are connected to the overproduction of the land and resources. We cannot talk about reclaiming our Black bodies, our ancestral bodies, and our collective bodies without also addressing our relationship to the earth, particularly in this time of environmental upheaval.

Our bodies are a reflection of the earth; however, we have become distorted in our reflection due to the separation we have from nature. We don't honor the grooves in our cellulite as we might celebrate the bark on a tree, or think about how the stretch marks that crisscross the earth's body are reflected in its lakes and rivers, or that its hair springs to life through the grasses and leaves.

The earth also has the capacity to return to itself, and even to be a regenerative resource in relation to us, but we must address our relationship with it. The land, which is earth's body, provides us with the nurturing and nourishment that are required for our own bodies. Food justice and sovereignty are connected to how we tend to the land, as well as how we source sustainably and support the conditions necessary for Mother Earth to return to herself. In order to live in harmony with the earth, we must see ourselves as an extension of it.

ADVICE FOR HEALTH PRACTITIONERS

The current treatment for eating imbalances relies heavily on therapy modalities that emphasize altering thoughts, feelings, and behaviors associated with the imbalance, in addition to other cognitive behavioral therapy techniques that focus on the thinking part of the brain and how it connects to behaviors associated with eating disorders.

I argue that the reason so many eating imbalances are left untreated is because there is a wider lens that we are missing when it comes to working with imbalanced eating. When Black women and femmes are seeking this type of care, our healing requires more than a focus on our bodies and how we think. Yet far too many health professionals in this field invalidate the real experiences Black women and femmes have endured from living in an oppressive society, by telling us to just change our thinking patterns or do mindset work. It is not that simple for us. It is also about the patriarchal messages that have been drilled into all non-men about what it means to control and restrict our bodies, and about the messages we have received from the media around diet culture and the thin ideal. And it is also about the problematic comments we receive from our families about our eating imbalances. Most modern eating imbalance treatment ignores these contributing factors.

When we view eating imbalances solely from a behavioral perspective, we miss the fact that even if we limit or stop all imbalanced eating behaviors, there are still bigger issues that keep eating imbalance thoughts and impulses active. Behavioral modification does not address the root issue; it merely serves as a Band-Aid. And it does not offer freedom from the thoughts, sensations, and feelings associated with the root of the eating imbalance. Rather, it creates another dynamic where we suppress the urges but don't fully excavate them. It also doesn't help that many health practitioners in this field themselves are dealing with their own imbalanced eating challenges—we just don't talk about it.

As Black women and femmes, we are more than just the person who is showing up in the flesh: Our experiences in our bodies are deeper, nuanced, and layered. We need a treatment and a healing model that meets us exactly where we are and doesn't require us to have to choose to leave out parts of what we need. We need a model of recovery that honors our wholeness and doesn't require that we show up fragmented. Even though I took a step back from meeting with therapy clients to write this book, I continued to pour into my business, and developed a comprehensive Reimagining Eating Disorders 101 course that offers a holistic model to recovery and healing from eating imbalances.

Whether you are a client or a health practitioner struggling with an eating imbalance, I encourage you to seek out treatment and care from folks who understand, and to share knowledge about your cultural background so that they can support you in curating space within yourself that makes you feel more at peace.

MOVING THE NEEDLE FORWARD

"Part of healing is taking care of your body and learning how to have a humane relationship with your body. I was broken and then I broke some more, and I am not yet healed but I am starting to believe I will be."

—ROXANE GAY, *Hunger: A Memoir of (My) Body*

The big question is: Can we heal from eating imbalances? Yes, we can—with a combination of holistic healing, intergenerational liberation, and culturally responsive care, as well as practices of embodiment and trauma-centered care. Throughout this book and in my own practice, I am intentional in naming that I am doing healing work. I distinguish healing work from treatment because I find that treatment often only addresses the symptoms of what people are experiencing. Treatment is concerned with using studies and research that is solely evidence-based. But as my colleague Jessica Wilson shared in her book *It's Always Been Ours: Rewriting the Narratives of Black Women's Bodies*, "When I look in the National Library of Medicine database, also known as PubMed, and type in 'eating disorders' and 'Black women,' only ten results from the last five years appear, and only one study of Black women exclusively. The majority compare Black women to white women, who are clearly defined as the norm or default sample population. Meanwhile, there are 8,173 results for 'eating disorders.' I don't think it is ethical to say that we're providing 'evidence-based' care to Black women with eating disorders when they are present in 0.001 percent of the research."

What we have been told about ourselves has been assigned to us by a people and a culture that has nothing to do with us. But our healing does not have to be prescriptive or pathologized in order for it to work. Treatment-focused care often teaches us to cope with and pacify the issue; a healing approach grounds us in our culture and recenters our indigenous and ancestral healing practices.

Unfortunately, the number of Black mental health therapists who work with eating imbalances is still quite small. Those of us in the field have been trained to treat symptoms and work in treatment-centered versus healing-centered environments. A lot of us didn't receive in-depth trauma, somatic, spiritual, or ancestral/lineage-based training in our programs. However, these are the modalities that are necessary for holistic healing for Black folks. The work we have been doing is good for stabilization, but the root of what we are working with is so much deeper. We are *not* the add-on to the work; rather, our experiences within the eating imbalance field need to also be centered.

My advice? We need to incorporate and see value in expanding our integrative teams beyond mental health therapists, dietitians, and psychiatrists. We need to fold in the knowledge and expertise of Reiki practitioners, yoga teachers, spiritual healers, and elders, and those trained in a variety of somatic practices, homeopathic medicine, and African and Black ancestral healing modalities. Our Western society thrives off our disconnection from our individual, collective, and spiritual bodies. It uplifts the Western model of being rooted solely in our thinking mind, and in what can be measured or labeled as proof that centers around one truth. This has caused us to downplay and ignore our bodies and intuition.

Healing for Black women and femmes looks like a model that centers lineage repair work, trauma-informed healing, reclamation of our ancestral and indigenous practices, spirituality, and somatic-embodied practice. Bringing up race or broaching the subject of race with Black women and femme clients in order to unpack our complexity should be part and parcel of all treatment of Black folks. Working with practitioners who understand our history, our embodied experiences, our resilience movements, and our healing practices that were stolen and appropriated is essential to our liberation.

GUIDED PRACTICE #10

Art therapy is frequently used in treating imbalanced eating as a way of helping us reframe our relationship with our bodies. It helps us get unstuck and realize that we are a part of something bigger, and that there are connections between us and the universe. As we expand the way we view our bodies, our relationship to food, and what it means to be nourished, we can break away from any limiting body ideals that have held us back, which makes room for more possibilities and choices to explore. This exercise is intended to help you understand how your body best needs to be nurtured and supported.

Before we get started, I invite you to notice your breathing, without feeling any pressure to change or shift its current state. After a few mindful inhales and exhales, notice your body again and ask yourself what it needs at this moment. Perhaps a break? Or you may need to get up and move around, or sit down. Your body will let you know what it needs—your "job" is to listen and tend to it with the capacity and accessibility available to you.

In this final guided practice, we will be working on drawing the body, also known as creating a bodyscape. It can be helpful to have something to draw with, and a piece of paper or canvas or digital space where you can create. If this activity does not feel aligned or resonate for you, that's okay! I respect your boundaries and what feels appropriate for you at this moment. Feel free to modify or identify something completely different that helps you to connect to your body.

Start by drawing an outline of your body on whatever surface you have to work with—and it doesn't need to be perfect. Envision your body as if it were a map of Mother Earth. Where do the grooves sit? Where do the rivers flow? Which sections of your body represent things like caves, mountains, crevasses, trees, animals, plants? Really spend some time with this and get creative! You can incorporate different textures, colors, materials, and mediums into your drawing, if that works for you. You can also approach this activity from the perspective of your inner child or teenager. How would your younger self answer these questions and interpret the ecology of your body at that age? In this approach, this ritual could be a way to heal your inner child by showing her that she's connected to something bigger, and that our bodies are vast, expansive, deep, open expressions of Mother Earth.

When you've completed the project to your satisfaction, take a long look to review what you drew. Consider each area of your bodyscape and describe what you see. Identify what parts of the body may contain different earthly elements—rain, water, sun, sand, dirt. Notice how you feel about your bodyscape, and what sensations come up when you think about your actual physical body. As you kindly interpret your drawing, think about why you drew a certain tree to represent sturdiness, or why you chose a flowing river to represent how emotions flow in and out of your heart.

Your answers may bring some enlightenment around the narratives you connect to your body. But this doesn't have to be a one-time practice: The more you explore earth or nature and form a better relationship of reciprocity, reverence, and curiosity, the more you will be able to come back to this representation and add in any new information you learn.

You will likely begin to see your body differently. You will have more to add, and more wisdom you've gathered from the process. Ashlee Bennett explains in her book *The Art of Body Acceptance: Strengthen Your Relationship with Yourself Through Therapeutic Creative Exercises* that the brain, which holds our body image "map," uses it to make sense of our bodies in space and time. So whenever your body changes, the brain receives new information that feeds into our sense of identity. As Bennett says, "This is a normal part of change. Embrace it, don't judge or label it. Our brain is in the process of integrating this new landscape for us to come home to."

QUESTIONS FOR REFLECTION

My hope is that this book has been fulfilling, edifying, and nourishing to your mind, body, soul, and spirit. Back in my home church there was a saying: "I am not leaving this place in the same way that I came in." This means that it is important to leave people, places, and things better than we found them. I am hopeful that we have created a safe space together that allows us to feel more connected to ourselves—and to one another—than we did when we began. With this in mind, I leave you with these final questions:

1. At the beginning of the book, I invited you to ask what embodiment looked like for you. What does it look like now?

How does embodiment look, feel, taste, smell, and sound to you at this moment?

2. What stories around embodiment or disembodiment in your family or culture have come to mind during this process?

3. What is one practice you can identify with today to begin to live into your embodied self?

4. Write down at least three takeaways from this book. Why are these things in particular important to you? What is next for you as a follow-up as we collectively move forward?

ADDITIONAL EMBODIED PRACTICES TO HELP YOU ALONG YOUR JOURNEY

THERE IS EVIDENCE TO support the case that within our cellular memory, our body stores ancestral trauma and burdens. It stands to reason, then, that our bodies must also store ancestral healing and blessings. For example, in my lineage my ancestors on my father's side were people who lived by the water. They were fishermen, and in relationship with the spirit of water. In my embodied practices, I have rituals on how I speak to water, how I take care of water, and how I ensure that water is clean. I recognize that water represents flow, abundance, cleansing, renewal, transformation, and expansion. And when I find that I am stuck in these areas I return to my relationship with water to learn about my body through the rivers, the oceans, the streams, the lakes, the rain, and the ponds.

Here are a few other practices to consider as we learn new ways to listen to our bodies:

ECOTHERAPY emphasizes connection to the land and nature, as well as plant medicine. It teaches us that increasing our access to land and food will reestablish our relationship to nourishment on a systemic and interpersonal level.

PRACTICES OF PRESENCE encourage us to consider our own safety, create boundaries, and make choices with self-compassion. It allows us to hold space for life's contradictions, with an understanding that we developed some of our conditions and tendencies as a means of survival. It gives us permission to accept that we are in a constant state of remembering and unlearning.

SPIRITUALITY offers healing on an individual and collective level because in spirit nothing is lost—it is just waiting to be remembered and reclaimed. For some of us, this means embracing the village and rejoining the community circle. For others, it may mean reconnecting to our indigenous healing practices and worldview orientation.

COMMUNITY HEALING that is trauma-informed by people who look like us can include tools such as rituals, spiritual baths using natural herbs, teas, and altars for offerings such as libations.

WORKS CITED AND SUGGESTED READING

INTRODUCTION

Giachin, G. (2023). Eating Disorder Statistics | General and Diversity Stats | ANAD. National Association of Anorexia Nervosa and Associated Disorders. anad.org/eating-disorders-statistics/.

Blüher, M. (2019). Obesity: global epidemiology and pathogenesis. *Nature Reviews Endocrinology, 15*(5), 288–298. doi.org/10.1038/s41574-019-0176-8.

Touyz, S., and Hay, P. (2015). Severe and enduring anorexia nervosa (SE-AN): in search of a new paradigm. *Journal of Eating Disorders* 3(1). doi.org/10.1186/s40337-015-0065-z.

Cachelin, F. M., Veisel, C., Barzegarnazari, E., and Striegel-Moore, R. H. (2000). Disordered eating, acculturation, and treatment-seeking in a community sample of Hispanic, Asian, Black, and White women. *Psychology of Women Quarterly, 24*(3), 244–253. doi.org/10.1111/j.1471-6402.2000.tb00206.x.

Goeree, M. S., Ham, J. C., and Iorio, D. (2009). *Caught in the Bulimic Trap: Do Eating Disorders Reflect Addictive Behavior?*.

Striegel-Moore, R. H., Dohm, F., Solomon, E. E., Fairburn, C. G., Pike, K. M., and Wilfley, D. E. (2000). Subthreshold binge eating disorder. *International Journal of Eating Disorders, 27*(3), 270–278. doi.org/10.1002/(sici)1098-108x(200004)27:3.

Rubin, L. R., Fitts, M., and Becker, A. E. (2003). "Whatever feels good in my soul": Body ethics and aesthetics among African American and Latina women. *Culture, Medicine and Psychiatry, 27*(1), 49–75. doi.org/10.1023/a:1023679821086.

Letseka, M. (2011). In defence of Ubuntu. *Studies in Philosophy and Education, 31*(1), 47–60. doi.org/10.1007/s11217-011-9267-2.

Strings, S. (2020b). Fearing the black body. In *New York University Press eBooks*. doi.org/10.18574/nyu/9781479891788.001.0001.

Roberts, D. E. (1997). *Killing the Black Body: Race, Reproduction, and the Meaning of Liberty*. ci.nii.ac.jp/ncid/BA50742008.

Lewis, L. (2011). African American Vernacular English. In *Springer eBooks* (p. 58). doi.org/10.1007/978-0-387-79061-9_4087.

Wilkerson, I. (2020b). *Caste: The Origins of Our Discontents*. Random House.

Menakem, R. (2022). *The Quaking of America: An Embodied Guide to Navigating Our Nation's Upheaval and Racial Reckoning*. Central Recovery Press.

Neville, H. A., Tynes, B. M., and Utsey, S. O. (2008). *Handbook of African American Psychology*. SAGE Publications, Incorporated.

ONE

About Gloria—Nalgona Positivity Pride. (n.d.). Nalgona Positivity Pride. nalgona -positivitypride.squarespace.com/about-gloria.

Fahy, J. (2022, August 17). *How Heirs' Property Fueled the 90 Percent Decline in Black-Owned Farmland*. Farm Aid. farmaid.org/blog/heirs-property-90-percent -decline-black-owned-farmland/.

The Transatlantic Slave Trade: 500 years Later the Diaspora Still Suffers. *New York Amsterdam News*. amsterdamnews.com/news/2019/01/05/transatlantic-slave-trade -500-years-later-diaspora/.

Bell, K. *Story*. (n.d.). rootedglobalvillage.com/story.

Historical Context: Facts About the Slave Trade and Slavery | Gilder Lehrman Institute of American History. (n.d.). gilderlehrman.org/history-resources/teacher -resources/historical-context-facts-about-slave-trade-and-slavery.

Gundaker, G. (2011). The Kongo Cosmogram in Historical Archaeology and the Moral Compass of Dave the Potter. *Historical Archaeology*, *45*(2), 176–183. doi .org/10.1007/bf03376840.

Tammen, S. A., Friso, S., and Choi, S. (2013). Epigenetics: The link between nature and nurture. *Molecular Aspects of Medicine*, *34*(4), 753–764. doi.org/10.1016/j .mam.2012.07.018.

Ellison, K. (2010). New Age or New Biology? *Frontiers in Ecology and the Environment*, *8*(2), 112. doi.org/10.1890/1540-9295-8.2.112.

Wolynn, M. (2022). *It Didn't Start with You: How Inherited Family Trauma Shapes Who We Are and How to End the Cycle*. Random House.

Sandoiu, A. (2021, February 26). 'Weathering': What are the health effects of stress and discrimination? *Medical News Today*. medicalnewstoday.com/articles/ weathering-what-are-the-health-effects-of-stress-and-discrimination#Allostatic -load-much-higher-in-Black-adults van der Kolk, B. A. (2014). *The Body Keeps the Score: Brain, Mind, and Body in the Healing of Trauma.* Penguin.

The Beginner's Guide to Trauma Responses. (2021, August 26). Healthline. healthline .com/health/mental-health/fight-flight-freeze-fawn.

TWO

Cleveland, C. (2022). *God Is a Black Woman.* HarperCollins.

hooks, b. (2004). *The Will to Change: Men, Masculinity, and Love.* Simon and Schuster.

History of Eating Disorders. (n.d.). *Psychology Today.* psychologytoday.com/us /blog/evolutionary-psychiatry/201112/history-eating-disorders#:~:text=The %20first%20descriptions%20of%20anorexia,and%20burned%20at%20the%20 stake.

THREE

Gay, R. (2017). *Hunger: A Memoir of (My) Body.* HarperCollins.

Epstein, R., Blake, J. J., and González, T. (2017b). Girlhood Interrupted: The Erasure of Black Girls' Childhood. *Social Science Research Network.* doi.org/10.2139/ ssrn.3000695.

Moses, H. (n.d.). *MOSES: Oversexualization of Black girls, women must stop.* Marquette Wire. marquettewire.org/4041391/featured/moses-oversexualization-of -black-girls-women-must-stop/.

White, D. G. (1985). *Ar'n't I a Woman?: Female Slaves in the Plantation South.* W. W. Norton.

London, L. S. O. (2022, July 26). *Linnaeus and Race.* The Linnean Society. linnean .org/learning/who-was-linnaeus/linnaeus-and-race.

Anschutz, D. J., Spruijt-Metz, D., Van Strien, T., and Engels, R. C. M. E. (2011). The direct effect of thin ideal focused adult television on young girls' ideal body figure. *Body Image, 8*(1), 26–33. doi.org/10.1016/j.bodyim.2010.11.003.

Larson, K. E., and Gosain, A. K. (2012). Cosmetic surgery in the adolescent patient. *Plastic and Reconstructive Surgery, 129*(1), 135e–141e. doi.org/10.1097/prs.0b013 e3182362bb8.

Gordon-Chipembere, N. (2011). *Representation and Black Womanhood: The Legacy of Sarah Baartman.* Springer.

Newton, J. (2003). *Out of the depths.*

Jones-Rogers, S. E. (2020). *They Were Her Property: White Women as Slave Owners in the American South.* Yale University Press.

DeGruy, J. (2017). *Post Traumatic Slave Syndrome: America's Legacy of Enduring Injury and Healing.* HarperCollins.

hooks, b. (2004). *The Will to Change: Men, Masculinity, and Love*. Simon and Schuster.

The Jezebel Stereotype—Jim Crow Museum. (n.d.). jimcrowmuseum.ferris.edu/jezebel/index.htm.

The National Intimate Partner and Sexual Violence Survey (NISVS) |Violence Prevention|Injury Center|CDC. (n.d.). cdc.gov/violenceprevention/datasources/nisvs/index.html.

https://ujimacommunity.org/?s=womens+violence+stats

FOUR

Lorde, A. (1988). *A Burst of Light: Essays*. Firebrand Books.

Nanton, B. (2022, January 7). "Lizzo celebrates weight gain with City Girls TikTok Dance Challenge." Girls United. girlsunited.essence.com/article/lizzo-weight-gain-tiktok-rodeo/.

Bailey, M. (2022). *Misogynoir Transformed: Black Women's Digital Resistance*. NYU Press.

Crenshaw, K. (n.d.). "Demarginalizing the Intersection of Race and Sex: A Black Feminist Critique of Antidiscrimination Doctrine, Feminist Theory and Anti-racist Politics." Chicago Unbound. chicagounbound.uchicago.edu/uclf/vol1989/iss1/8.

Ochefu, A. (2021). The history of intersectionality and the Black feminists behind it—Assembly | Malala Fund. *Assembly*. assembly.malala.org/stories/the-history-of-intersectionality-and-the-black-feminists-behind-it.

The Mammy Caricature—Anti-black imagery—Jim Crow Museum. (n.d.). jimcrowmuseum.ferris.edu/mammies/homepage.htm.

Weintraub, A., Robinson, K., Tam, P., and Perkin, E. (2023, September 29). Ex-Lizzo staffer speaks out after filing lawsuit against singer alleging hostile work environment. *ABC News*. abcnews.go.com/US/asha-daniels-lizzo-staffer-speaks-after-filing-lawsuit/story?id=103490699#:~:text=Like%20Daniels%2C%20the%20three%20former,at%20a%20club%20in%20Amsterdam.

The Sapphire caricature—Anti-black imagery—Jim Crow Museum. (n.d.). jimcrowmuseum.ferris.edu/antiblack/sapphire.htm.

FIVE

About. (2023, August 3). Gabes Torres. gabestorres.com/about/.

Gutin, I. In BMI We Trust: Reframing the Body Mass Index as a Measure of Health. Soc Theory Health. 2018; Aug;16(3):256-271. doi: 10.1057/s41285-017-0055-0. Epub 2017 Oct 25. PMID: 31007613; PMCID: PMC6469873.

Stern, C. (2021, May 8). Why BMI is a flawed health standard, especially for people

of color. *Washington Post*. washingtonpost.com/lifestyle/wellness/healthy-bmi
-obesity-race-/2021/05/04/655390f0-ad0d-11eb-acd3-24b44a57093a_story.html.

McGee, D. L., and Diverse Populations Collaboration (2005). Body mass index and
mortality: a meta-analysis based on person-level data from twenty-six observa-
tional studies. *Annals of Epidemiology, 15*(2), 87–97. doi.org/10.1016/j.annepidem
.2004.05.012.

Mann, T., Tomiyama, A. J., Westling, E., Lew, A. M., Samuels, B., and Chatman, J.
(2007). Medicare's search for effective obesity treatments: diets are not the answer. *American Psychologist, 62*(3), 220–233. doi.org/10.1037/0003-066X.62.3.220.

Tomiyama, A. J., and Mann, T. (2008). Focusing on weight is not the answer to America's obesity epidemic. *American Psychologist, 63*(3), 203–204. doi.org/10.1037/
0003-066X.63.3.203.

Miller, W. C., Koceja, D. M., and Hamilton, E. J. (1997). A meta-analysis of the past
25 years of weight loss research using diet, exercise or diet plus exercise intervention. *International Journal of Obesity and Related Metabolic Disorder; Journal of
the International Association for the Study of Obesity, 21*(10), 941–947. doi
.org/10.1038/sj.ijo.0800499.

Tylka, T. L., Annunziato, R. A., Burgard, D., Daníelsdóttir, S., Shuman, E., Davis, C.,
and Calogero, R. M. (2014). The weight-inclusive versus weight-normative approach to health: evaluating the evidence for prioritizing well-being over weight
loss. *Journal of Obesity, 2014*, 983495. doi.org/10.1155/2014/983495.

Bacon, L., and Aphramor, L. (2011). Weight science: evaluating the evidence for a
paradigm shift. *Nutrition Journal*, 10, 9. doi.org/10.1186/1475-2891-10-9.

National Eating Disorders Association. (2021, July 14). nationaleatingdisorders.org/
statistics-research, Statistics and Research on Eating Disorders.

Tester, J., Lang, T., & Laraia, B. (2016). Disordered eating behaviours and food insecurity: A qualitative study about children with obesity in low-income households.
Obesity Research & Clinical Practice, 10(5), 544-552. http://dx.doi.org/10.1016/j
.orcp.2015.11.007. escholarship.org/uc/item/4g25k9td

Harrison, D. L. (2021). *Belly of the Beast: The Politics of Anti-Fatness as Anti-
Blackness*. National Geographic Books.

Wilson, J. (2023). *It's Always Been Ours: Reclaiming the Story of Black Women's Bodies*. Hay House, Inc.

Freedhoff, Y. (2015). *The Diet Fix: Why Diets Fail and How to Make Yours Work*.
Harmony.

Puhl, R. M. and Heuer, C. A. (2010). Obesity stigma: important considerations for
public health. *American Journal of Public Health, 100*(6), 1019–1028. doi.org/
10.2105/AJPH.2009.159491.

Salas, Ximena Ramos. (2015). The ineffectiveness and unintended consequences
of the public health war on obesity. *Canadian Journal of Public Health, 106*(2),
e79–e81. doi.org/10.17269/cjph.106.4757.

Sarah E. Hampl, Sandra G. Hassink, Asheley C. Skinner, Sarah C. Armstrong, Sarah E. Barlow, Christopher F. Bolling, Kimberly C. Avila Edwards, Ihuoma Eneli, Robin Hamre, Madeline M. Joseph, Doug Lunsford, Eneida Mendonca, Marc P. Michalsky, Nazrat Mirza, Eduardo R. Ochoa, Mona Sharifi, Amanda E. Staiano, Ashley E. Weedn, Susan K. Flinn, Jeanne Lindros, Kymika Okechukwu; Clinical Practice Guideline for the Evaluation and Treatment of Children and Adolescents With Obesity. *Pediatrics* February 2023, *151*(2), e2022060640. 10.1542/peds.2022 -060640.

Tinagli, P. (1997). *Women in Italian Renaissance Art: Gender, Representation and Identity.* Manchester University Press.

Kiely, A. (2022). The Mysterious Venus of Willendorf: What Does It Mean? *The Collector.* thecollector.com/venus-of-willendorf/.

Harvard Health. (2019, June 24). *Why people become overweight.* health.harvard .edu/staying-healthy/why-people-become-overweight#:~:text=To%20 date%2C%20more%20than%20400,appear%20to%20be%20major%20players.

Strings, S. (2019). *Fearing the Black Body.* New York University Press.

Bourdieu, P. (2013). *Distinction: A Social Critique of the Judgement of Taste.* Routledge.

Vandereycken, W., and Noordenbos, G. (1998). *The Prevention of Eating Disorders: Ethical, Legal, and Personal Issues.* NYU Press.

SIX

About—Lyvonne. (n.d.). Lyvonne. lyvonnep.com/what-i-do.

GoodRX. (n.d.). goodrx.com/healthcare-access/patient-advocacy/what-is-healthism.

Terry, B. (2021). *Black Food: Stories, Art, and Recipes from Across the African Diaspora [A Cookbook].* 4 Color Books.

Penniman, L. (2018). *Farming While Black: Soul Fire Farm's Practical Guide to Liberation on the Land.* Chelsea Green Publishing.

CDC Newsroom. (2016, January 1). CDC. cdc.gov/media/releases/2017/p0502-aa -health.html.

Cunningham, T. J., Croft, J. B., Liu, Y., Lu, H., Eke, P. I., and Giles, W. H. Vital Signs: Racial Disparities in Age-Specific Mortality Among Blacks or African Americans— United States, 1999–2015. *MMWR Morb Mortal Wkly Rep, 2017*(66), 444–456. doi: dx.doi.org/10.15585/mmwr.mm6617e1.

Dunn, T. M., and Bratman, S. V. (2016). On orthorexia nervosa: A review of the literature and proposed diagnostic criteria. *Eating Behaviors, 21,* 11–17. doi.org/ 10.1016/j.eatbeh.2015.12.006.

Mercedes, M. (2021, December 16). Public Health's Power-Neutral, Fatphobic Obsession with "Food Deserts." *Medium.* marquisele.medium.com/public-healths -power-neutral-fatphobic-obsession-with-food-deserts-a8d740dea81.

Brones, A. (2018, May 10). Karen Washington: It's Not a Food Desert, It's Food Apartheid. *Guernica.* guernicamag.com/karen-washington-its-not-a-food-desert-its-food-apartheid.

The Original Intuitive Eating Pros. (2019, June 3). Homepage—Intuitive eating. Intuitive Eating. intuitiveeating.org/#:~:text=Intuitive%20Eating%20is%20a%20self,and%20Elyse%20Resch%20in%201995.

Angelou, M. "Our Grandmothers." AfroPoets Famous Writers. (n.d.). afropoets.net/mayaangelou25.html.

About. (n.d.). Dara Cooper. daracooper.com/about.html.

SEVEN

www.naacpldf.org/brown-vs-board/significance-doll-test/#:~:text=In%20the%20 1940s%2C%20psychologists%20Kenneth,to%20test%20children's%20racial%20 perceptions.

Chamorro-Premuzic, T. (2019, October 31). Attractive People Get Unfair Advantages at Work. AI Can Help. *Harvard Business Review.* hbr.org/2019/10/attractive-people-get-unfair-advantages-at-work-ai-can-help.

Harrison, D. L. (2021b). *Belly of the Beast: The Politics of Anti-Fatness as Anti-Blackness.* National Geographic Books.

Corry, K. (2021, January 29). Is Hip-Hop Ready to Address Its Colorism Problem? *Vice.* vice.com/en/article/4ad5pw/is-hip-hop-ready-to-address-its-colorism-problem-danileigh-yellow-bone.

Kerr, A. E. (2005). The Paper Bag Principle: Of the Myth and the Motion of Colorism. *Journal of American Folklore, 118*(469), 271-289. doi.org/10.1353/jaf.2005.0031.

HOME | My Site 2. (n.d.). My Site 2. mayowasworld.com/.

Callender, B. S. (2020, October 24). The Tignon Laws Set the Precedent for the Appropriation and Misconception Around Black Hair. *Essence.* essence.com/hair/tignon-laws-cultural-appropriation-black-natural-hair/.

The Official CROWN Act. (n.d.). thecrownact.com/.

Children as young as 3 unhappy with their bodies. (2023, September 29). pacey.org.uk/news-and-views/news/archive/2016-news/august-2016/children-as-young-as-3-unhappy-with-their-bodies/.

Kong, S. L. (2022). For her next trick, Kim Kardashian will be cosplaying as a white woman. | Friday Things, fridaythings.com/recent-posts/kim-kardashian-race-whiteness-new-look.

McKinley, C. E. (2021*). The African Lookbook: A Visual History of 100 Years of African Women.* Bloomsbury Publishing USA.

EIGHT

ABOUT. (n.d.). Decolonizing Fitness. https://decolonizingfitness.com/pages/about -ilya.

Unpacking the History of Anti-Blackness in the Fitness Industry. (2022, January 17). Decolonizing Fitness. decolonizingfitness.com/blogs/decolonizing-fitness/unpacking -the-history-of-anti-blackness-in-the-fitness-industry.

Galton, F. (1870). *Hereditary Genius: An Inquiry into its Laws and Consequences*.

Lelliott, J. (2004). War Against the Weak: Eugenics and America's Campaign to Create a Master Race. *BMJ: British Medical Journal, 328*(7436), 411.

Meet Coach Ve | The Strong Academy. (n.d.). The Strong Academy. thestrongacademy .com/meet-coach-ve#:~:text=Venus%20(Ve)%20Davis%20is%20the,for%20 professionals%20and%20committed%20individuals.

Erika Totten | Healer. activist. facilitator. (2023, September 26). Healer. Activist. Facilitator. erikatotten.com/.

About. (2022, May 15). Leaving Evidence. leavingevidence.wordpress.com/about-2/

Our team—sins invalid. (n.d.). Sins Invalid. sinsinvalid.org/staff.

RING SHOUT—Jazz History Tree. (n.d.). jazzhistorytree.com/ring-shout/.

University, S. S. P. O. H. N. (1987). *Slave Culture: Nationalist Theory and the Foundations of Black America*. Oxford University Press, USA.

About—Positive Force Movement. (n.d.). Wild Within Acres. positiveforcemovement .org/about#lore.

NINE

Harrison, D. L. (2021c). *Belly of the Beast: The Politics of Anti-Fatness as Anti-Blackness*. National Geographic Books.

naafa. (n.d.). Naafa. naafa.org.

Who Is Simone? (2023, August 28). Simone Mariposa. thesimonemariposa.com/ about/.

Kight, D. (2014). Uncovering the History of Fat Acceptance: Lew Louderback's 1967 Article. Powerful Hunger. powerfulhunger.com/powerful_hunger_blog/history-of -fat-acceptance-lew-louderback-1967-article/.

Louderback, L. (1970). *Fat Power: Whatever You Weigh Is Right*. Hawthorn Books.

Fishman, B. and Golda, S. "Life in the Fat Underground." *Radiance Magazine Online*, radiancemagazine.com/issues/1998/winter_98/fat_underground.html.

Library Guides: FAT Activism: FAT Liberation Manifesto. (n.d.). guides.lib.uw.edu/ FatActivism/Manifesto.

Agel, J. (1971). *The Radical Therapist: Therapy Means Change Not Adjustment*. Ballantine Books.

Rothblum, E. D., and Solovay, S. (2009). *The Fat Studies Reader*. NYU Press.

Eye of the Tigress. (n.d.). Smith College. smith.edu/news/2023-eye-of-the-tigress.

Hunter Ashleigh Shackelford—Forward Together. (2020, February 11.) Forward Together. forwardtogether.org/?team=ashleigh-shackelford.

Lupton, D. (1996). *Food, the Body and the Self*. SAGE Publications Ltd.

Fat Women of Color | Sisterhood, support, and sanctuary for Black and Brown women of size. (n.d.). fatwomenofcolor.com/#:~:text=Fat%20Women%20Of%20Color%20%7C%20Sisterhood,and%20Brown%20women%20of%20size.&text=Black%20and%20Brown%20women%20of%20size%2C%20we%20create%20online%20and,an%20attempt%20to%20marginalize%20you.

TEN

Kumai, C. (2018). *Kintsugi Wellness: The Japanese Art of Nourishing Mind, Body, and Spirit*. HarperCollins.

ACKNOWLEDGMENTS

Land Acknowledgment and Life Honoring Practice: I wrote this book on the land of the Piscataway and Nacotchtank (Anacostan) peoples. I show reverence for the stewards of Turtle Island, and offer my deepest gratitude to the Black, Brown and Indigenous folks who were forcibly removed from their land who tended to and fostered a regenerative relationship with Turtle Island and Indigenous land globally. Thank you God and goddess for divine favor and guidance. I honor the elevated ancestors who are also integrated within me. My higher self, my spirit guides and all other entities that journey with me in this lifetime. I revere mama earth, the elementals, elder species, plants, animals, cosmic matter seen and unseen. I am one piece of the collective tapestry and Sankofa that connects both past, present, and future and I honor our beingness and connectedness in flowing together.

—ASE

To my parents, Harvey McCullough and Michelle McCullough: Thank you for your unwavering support of this book writing process, from offering context about the family story to reviewing multiple drafts of the manuscript throughout the creation of this book. Thank you for taking care of Zora (my dog), during the times where I needed solitude to go deeper into the writing process. To my siblings, Amber McCullough and Harvey

McCullough, Jr., thank you for your support, validation, and empowerment to stand in my truth.

I am also appreciative of my grandparents, aunts, uncles, and cousins who have always offered encouraging words and check-ins about my work over the years. Thank you to my friends and colleagues who consistently asked, "How's the book going?" and would genuinely listen to the ups and downs and let me know how excited they were to purchase the book, even when I had just received the book deal! I am so grateful to be surrounded by an overflow of love and care throughout this birthing experience.

Cherise Fisher, you are the world's best book agent! Thank you so much for being in my corner over the last four years. You saw the vision and potential of this work from day one, and have relentlessly advocated for my well-being both personally and professionally. I am so grateful for your nurturing spirit and to call you a friend. Maya Millett, I truly received my dream editor when I signed with The Dial Press. Since connecting with you I have experienced your intentionality and care for this book and my personhood. I could not have asked for a better editor and friend to trust with the guidance and manifestation of this book. Vanessa De Luca, thank you so much for being an amazing book consultant. Your energy always encouraged me to keep going, knowing that we would take an idea or an experience and alchemize it into this beautiful offering that I get to share with the world.

Thank you to my own therapist for holding space for me to become undone and put back together again and again throughout the writing process. To my clients, thank you for offering me the privilege of holding space for your stories and trusting me to support you along your journey.

Thank you to my team at The Dial Press (Whitney Frick, Debbie Aroff, Michelle Jasmine, Jordan Forney) and the larger team at Random House.

Book contributors and friends

Ilya Parker, Brittany Cannon, Kanolani Patterson, Gloria Lucas, and Shana McDavis-Conway, I am deeply grateful for your vulnerable contributions to this book and for your pouring your wisdom, love, and generosity into supporting this writing process.

Shout out to my fellow healers, liberators, disrupters, wise counsel, and author village

Jennifer Mullan: I appreciate you, Sis, for being an early beacon of light, healing, and disruption within the mental health field. When we first connected in 2019 I finally aligned with someone who was already embodying the essence of "Decolonizing Therapy." You pushed me to continue to challenge the dominant narratives within mental health. Your work helped me marry ancestral healing, historical trauma, and the sacred assignment of healing with the work that I was doing as a mental health therapist. I have so much reverence for our sisterhood.

Jessica Wilson: What can I say, friend, it all started with our connection through the AmplifyMelanatedVoices movement. It was ordained for us to meet, and we were destined to have these sacred books that will forever transform the field in all of the ways that we needed when we first started out. While it has been an uphill battle to have our voices heard and work respected, this is our legacy to the eating disorders field. We built our own table outside of the dominant system!

Shawna Murray Browne: Shawna! Wow, what a journey we have been on. Thank you so much for showing up and being intentional with your presence. Your multifaceted work introduced me to Ancestral Healing and then Decolonizing Therapy for Black Folks, which validated my passion and offered a soft landing place in the liberation-centered mental health community, which forever changed me as a person and practitioner. I appreciate your unwavering support of my work and being.

Rachel Ricketts: Sis! This book would not be possible without you, It was through your generosity that I was introduced to the publishing field. I am overflowing with gratitude for you. Our being and birthing exist in such an experiential space that words do not truly encapsulate it. Thank you for your audaciousness, for community care, and for self-preservation.

Lyvonne Briggs: My good sis! I am so, so grateful for you. Your being and creation of The Proverbial Experience is what allowed me to redefine myself as the divine, and break out of the limiting barriers that I had been indoctrinated into. Through your ministry I strengthened my voice and developed a deeper relationship with my sensuality. I am so proud of you and grateful for our sisterhood.

Mariel Buque: Sis, I am so glad that we were able to connect through that mental health event during the height of the pandemic. Since our connection you have been such a supportive kindred spirit, and it has been so encouraging to have a friend on a similar path attracting abundance and light along the journey.

shena young: shena, my gentle spirit, intuitive, warrior friend. Thank you so much for guiding me with the writing process very early on and calling me back to my body. Your living, your work, and your energy naturally offer spaciousness for transformation and healing.

Chrissy King: Chrissy! My heart is so full, feeling how our work truly brings people back into their bodies in safe and affirming ways. I am so grateful for your integrity and light energy. You encourage all to always remember our deservability and never settle. I have taken those lessons with me in the birth of this book.

Jacquelyn Ogorchukwu Iyamah: Jacquelyn, I am so deeply grateful for your voice and being. Connecting with you gave me permission to boldly sit in the center of being the artist, the culture shifter, and healer. I am continually inspired by your grace and genuine energy.

Natalie Gutierrez: My sister, I am inspired by the depth of your healing energy. Thank you for your encouragement and reminder that I needed to rest and receive ease throughout the writing process and beyond.

Ash Johns: To my coach, sister, and friend, thank you for ushering me into my power as a creational woman, and facilitating deeper alignment with my ancestors. I am so inspired by your regenerative nature and deep listening to spirit. You have shown me how to dream unbounded and then call forth the physical manifestations of those dreams and heart desires.

Kenyatta Muzzanni Robles: Thank you for being an amazing business partner and strategist. You have truly been my solid support system and have taken my business Black and Embodied to the next level! We could not have launched this book without your wisdom, guidance, and deep commitment to community care.

Thank you to the teachers, somatic healers, activists, leaders, and liberators devoted to this work, especially Erika Totten, Christina Cleveland, Ivy Felicia, Whitney Trotter, Safiya McHale, Gabes Torres, Tasha Bailey, Dr. Joy Degruy, Tricia Hersey, Da'Shaun Harrison, Marquisele Mercedes, Sonya Renee Taylor, Dr. Sabrina Strings, Resmaa Menakem, Rev. Angel Kyodo Williams, Dr. Sara' King, and Dr. Asher Larmie.

Finally, thank you to all of my community in the mental health and eating disorder fields, in somatic and spiritual healing, and in social justice and activism. Much love to "The Fam," "Elevate Sisterhood," the Black and Embodied village, and a special shout-out to Dorenza Frederick, Ilya Parker, and Chris Roberts for being my voice note support group in the thick of the messy writing and living process.

I am because we are.

ABOUT THE AUTHOR

ALISHIA MCCULLOUGH (she/her) is a licensed clinical mental health therapist and the founder of Black and Embodied Consulting PLLC. She specializes in somatic therapy, trauma healing, and eating disorder treatment, with a focus on cultivating embodiment and fostering liberation. Alishia also runs the self-paced online course Reimagining Eating Disorders 101.

blackandembodied.com
Instagram: @blackandembodied

ABOUT THE TYPE

This book was set in Caledonia, a typeface designed in 1939 by W. A. Dwiggins (1880–1956) for the Merganthaler Linotype Company. Its name is the ancient Roman term for Scotland, because the face was intended to have a Scottish-Roman flavor. Caledonia is considered to be a well-proportioned, businesslike face with little contrast between its thick and thin lines.

Books Driven by the Heart

Sign up for our newsletter and find more you'll love:

thedialpress.com

⊙ @THEDIALPRESS

▶ @THEDIALPRESS